Edinburgh
Information and Technology Series

AUTOLOGIC

NEIL TENNANT

AUTOLOGIC

EDINBURGH UNIVERSITY PRESS

© Neil Tennant, 1992
Edinburgh University Press
22 George Square, Edinburgh

Typeset by the author using LaTeX and
printed in Great Britain by
Hartnoll Ltd., Bodmin

A CIP record for this book is available from the British Library.

ISBN 0 7486 0358 1

Contents

v

Preface

I hope there is something in this book for computational logicians; for proof-theorists; for cognitive scientists; for workers in artificial intelligence; and for the Prolog and logic programming community.

It has long seemed obvious to me that one should be able to program on a computer the effective skills taught in introductory and intermediate logic courses. After all, if one can teach students reasonable methods for finding proofs (in a system of natural deduction), why should one not be able to express those methods in a programming language?

When I became interested in the computational aspects of logic, I had philosophical reasons for rejecting classical logic. In my book *Anti-Realism and Logic*, I gave arguments in favour of a system that I called *intuitionistic relevant logic*. These arguments were philosophical, methodological and metamathematical. I found from working within this system that I could find proofs *more easily* because of the constraint of relevance between their premises and their conclusions. In this new kind of relevance logic, however, the constraint of relevance is realized in a way radically different from that which derives from the Anderson-Belnap tradition.

The Anderson-Belnap systems of relevant logic have proved horribly intractable. They have a messy proof theory. I put it to colleagues in the Automated Reasoning Project of the Australian National University that the choice of these systems was theoretically ill-informed. A look at Prawitz's formulation of natural deduction for this kind of relevance logic would quickly convince one that proof-search would be super-exponential. This view did not find favour in one quarter. A great deal of effort and funding had been put into the design and implementation of an algorithm, coded in *C*, that quickly seized up on problems of medium length. Moreover, the search methods were based on sequent rejection via algebraic countermodelling: hardly what would be going on inside the expert human reasoner's head.

I was interested in the cognitive scientific project of *emulation by simulation* of human cognitive capacities. I had also been looking at ways of throwing light on problems in philosophical logic by applying proof theory rather than model-theoretic semantics. It occurred to me that I ought to try devising a proof-finder for my system *IR* of intuitionistic relevant logic, one that would work according to purely proof-theoretic principles. After all, if I could find proofs in the system, couldn't I simply excogitate what it was that guided me? And couldn't a machine then do it the same way, only much faster? If such a proof-finder worked well in comparison with those for the Anderson-Belnap systems, this would be yet more evidence that the choice of *IR* was preferable to its rivals. To the philosophical, methodological and metamathematical considerations would now be added *computational* considerations.

The project meant programming in a flexible language for fast prototyping, one that was amenable to a logician. What better language than Prolog? As I worked with Prolog I came to realise that my project had relevance for logic programming generally. Success in this project holds out the promise of treating negation as *denial*, and not as *failure*, within Prolog itself as a programming language. There is a nice irony about what I was setting out to do. I was trying to use negation-deficient Prolog (with negation interpreted as failure) as the metalogic to write a proof-finder for an object logic whose own negation operator was to be construed properly as denial. One day, I hope, this proper treatment of negation will be bootstrapped up into the programming language itself. I hope therefore that it will be of interest to the Prolog and logic programming communities.

What proof-theorists might find interesting is the *hybrid* systems of logic that I have developed here in response to the exigencies of efficient computation. A hybrid system is mid-way between a natural deduction system and the corresponding sequent system. Hybrid proofs, like sequent proofs, are easy to find and are economical to display; and, like natural deductions, represent clearly the 'lines of reasoning' within a proof. By varying the discharge conventions governing their rules of inference, one can generate a variety of related systems of logic.

Another aspect of this project that may be of interest to proof-theorists is the range of *normal form* and *filtering* theorems established for the systems of minimal and intuitionistic relevant logic. These theorems help to focus proof search, and were born of the need to do so.

For reasons explained in the text, I started my project not with the system *IR*, but with the system *M* of minimal logic. There is enough to deal with in that more familiar setting, before effecting the transition to the less familiar. My methods have been devised so as to survive such transition. Their application to *IR* itself is material for another monograph. This one is by way of preliminary report on the fruitfulness of natural deduction methods for non-classical computational logic.

When I looked at the literature on computational logic, I found it largely unhelpful. Almost all of it concerned only classical logic, and precious little of it was informed by proof-theoretic considerations. So I had to strike out on my own. In doing so I came into email contact with the odd worker here and there — Lund, Pittsburgh, St Andrews, Tucson — who had embarked on roughly similar approaches. *Natural deduction based sub-classical computational logic* seemed to be gathering a head of steam. It is time now to let some of it off. Hence this book.

Acknowledgements

I would like to thank an anonymous referee for constructive comments on an earlier draft.

The work described here was carried out in the Department of Computer Science in the Faculty of Science at the Australian National University. External support came from two sources. The Australian National University granted me a semester-long Outside Studies Period. The Australian Research Council provided a grant for six months' relief from other duties in order to pursue research on a project entitled 'Computer implementation of systems of constructive and relevant reasoning'. I am grateful to both organisations for that support.

It gives me especial pleasure, however, to acknowledge the internal support that I have enjoyed for two years as an informal guest among colleagues in the Department of Computer Science. They have been an unstinting and friendly source of all manner of advice, from theoretical know-that to practical know-how. They have also proved themselves, by virtue of their training as computer scientists and their general rigour of outlook, to be some of the most stimulating *philosophical* colleagues with whom I have had the pleasure of working.

My first debt of gratitude is to Robin Stanton, who as Head of Department made me welcome and encouraged me to avail myself of the facilities in his Department. My second debt of gratitude is to Seppo Keronen, who has been an unfailing source of help and advice as I learned to program in Prolog. Seppo's own interest in proof theory and its relevance to computational logic helped to keep me focused on the project even at times when I was suffering from bugs. My third debt of gratitude is to other colleagues such as Brendan Mackay, Malcolm Newey, Brian Molinari, and Robert Edmondson who have always been prepared to share their knowledge of relevant theoretical matters. My fourth debt of gratitude is to the programming staff of the Department: David Hawking, Drew Corrigan, Steven Ball, Peter Farmer and Ivan Dean, for their cheerful and efficient instruction in Unix, for their recovery of lost files, and for countless other favours.

Trevor Vickers has been a great help with LaTeX.

My work has benefited from exchange of ideas with John Pollock, Dov Gabbay, Wilfried Sieg, Richard Schienes, Roy Dyckhoff, Torkel Franzen, Timothy Smiley, Peter Schroeder-Heister and John Slaney. I must also thank Alan Robinson and Bob Meyer for their encouragement. My thinking has been helped by audiences at various seminars on this work, given to the Departments of Computational Logic and of Artificial Intelligence at the University of Edinburgh, the Seminar für natürliche Sprachsysteme at the University of Tübingen, the Department of Philosophy and the Research Center in Cognitive Science at The Ohio State University, and the Department of Computer Science and the Automated Reasoning Project at the Australian National University.

There is, however, no source of inspiration better than cynics when work is in its infancy in a rival paradigm to that of their own. One of these, who will remain nameless, will be interested in the following progress indicator for Prolog-based proof-finders for subclassical logics. When I first embarked on their development, he invited me to try to decide whether 'Meyer's formula' is a theorem of minimal logic. This is the answer from a Sun 4/40:

```
NU-Prolog 1.3
1?- Loading squish.no.
done
true.
2?- t(meyer).


PROBLEM NUMBER 1:

[] ?- if(if(if(if(if(a,b),b),a),c),if(if(if(if(if(b,a),a),b),c),c))

The length of this problem is 21

I take only 0 ms to decide that there is NO DERIVATION

Thank you for your attention.
```

I ought to end with the usual caveats about errors. The *computational* work was done, as remarked above, on a Sun 4/40 machine, with 20 megabytes of RAM. The *theoretical* work was done on a neural network, with about 10^{14} neurons[1] and not a little $N(CH_3)CON(CH_3)C : CCON : CHN(CH_3) + H_2O$[2]. Any errors that remain are entirely the fault of these machines, and *I* refuse to accept responsibility for them.

I dedicate this book to my daughters Liz and Kate.

---

[1] and decreasing!

[2] not to mention the β-endorphins when the programs ran fast.

Chapter 1

Introduction

1.1 Computational logic and Prolog

Logic, said Quine, is an ancient subject, and since 1879 has been a great one[1]. One might add that recently it has become a fast one.
For logic has taken the computational turn[2].
I treat here of decidable propositional logics. A *propositional* logic deals only with logical operators that form sentences from one or more sentences[3]. The most familiar of these are ¬ (negation), ∧ (conjunction), ∨ (disjunction) and ⊃ (implication). A logic is *decidable* when there is an effective method for deciding, of any finite set of premises and a conclusion, whether the latter can be deduced from the former within that logic.

I seek efficient algorithms for finding proofs of such deductive problems within a decidable logical system. I hope thereby to quicken both logic and interest in it.

Algorithms are more or less invariant across change of programming language, give or take the various tweaks that may exploit special features of a particular language. The algorithm is the intellectual object that matters.

I use Prolog as my programming language[4].

---

[1] He was referring, of course, to the publication of Frege's *Begriffsschrift*.

[2] For the early history of computational logic, see W.W.Bledsoe and D.W.Loveland, *Automated theorem proving: after 25 years*, American Mathematical Society, Providence, RI, 1983.

[3] These are often called *connectives*.

[4] The *loci classici* are A.Colmerauer, H.Kanoui, R.Pasero and P.Roussel, *Un Système de Communication Homme-machine en Français*, Research Report, Groupe d'Intelligence Artificielle Université d'Aix-Marseille II, 1973; and R.Kowalski, 'Predicate Logic as a Pro-

I do so for both practical and aesthetic reasons. First, Prolog is marvellously accessible to logicians. A Prolog program consists of clauses that can be understood as inference rules of the form 'if $P_1, \ldots, P_n$, then Q', where Q is an atomic sentence and each of $P_1, \ldots, P_n$ is an atomic or negated atomic sentence. (These negations are interpreted as failure: $not(P)$ succeeds if and only if P fails.) The declarative meaning of a program in Prolog is just the set of consequences that can be drawn from its clauses by using them as rules. Secondly, Prolog allows one to write reasonably short programs for hard problems, and thus lends itself to fast prototyping. This is especially important in computational logic, where experimentation with theoretically motivated constraints on proof-search can yield great speed-up. Prolog narrows the gap between having a theoretical insight and implementing constraints based on it. It allows the logician to be the programmer. At any stage of its development a Prolog program is an adaptable, flexible product. Programming at this level reduces the danger of being locked in to any one approach at the expense of alternatives that might suggest themselves.

Computation grew out of the foundations of logic laid by Gödel, Turing, Church and others from the early 1930's. A high-level programming language like Prolog grew directly out of a limited fragment of first-order logic. Prolog's own control structure is an inference engine for this fragment. And as a high-level programming language Prolog can be used to design proof-finders (inference engines) for various logical systems in various formal languages. An overarching irony is that Prolog's inference engine is at present the *SLD*-resolution method; and I propose to use Prolog to devise proof-finders, for various systems of (propositional) logic, that I would wish to maintain are better than the resolution system. This is like driving a car with a poor engine to find a better engine. But if I am right, and if the methods I develop *do* generalize nicely to first-order languages[5], we shall then be in a position to consider taking the old engine out and putting the new engine in. One will then be able to drive ever faster to ever better engines. Prolog's new implementation would be able to exploit the proof-finders first

---

gramming Language', *Proc. IFIP Congress*, North-Holland, Stockholm 1974. See also M. van Emden and R.Kowalski, 'The Semantics of Predicate Logic as a Programming Language', *J. ACM* 23, 1976, pp. 733-742. Good texts on Prolog are R.Kowalski, *Logic for Problem Solving*, North-Holland, 1979; W.F.Clocksin and C.S.Mellish, *Programming in Prolog*, Springer, 1981; I.Bratko, *Prolog Programming for Artificial Intelligence*, Addison-Wesley, 1986; and L.Sterling and E.Shapiro, *The Art of Prolog*, MIT Press, 1986. The latter has an excellent chapter on red and green cuts.

[5] See section 7 below for discussion of this consideration.

developed with its old implementation (*SLD*-resolution).

One very distant theoretical possibility is that one might be able, by means of the methods developed here, to create versions of Prolog in which negation is interpreted correctly as denial, and not incorrectly as failure. In the logical systems we shall be investigating, the negation of P is deducible only when P is refutable. This is how it should be. In current versions of Prolog, however, the negation of P succeeds as a goal when P fails, regardless of whether some consistent extension of the program might make P succeed. If our proof-finders, in which negation is *denial*, were to become the inference engine for Prolog, this situation could be remedied.

1.2   Three well-known systems of logic

Classical logic properly contains intuitionistic logic, which properly contains minimal logic[6]:

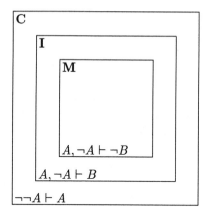

Minimal logic, consisting as it does of just the introduction and elimination rules for the logical operators, has a nice internal symmetry. The elimination rules exactly balance the introduction rules. The introduction rules tell us what goes into the justification of an assertion; the elimination rules tell us

---

[6]The nicest account of this containment is in D.Prawitz, *Natural Deduction: A Proof-Theoretical Study*, Almqvist and Wiksell, Stockholm, 1975.

what we can glean from one. Intuitionistic logic ventures further to add the absurdity rule, allowing us to infer anything from a contradiction. Classical logic goes even further by adding one of the classical rules of negation: the law of double negation, or classical reductio, or the rule of dilemma, or the law of excluded middle.

1.3   Computational logic and complexity

Because of these extra rules, classical logic has the tamest decision problem of all: it is NP-complete[7].

What does it mean when one says that a computational problem class (such as deciding whether a given deductive problem admits of proof) is NP-complete? It means that it *can be solved* in *non-deterministic polynomial* time (that is, it is NP-*easy*); and that any other problem class that can be so solved can be transformed into the one at hand in *(deterministic) polynomial* time (that is, it is NP-*hard*). This in turn raises definitional demands regarding *non-deterministic polynomial time* and *(deterministic) polynomial* time. We take the latter first. A problem class can be solved in *(deterministic) polynomial* time if there is a polynomial function $f(\_)$ such that any problem of length n in the given class can be solved in $f(n)$ units of time. These are also known conventionally as the 'tractable' problems. Now for the former. A problem class can be solved in *non-deterministic polynomial* time just in case there is an algorithm α for solving it, and a polynomial function $f(\_)$, such that for any input problem π of length n, the search tree generated by the branching (choice) points of the algorithm α applied to the problem π contains a solution at the end of a branch of length less than $f(n)$. An intuitive way of thinking of this is that if, in the execution of the algorithm α (which requires us at branching points to make single choices from a range of possible alternatives) we were so *lucky* as always to choose 'correctly' — and thereby solve the problem as quickly as possible — then indeed we would do so in no more than $f(n)$ units of time.

That we should be so lucky! ... P is the class of problems (more exactly: problem classes) that can be computed in polynomial time. NP is the class of problem classes that can be computed in non-deterministic polynomial time. It is an open problem whether $P=NP$. The orthodox conjecture is

---

[7]S.A.Cook, 'The Complexity of Theorem-Proving Procedures', *Proc. 3rd Annual ACM Symposium on Theory of Computing*, 1971, pp.151-158.

that $P \neq NP$; for no-one has ever provided, for any one of the hundreds of problem classes now known to be NP-complete, an algorithm that runs in polynomial time[8]. Classical logic is NP-complete because it provides a very replete set of proof methods. Both intuitionistic logic and minimal logic, by contrast, are PSPACE-complete[9], which is *prima facie* worse.

1.4 The choice of minimal logic

I start on minimal logic.

This immediately produces a problem. There are no such results as conjunctive normal form or disjunctive normal form theorems for minimal logic. Familiar de Morgan laws and dualities break down. Double negations cannot in general be spirited away. This sparseness of inner relations among sentences in minimal logic drastically curtails the extent to which one can crush a problem by normal-forming, or pre-processing, its premisses and conclusion before embarking in earnest on proof-search for the dregs. In minimal logic one has to take one's input raw. And in such circumstances it becomes much easier to bite off more than one can chew. This difficulty, however, is to me a welcome one; it keeps one's toil honest. I note the difficulty in passing, and note also that the resolution method, insofar as it relies on such normal-forming of formulae, is provincial to classical logic[10].

My main reasons for starting on minimal logic are threefold. First, as just indicated, it is a tough nut to crack computationally. Its logical rules generate as much complexity as we might desire, and no more than we should fear, in a propositional logical system. Secondly, it is well-known and is located in the proof-theoretic taxonomy of important systems in such a way as to provide computational access to important containing or otherwise related systems.

---

[8] For a lucid introduction to the theory of complexity see M.R.Garey and D.S.Johnson, *Computers and Intractability*, W.H.Freeman, San Francisco, 1979. I shall be discussing in a later chapter some practical concerns about complexity in computational logic.

[9] R.Statman, 'Intuitionistic Propositional Logic is Polynomial Space Complete', *Theoretical Computer Science*, 9, 1979, pp.67-72. The proof given there can be adapted to deal also with minimal logic.

[10] A classic source on the failure of normal-forming for formulae in sub-classical logics is G.E.Minc, 'The Skolem method in intuitionistic calculi', *Proceedings of the Steklov Institute of Mathematics 121, 1972: Logical and Logico-Mathematical Calculi, 2* (American Mathematical Society, 1974), pp.73-109.

I have a special final reason to start with minimal logic, which has to do with the overall aims of the discipline of computational logic. Looking further ahead, we wish to handle *quantifiers*; and we wish to develop proof-search methods that can benefit from paying heed to the notion of *relevance* of premises to conclusion, rather than be hindered by so doing.

On *quantifiers* there is little I can offer at this stage by way of special justification for minimal logic as opposed to, say, classical logic. The first-order versions of either of these logics are undecidable anyway. I do believe, however, that a deeper understanding of algorithms for handling disjunctive conclusions and premises can help when one comes to algorithms for handling constructive existential quantification. But that is another story.

1.5 Relevance

On *relevance* I can say a little more. Indeed, I should say straightaway that the present work on minimal logic is only a prolegomenon to work that I plan to do on a closely related system of constructive and relevant reasoning. Through minimal logic as a testing ground for proof-finding programs, I can chart an easy theoretical transition to *intuitionistic relevant* logic. This system, I have argued elsewhere[11], has strong meaning-theoretic, epistemological and methodological claims to adequacy and correctness. I call the system *IR. IR is the right logic.* And I am able also to show[12] that its computational credentials are as compelling as its philosophical and meta-mathematical ones. By this I mean that its exploitation of the notion of relevance will not make it strictly more difficult to find proofs than it already is in intuitionistic logic. *My method of relevantising a system of logic will produce a relevant system whose decision problem is no more complex than the decision problem of the parent system.* The method of relevantising the system *I* of intuitionistic logic to get the system *IR* also produces, in a exactly similar fashion, the system *CR* of *classical relevant logic* from the system *C* of classical logic. Both *IR* and *CR* are decidable, and have decision problems no more complex than those of *I* and of *C* respectively.

---

[11] See my *Anti-Realism and Logic*, Oxford University Press, 1987. A summary of the main proof-theoretic ideas, and a list of *desiderata* for proof systems, can be found in my paper 'Delicate Proof Theory', in J.Copeland (ed.) *Proceedings of the Arthur Prior Memorial Conference*, forthcoming.

[12] See the metatheorem on p.189.

Chapter 2

The Relevance of Relevance

2.1 Complexity considerations

As I said at the end of the previous chapter, the relevance logics IR and CR are decidable. By contrast, the propositional relevance logic R of Anderson and Belnap[1] is undecidable[2]. Its well-known decidable fragment LR[3], obtained by dropping the distributivity axiom, has an awesomely complex decision problem: at best ESPACE hard, at worst space-hard in a function that is primitive recursive in the generalised Ackerman exponential[4]. From NP to ESPACE or worse, courtesy of 'relevance'! — so much the worse, then, for *this* brand of relevance.

These complexity results for LR (and the undecidability of R itself) bring out an important tension between one *motivation* for studying relevance, and the *Anderson-Belnap paradigm* for treating it. The *motivation* is that a proof system obeying some constraint of relevance of assumptions to conclusion would admit of faster proof search. The untutored idea is that a suitable relevance constraint will somehow narrow the search space. The *Anderson-Belnap paradigm* for treating relevance is their family of systems,

---

[1] A.R.Anderson and N.D.Belnap, Jnr., *Entailment: The Logic of Relevance and Necessity, Vol.1*, Princeton University Press, 1975.

[2] A.Urquhart, 'The undecidability of entailment and relevant implication', *Journal of Symbolic Logic* 49, 1984, pp.1059-1073.

[3] P.B.Thistlethwaite, M.A. McRobbie, and R.K.Meyer, *Automated Theorem-Proving in Non-Classical Logic*, Research Notes in Theoretical Computer Science, Pitman, London and Wiley, New York, 1987.

[4] A.Urquhart, 'The Complexity of Decision Procedures in Relevance Logic', unpublished typescript.

clustering around R, that enjoy unrestricted transitivity of proof, eschew disjunctive syllogism, and involve so-called 'intensional' connectives. If the motivation and the untutored idea are sound, we must conclude, in the light of the complexity results, that the Anderson-Belnap approach to relevance is not. The possibility remains that some other characterization of relevance will yield the sought reduction in complexity of proof search (or, at least, no increase). Here is an opportunity for computational concerns to inform philosophical preferences for one system of relevance logic over another.

2.2 The design of expert systems

Many writers have stressed the importance of the relation of relevance between premisses and conclusion in such applications as the querying of data bases. The data base, and the method of answering queries, form a so-called *knowledge-based expert system*. In an expert system the data base is the set of available premisses. When one poses a query, the sentence queried is posed as a potential conclusion. It is the task of the deductive component of the expert system to search for a proof of that conclusion from those premisses, in order to produce an affirmative answer to the query (if there is one). Now one would not want an affirmative answer to *any* and *every* query *just because the deductive component had happened upon a localized inconsistency in the data*. For it is all too easy for such inconsistencies to creep in undetected, when a data base gathers its data from several suppliers. Rather than suffer an attack of theorrhoea, a good expert system would *clam up*, and alert the user to the presence of the inconsistency detected. We shall see that the systems *IR* and *CR* embody relevance in a way precisely tailored to such epistemic need.

Quite apart from this obvious desideratum, a system embodying a proper analysis of relevance is likely to fare better in computational implementations and as a representation of human reasoning. There is no doubt that expert human reasoners can detect in a trice when a premiss is glaringly irrelevant to the production of a sought conclusion. The challenge is to identify the syntactic cues that expert human reasoners must be exploiting in order to do this. If we succeed, then the computational payoff should be significant. Our proof-finders will not explore blind (because irrelevant) alleys. The search will keep focused on the *relevant*, hence potentially productive, premisses in hand.

A metatheorem showing just how fruitful our analysis of relevance is in this regard will be proved in Chapter 9.

2.3   Relevantising mathematics

The motivation and proclaimed intuitions behind the Anderson-Belnap systems of relevance logic are completely unconvincing. What mathematician anxious to 'relevantise' a mathematical theory presumed (if not known) to be consistent, would ever relinquish disjunctive syllogism and hold on to unrestricted transitivity of deduction? Those who would 'relevantise' mathematics in R have to do so piecemeal. They have laboriously to re-derive in R well-known mathematical theorems from the accepted axioms. They have no general metatheorem to the effect that if a result holds classically, then by such-and-such methods one can obtain a relevant proof of it.

There is no easy generalisation of the semantics of propositional R to a semantics for first-order R^5. And the rule Gamma (for a system S):

$$\frac{A \text{ is a theorem of } S \quad (A \supset B) \text{ is a theorem of } S}{B \text{ is a theorem of } S}$$

turns out not to hold for $R\#$, the system of Peano arithmetic based on R^6. This has dashed hopes to use R-based computational logics in the computer generation of a proof of, say, Fermat's last theorem.

By contrast with R, the systems of relevance logic that I have developed admit of metatheorems guaranteeing the relevantisability of consistent mathematical theories — both constructive and classical[7]:

THEOREM: Any proof in I of a conclusion A from a set X of premises can be transformed into a proof in IR of either A or $\perp$ (absurdity) from (some subset of) X

---

[5] K.Fine, 'Incompleteness for Quantified Relevance Logic', in ed. R.Sylvan, *Directions in Relevance Logic*, forthcoming; and 'Semantics for Quantified Relevance Logic', *Journal of Philosophical Logic* 17, 1988, pp.27-59.

[6] H.Friedman and R.K.Meyer, 'Can we implement relevant arithmetic?', Technical Report TR-ARP-12/88, Automated Reasoning Project, Research School of Social Sciences, Australian National University, 1988.

[7] See my 'Perfect Validity, Entailment and Paraconsistency', *Studia Logica* XLIII, 1984, pp.179-198, and 'Intuitionistic mathematics does not need *ex falso quodlibet*', typescript.

THEOREM: Any proof in C of a conclusion A from a set X of premisses can be transformed into a proof in CR of either A or $\perp$ (absurdity) from (some subset of) X

These two metatheorems guarantee *epistemic gain*. On relevantising any classical or intuitionistic proof, one obtains *either* a proof of the sought conclusion from the set X of original premisses; *or* a proof of that conclusion from some *proper subset* of X; *or* a proof that (some subset of) X is *inconsistent*. We may sum up by saying:

1. *we may relevantise without loss on consistent sets of premisses*

2. *we may relevantise without loss on logical truths (i.e., on the empty set of premisses)*

3. *we may relevantise without loss on inconsistent sets of premisses*

So on the assumption that mathematics is consistent, we are assured that every mathematical theorem (classical or intuitionistic) admits of the corresponding kind of *relevant* proof. And if mathematics is *not* consistent, we are assured further that we shall be able to prove this *relevantly*. We are assured, moreover, that every logical truth can be proved in relevant logic. Finally, we are assured that the *hypothetico-deductive method of science*, which involves the logical pursuit of inconsistencies between hypotheses and observational evidence, can be carried out using relevant logic.

In summary, the systems IR and CR can do everything that any intuitionist or classicist, respectively, could wish their logic to do. Furthermore, we have now the prospect of exploiting the relevance relation (as these systems explicate it) so as to *speed up* proof-search — or, at the very least, *not slow it down*. Propositional CR should be no harder than NP; propositional IR no harder than PSPACE.

2.4   A clash of paradigms

To summarise, then, we have the following contrasts between the Anderson-Belnap approach to relevance and the approach that I favour:

1. They can relevantise mathematics only piecemeal. By contrast, I have metatheorems guaranteeing the relevantisability of mathematics.

2. They keep unrestricted transitivity of deduction, and abandon disjunctive syllogism. By contrast, I control transitivity of deduction in an epistemically gainful way, and retain disjunctive syllogism.

3. Their propositional logics are either undecidable or have decision problems of awesome complexity, compared to those of their parent systems. By contrast, my propositional logics lead to no increase in the complexity of the decision problem.

On balance, then, I believe it would be worthwile to press on with computational investigations of *CR* and *IR*.

Chapter 3

Logic and Cognitive Science

3.1 On inference engines

The results of these investigations promise to fit in well with the overall aims of computational logic. As a central normative component of cognitive science, computational logic should direct its interests first and foremost to the design of ideal inference engines for artificial intelligence. We should be seeking cybernetic extension of our deductively extracted beliefs. This includes cybernetic development of the logical consequences of sets of mathematical axioms; cybernetic unfolding of the predictive content of our scientific hypotheses; and cybernetic revision of those theories in the light of contradictions discovered, whether internally or with recalcitrant observation. In short, wherever logical reasoning features in our own framing, testing and revision of theories, we should aim to have computational surrogates for that exercise of our own logical intelligence.

Computational logic then, even conceived as a part of cognitive science, is a normative enterprise. One is seeking a model of *competence*, not of performance. The methodology is *a priori*, and involves expert introspection. The challenge is to identify, formulate and implement constraints governing search for proofs.

In a project like this, one has to get three things right:

1. a theoretically well-informed *choice of logic* (where the theoretical considerations can concern such matters as computational complexity, philosophical grounding, adequacy for science and mathematics, etc.)

2. a *decision algorithm* that is no more complex than it has to be for the logic in question (where the algorithm can be one that searches for proofs and/or counterexamples; and where the proofs can be in various formats: Hilbert-style axiomatic proofs, Fitch-style natural deductions, Gentzen sequent proofs, Prawitz-style natural deductions, Beth tableaux, Robinson-style refutations, etc.)

3. an *implementation* of that algorithm that is as efficient as possible (where the implementation should be suitably general and uniform across all possible input problems; that is, it should not involve any *ad hoc* methods whose efficiency depends crucially on the nature of whatever class of test-problems may have been given[1])

3.2   Methodological choices

The dominant recent approach of resolution-based theorem proving is not necessarily the best, heuristically or intrisically. Even without knowing whether $P=NP$, we know that the resolution method for classical logic is intractable[2]. It also does not transfer to other logics, since it is based (as already remarked above) on normal-forming methods provincial to classical logic.

A central methodological question poses itself in connection with any logic we may try to treat computationally:

Do we search for proofs by brute methods or by refined ones? By machine-driven merry dance, *à la* resolution or model elimination methods, or by somehow emulating or simulating competent human interests and methods?

The brute methods are widespread because of the history of the discipline. Intellectual migration into computational logic has come from computer science, mathematics, cognitive science and logic. The computer scien-

---

[1] An example of such an *ad hoc* method would be a method for quick detection of membership or inclusion in a set of sentences that exploits the fact that, say, at most three propositional atoms are involved in the sentences. One can hack up such membership or inclusion tests at machine level by exploiting the numerical limitation in question so as to confine the calculation to the smallest possible region of the hardware. When a proof-finding algorithm owes much of its speed on appropriately restricted test problems to such 'limitation of size' strategies, it is to be viewed with suspicion. Increasing the size of the problem in that crucial respect may lead to computational explosion.

[2] A.Haken, 'The intractability of resolution', *Theoretical Computer Science* 39, 1985, pp.297-308.

tists got there first; the logicians last. The result is a dominant paradigm — resolution theorem proving[3] — whose outputs bear no discernible relation to the protocols human reasoners produce. With growing contemporary interest in cognitive science, and the concern to emulate (if not simulate) human problem-solving abilities, the time is ripe for a change.

Considered as part of *cognitive science*, computational logic faces a double challenge. First, one still has the old challenge of using computers as prosthetic devices. That is, one programs computers to find solutions to difficult problems *faster* and *much more accurately* than the unaided human mind. One can meet this challenge without any concern for naturalness, simplicity, elegance or 'human-like' features of one's search algorithms, except insofar as these features might conduce anyway to greater speed and efficiency in the execution of the programs on the available hardware.

Among logicians, there are those whose background is mainly in algebraic semantics and model theory, and there are those whose background is mainly in proof theory. When trying to decide a deductive problem, the former tend to favour searching for countermodels; the latter, searching for proofs. In an ideal world, they would enter a mutually recursive partnership. The best implemented decision algorithm, surely, would be one which provided, for any input problem $X?\text{-}A$, a proof of A from the set X of premises, if one exists; or a countermodel forcing all of X, but not A, if no such proof exists. And, it should go without saying, one would want the countermodels to come from a semantics with respect to which the proof system is both sound and complete, so that every argument $X{:}A$ has either a proof or a countermodel but not both. Each method — finding proofs or finding countermodels — stands to gain from refinements of the other. Find a proof more quickly of $X{:}A$, and you can shut down the parallel search for a counterexample; find a countermodel, on the other hand, and you can shut down the parallel search for a proof. Speed-up with either kind of search should induce speed-up with the other.

---

[3] J.A.Robinson, 'A machine-oriented logic based on the resolution principle', *Journal of the Association of Computing Machinery* 12, 1965, pp.23-41. For a mature exposition, see J.A.Robinson, *Logic: Form and Function. The Mechanization of Deductive Reasoning*, Edinburgh University Press, 1979. The method was inspired by Prawitz's seminal paper on the unification algorithm, which, happily, requires only linear time; see Prawitz, 'An improved proof procedure', *Theoria* 26, 1960, pp.102-139.

3.3   Emulation by simulation

As part of cognitive science, computational logic faces a new challenge: that of programming the machines to *emulate human reasoning by simulating it*. That is, one tries to design algorithms for proof search, to be executed by the machines, that are *as isomorphic as possible* to whatever collection of methods is employed by competent human reasoners in search of suasive arguments. To face this new challenge, as a cognitive scientist, is to give hostage to fortune in the competition to design proof-finders that do their work simply *as fast as possible*. For the available hardware, because of its radically different physical construction from the human brain, might be much better at some tasks than the human being; and, correlatively, might be much worse at others.

The human brain, as a product of natural selection, has highly evolved abilities to recall and match visual patterns. This ability no doubt features crucially in 'higher order' human competence in schematic reasoning — at least on *reasonably short* problems. Likewise, we are able to *remember* past attempted moves and their outcomes when solving a problem. (And the word 'remember', remember, is ambiguous between *record* and *recall*.) Our relatively effortless memory of what we have recently done enables us to learn rapidly from past mistakes.

In both these respects we are, arguably, somewhat different from to-day's programmable hardware. Depending on one's programming language, there may be a disproportionately higher 'cost', in the case of a machine, associated with recording and consulting results of recently past computations. And pattern-matching and other forms of associative learning may be severely hampered by the physical design of the hardware. We may have to wait for an engineering revolution in the design of neural networks before our prosthetic devices' profile of relative competences begins to match our own. Just having the theoretical assurance that any Turing machine can be modelled by one of today's digital computers offers no comfort to the cognitive scientist endeavouring to use those computers to simulate our own range of competences in a way that would be *real-time faithful*.

With the human profile of competence possibly drastically skewed with respect to that of the digital computer, it may turn out that unnatural algorithms can be executed faster than the natural ones that reflect specifically *human* techniques, abilities, interests and methods. This must constantly be borne in mind when assessing the models of reasoning, or of proof search, offered by computational logic as a branch of cognitive science. But at the same time it lends a certain *frisson* to the rivalry between those who are happy to employ any brute-force or machine-friendly method, and those who want to 'make the machine think the way we do'. If the latter can come close to matching the achievements of the former as far as *execution times* are concerned, that would already be cause for considerable satisfaction. (Especially when one considers how late has been the entry of 'natural deduction'-minded logicians into the field of computational logic.) But there is the exciting prospect also of achieving the added benefit of, say, *finding the very proofs that human beings would find, by following methods that human beings themselves deploy.* So I would venture to suggest that, in addition to execution times, one consider the *nature of the process* and *features of the output* — in particular, the *length and structure of a natural deduction* — before entering a decision as to which computational logic program is optimal as a model of human deductive reasoning.

3.4   Computational logic and proof theory

Deductive logic is the centrepiece of any model of (ideal) cognition and reasoning. One's metaphysical stance can influence choice of methodology: e.g. choice of syntactic, proof-theoretic methods over semantic, model-theoretic methods which in their full extent can deal with infinitary objects. A cognitive scientist whose metaphysical position is basically materialist, and who is impressed by the finitude of the neural network, will incline towards models of cognition and reasoning that involve effective transformation of finitary representations.

Now from the standpoint of one interested in human cognitive competence — and in particular the ability to reason logically — 'natural proof search' methods seem strikingly underdeveloped[4]. Computational logic needs to explore the algorithmic gains in efficiency on offer from over five decades

---

[4]Interesting beginnings have, however, been made by L.C.Paulson, 'A Generic Theorem Prover', *Journal of Automated Reasoning* 5, 1989, pp.363-397; R.Schienes and W.Sieg, 'Searching for Proofs', to appear in *Proceedings of the 4th Annual Conference on Computers and Philosophy*; J.Pelletier, 'Completely Non-Clausal, Completely Heuristically Driven Automatic Theorem Proving', Technical Report 82-7, Department of Computing Science, University of Alberta; J.Pollock, 'Interest-Driven Reasoning', *Synthèse* 74, 1988, pp.369-390; D.Miller and A.Felty, 'An Integration of Resolution and Natural Deduction Proving', *Proceedings aaai-86, Fifth National Conference on Artificial Intelligence*, Vol.1: Science, Morgan Kaufmann, Los Altos, 1986, pp.198-202; T.Franzen, 'Algorithmic aspects of intuitionistic propositional logic', I and II, Swedish Institute of Computer Science Research Reports R87010B, 1987 and R89006, 1989.

of proof theory. The kind of proof theory I have in mind here is what might be called *intra-systematic* proof theory. Its main concern is to achieve a thorough understanding of what a given proof system is like 'from the inside', so to speak. It studies the structure, in the system, of proofs in normal form. The system is characterized by its rules of inference and by the way steps according to them can be patterned so as to form proofs.

It is the central concern of this work to explore what proof theory can offer computational logic. We discover how fast successful proof-search can be, when it is guided by constraints deriving from a deeper understanding of the structure of proofs in normal form. In the course of doing so, we also discover some unexpected benefits for proof theory in confronting the exigencies of computation. The main one is a hybrid system of proof that can be characterised as midway between a Gentzen sequent system and a Prawitz-style natural deduction system. But more of that later.

Another closely connected concern is to develop methods to deal with *propositional* logic that will generalise smoothly to *first order logic*. We wish emphatically to avoid any hacker's devices that will not survive the lift to first order. This includes, for example, the use of low-level programming tricks to speed up membership tests, when such tests are possible only because the number of propositional atoms is kept very small. We want, as far as possible, to *keep our algorithmic principles uniform across the whole class of input problems*. It is this concern that gives us further reason to explore systems of natural deduction, and attack the problem of how to find or generate proofs as suitably structured patterns of sentences.

When searching for proofs we are seeking to construct tree-like arrays of sentences satisfying local or global constraints on their syntactic patterning. Intelligent — that is, highly constrained — search would be best secured by applying the knowledge we have from proof theory about the shape of proofs in normal form, and the transformations that convert proofs into normal form. If reason somehow resides in cerebral symbol-shunting, I have a hunch that it is has to do with shunting those sentences, and their syntactic constituents, that arise directly from the deductive problem at hand (or in mind!). I think it is highly unlikely that the cortex generates arcane matrices to knock out invalid sequents during the mental rites of inferential passage[5]. Of course, this (introspective) hunch concerns only human

---

[5] J.Slaney and G.Meglicki, 'MaGIC, Matrix Generator for Implication Connectives', Technical Report TR-ARP-10/89, August 1990; and J.Slaney, 'Finite Models for Some Non-Classical Logics', Technical Report TR-ARP-2/90, 1990; both from Research School of Social Sciences, Australian National University.

computers. It may be that currently available hardware may be better off executing the brute force methods. The danger lurking in this accidental historical advantage would then be that the quest for an understanding of human logical competence might be diverted into refinements and extensions of techniques that have nothing to do with the way competent logicians and mathematicians actually reason.

This danger has to be borne in mind when we ask ourselves what we aspire to achieve in the computational treatment of logic. As urged above, should it not be to get cybernetic surrogates to the point where they can deductively extend the frontiers of our (conjectural) knowledge? Knowledge that we ourselves find worthwhile and interesting, and the cybernetically blazed path to which we could in principle follow? By 'path' here I mean not only the route within the proof from premisses to conclusion, but also the route of discovery to the proof itself.

This is not, however, to undervalue the route within the proof from premisses to conclusion. On the contrary — this is a further 'plus' in favour of natural deduction-based computational logic as opposed to, say, the resolution method. For with the resolution method nothing remotely approximating a suasive proof is produced. The end-product of the search is not an epistemically satisfying object. But on our approach it will be. Our searches will produce highly readable proofs that are rigorous and detailed formalizations of intuitive lines of human reasoning. The more succinct arguments that human reasoners would produce in actual logical or mathematical discourse will be homomorphs of these formal proofs under a very natural projection.

Another advantage for a computational logician in working with systems of natural deduction rather than, say, with Beth tableaux or the resolution method, is that *debugging one's proof-finding programs is much easier.* Suppose, for example, that one discovers a provable problem that one's program fails to prove. When one examines the trace of the computation one is much better able, in a natural deduction system, to locate and isolate the characteristic errors through failure to construct various subproofs of the would-be proof. Clauses of the program correspond to rules of inference; calls of clauses correspond to attempted applications of these rules of inference. The subproblems generated correspond to the subproofs required for successful application of those rules of inference. Diagnosis and debugging are very easy in such a nested environment.

3.5   Compossible constraints

Systems of natural deduction offer a rich variety of what might be called *completeness-conserving constraints on proof search*. The main theoretical investigations to be presented below concern the existence of various kinds of *normal forms* for proofs of given problems. A deductive problem is of the form $X?\text{-}A$ where X is a finite set of sentences (the *premisses*) and A is a sentence (the *conclusion*). Suppose P is an effectively decidable property of (X, A) and F is an effectively decidable *and non-trivial — that is, constraining* — property of proofs. Then what I shall call a PF-*normal form theorem* is a result of the following form:

> for all X for all A if $P(X, A)$ then for all proofs Π of A from any subset Y of X, there is a proof Σ of A from some subset Z of Y such that $F(Z, A, \Sigma)$

Such a theorem gives constraining heuristic guidance in the search for proofs for the problem $X?\text{-}A$. One checks whether $P(X, A)$. If so, then one confines one's search to proofs with property F.

Ordinary normalization theorems are special cases of results of the above form:

> for all X for all A for all proofs Π of A from any subset Y of X, there is a proof Σ of A from some subset Z of Y such that Σ is in normal form

Note that the precondition P in their statement is trivial, and F is the property of normality as usually understood (that is, 'not containing any maximal formula occurrence — an occurrence standing as the conclusion of an introduction rule and as the major premiss of the corresponding elimination rule'). We shall of course exploit this conventional normal form theorem, in that we shall seek only proofs in such conventional normal form. But we shall supplement this obvious focusing of our search with further PF-normal form theorems, for non-trivial preconditions P, tailored for service in computational logic.

Another special case of PF-normal form theorems is where the relational property F is restricted to the arguments Z, A, and is *persistent*, in the sense that if $F(Z, A)$ and Z is a subset of Y, then $F(Y, A)$:

> for all X for all A if $P(X, A)$ then for all proofs Π of A from any subset Y of X, there is a proof Σ of A from some subset Z of Y such that $F(Z, A)$

Results like this are called *filters*. They say, essentially, that if $P(X, A)$ then the problem $X?\text{-}A$ has a proof only if $F(X, A)$. So if we are given $X?\text{-}A$, and can determine that it has property P but lacks property F, then we know that there is no proof to be had.

One has to be careful to prosecute the enquiry into constraints with controlled *acharnement*, on pain of producing an incomplete proof-finder for one's chosen logical system. One has to pay attention, that is, to the *compossibility of constraints*. For suppose one has a series of $P_i F_i$-normal form theorems $(i=1,\ldots,n)$. One may have a provable problem that satisfies all the P_i. If one has constrained one's search by using all of the corresponding F_i, then one must be assured that *the F_i are compossible* — that is, that there will indeed be a proof satisfying all the properties F_i.

Think of a completeness-conserving contraint F as a spotlight on a surface whose points are proofs. Compossibility then amounts to this: with several spotlights in play, one wants to be sure that there is a region that they *all* illuminate. When one's contraints are *not* thus compossible, then *one is forced to choose different combinations from among them that are*. And here lies the prospect (for computational logic as a branch of cognitive science) of being more or less faithful to the repertoire of human logical competence. Some completeness-conserving constraints may force proofs into a form that is highly unlikely to be happened upon by those caravans in the desert that correspond to human cogitation. Others may turn proofs into veritable oases, suasive Romes on which all human roads converge. Our investigations are but a first feeble attempt to map this cognitive basin.

3.6 'My program is better than your program'

Computational logic, like any other discipline, stands to gain most from a fertile proliferation of alternative approaches, which it can then sift and combine to fashion the best techniques of the discipline. We should remain aware of the broad parameters set to our projects by theoretical results (such as those concerning extreme intractability) and of important distinctions such as that between an abstract algorithm and any of its implementations in a particular language on a particular machine.

This brings me to a final question: how do we judge how well an algorithm performs?

The discipline of computational logic has reached the point where it would benefit from a set of 'international standards'. This would enable one to compare different algorithms implemented in the same language and on the same machine, and to compare different implementations of the same algorithm, be they in different languages or on different machines. But at present there is no such set of standards. I can only describe how my algorithm, in its present Prolog implementation, performs on sundry problems drawn from the literature. Critics and detractors are cordially invited not to condemn the algorithm on the basis of apparent performance limitations of its (present) Prolog implementation. For there is reason to believe that these have more to do with Prolog's computational overheads than with deficiencies in the algorithm as such.

But I believe that anyone with a taste for elegance would like the Prolog proof-finding programs that result from proof-theoretic investigations. They write themselves. Their elegance derives from the exigencies of the logic itself. They are a metalinguistic, inferential codification, in the sparsest possible fragment of first-order language, of a theory of inference for the object language. I would offer them to the reader for reflection and, no doubt, further improvement, were it not for limitations of space and a measure of proprietorial reluctance to divulge![6]

A final word in closing this chapter: let the reader not underestimate the difficulty of the project. Searching for proofs is *hard*. It is hard enough to get a computer program that will find some short proofs as quickly as a well-trained logician can. It is *wonderful* when a computer program finds proofs, typically hundreds of steps long, in fractions of a second, for problems as long and complicated as these:

$[\supset\supset \neg p \neg \supset\supset \neg q \neg r \supset\supset qrq \supset\supset p \supset\supset \neg q \neg r \supset\supset qrqp]$
?-
$\supset\supset \neg \supset\supset \neg p \neg q \supset\supset pqp \neg r \supset\supset\supset \neg p \neg q \supset\supset pqpr \supset\supset \neg p \neg q \supset\supset pqp.$

$[\supset \vee\neg \supset \vee\neg p \supset pq \supset\supset qpq \supset\supset \vee\neg p \supset pq \supset\supset qpqr \supset\supset r \supset \vee\neg p \supset pq \supset\supset qpqr]$
?-
$\supset \vee\neg p \supset p \supset \vee\neg q \supset qr \supset\supset rqr \supset\supset\supset \vee\neg q \supset qr \supset\supset rqrp \supset \vee\neg q \supset qr \supset\supset rqr.$

---

[6]This reluctance is conveniently served by the prevailing convention in the field of computing according to which one sketches an algorithm, but does not reveal detailed implementations. Colleagues in computer science assure me that such *gaucherie* would be an invitation to ridicule by bug-hunters, nit-pickers and tweakers.

$[\supset \neg \supset \subset \neg \supset pq \lor p \neg\neg qr \lor \supset \neg \supset pq \lor p \neg\neg q \neg\neg r]$
?-
$\supset \neg \supset p \supset \neg \supset qr \lor q \neg\neg r \lor p \neg\neg \supset \neg \supset qr \lor q \neg\neg r.$

$[\supset\supset\supset\supset\supset pqp \lor p \neg\neg qr \supset\supset\supset pqp \lor p \neg\neg q \lor \supset\supset\supset pqp \lor p \neg\neg q \neg\neg r]$
?-
$\supset\supset\supset p \supset\supset\supset qrq \lor q \neg\neg rp \lor p \neg\neg \supset\supset\supset qrq \lor q \neg\neg r.$

$[\supset\subset \neg\neg p \supset\subset \neg\neg qr \supset \neg rq \supset \neg \supset\subset \neg\neg qr \supset \neg rqp]$
?-
$\supset\subset \neg\neg \supset\subset \neg\neg pq \supset \neg qpr \supset \neg r \supset\subset \neg\neg pq \supset \neg qp.$

$[\supset\subset \neg\neg \supset\subset \neg\neg pq \supset\supset qppr \supset\supset r \supset\subset \neg\neg pq \supset\supset qpp \supset\subset \neg\neg pq \supset\supset qpp]$
?-
$\supset\subset \neg\neg p \supset\subset \neg\neg qr \supset\supset rqq \supset\subset\subset \neg\neg qr \supset\supset rqqpp.$

$[\supset\subset \neg\neg p \supset\subset \neg\neg qr \lor r \supset rq \lor \supset\subset \neg\neg qr \lor r \supset rq \supset\subset\subset \neg\neg qr \lor r \supset rqp]$
?-
$\supset\subset \neg\neg \supset\subset \neg\neg pq \lor q \supset qpr \lor r \supset r \supset\subset \neg\neg pq \lor q \supset qp.$

$[\lor \supset \neg\lor \supset \neg p \land qp \lor\neg p \neg\neg q \land r \lor \supset \neg p \land qp \lor\neg p \neg\neg q \lor\neg\lor \supset \neg p \land qp \lor\neg p \neg\neg q \neg\neg r]$
?-
$\lor \supset \neg p \land\lor \supset \neg q \land rq \lor\neg q \neg\neg rp \lor\neg p \neg\neg\lor \supset \neg q \land rq \lor\neg q \neg\neg r.$

$[\supset \lor \subset \lor \supset pq \neg\neg p \supset\subset qppr \neg\neg \supset \lor \supset pq \neg\neg p \supset\subset qpp \supset\subset r \supset \lor \supset pq \neg\neg p \supset\subset qpp \supset \lor \supset pq \neg\neg p \supset\subset qpp]$
?-
$\supset \lor \supset p \supset \lor \supset qr \neg\neg q \supset\subset rqq \neg\neg p \supset\subset\subset \lor \supset qr \neg\neg q \supset\subset rqqpp.$

$[\lor \supset \neg\lor \supset \neg pq \lor \supset pq \neg\neg qr \lor \supset \lor \supset \neg pq \lor \supset pq \neg\neg qr \neg\neg r]$
?-
$\lor \supset \neg p \lor \supset \neg qr \lor \supset qr \neg\neg r \lor \supset p \lor \supset \neg qr \lor \supset qr \neg\neg r \neg\neg\lor \supset \neg qr \lor \supset qr \neg\neg r.$

$[\lor \supset \neg\lor \supset \neg p \land qp \lor \supset pq \neg\neg q \land r \lor \supset \neg p \land qp \lor \supset pq \neg\neg q \lor \supset \lor \supset \neg p \land qp \lor \supset pq \neg\neg qr \neg\neg r]$
?-
$\lor \supset \neg p \land\lor \supset \neg q \land rq \lor \supset qr \neg\neg rp \lor \supset p \lor \supset \neg q \land rq \lor \supset qr \neg\neg r \neg\neg\lor \supset \neg q \land rq \lor \supset qr \neg\neg r.$

24 AUTOLOGIC

[⊃⊂ ∨ ⊃⊂ ⊃⊂ ∨p ¬pq ⊃⊃qpp ¬ ⊃⊂ ∨p ¬pq ⊃⊃qppr ⊃⊂r ⊃⊂ ∨p ¬pq ⊃⊃qpp ⊃⊂ ∨p
¬pq ⊃⊃qpp]
?-
⊃⊂ ∨p ¬p ⊃⊂ ∨q ¬qr ⊃⊃rqq ⊃⊃⊂ ⊃⊃⊂⊃ ∨q ¬qr ⊃⊃rqqpp.

[⊃ ∨ ⊃p ⊃ ∨ ⊃qr ¬¬r ¬⊃r¬r ⊃ ∨r ¬rq ¬¬r ⊃ ∨ ⊃qr ¬¬r¬r ⊃ ∨r ¬rq ⊃ ∨ ⊃ ∨ ⊃qr ¬¬r
⊃ ∨r ¬rq ¬ ⊃ ∨ ⊃qr ¬¬r¬r ⊃ ∨r ¬rqp]
?-
⊃ ∨ ⊃⊂ ∨ ⊃pq ¬¬q ⊃ ∨q ¬qpr ¬¬r ⊃ ∨r ¬r ⊃ ∨ ⊃pq ¬¬q ⊃ ∨q ¬qp.

[⊃ ∨ ⊃⊂ ∨ ⊃pq ¬¬¬p ⊃⊃qp ∨p ¬pr ¬ ⊃ ¬¬r ⊃ ∨ ⊃pq ¬¬¬p ⊃⊃qp ∨p ¬p ⊃⊂r ⊃ ∨ ⊃pq
¬¬¬p ⊃⊃qp ∨p ¬p ∨ ⊃ ∨ ⊃pq ¬¬¬p ⊃⊃qp ∨p ¬p ¬ ⊃ ∨ ⊃pq ¬¬¬p ⊃⊃qp ∨p ¬p]
?-
⊃ ∨ ⊃p ⊃ ∨ ⊃qr ¬¬¬q ⊃⊃rq ∨q ¬q ¬¬¬p ⊃⊃⊂ ∨ ⊃qr ¬¬¬q ⊃⊃rq ∨q ¬qp ∨p ¬p.

[∨ ⊃⊃p ∨ ⊃⊃qr ∨r ¬¬r ⊃⊂ ¬rrr ∨∨ ⊃⊃qr ∨r ¬¬r ⊃⊂ ¬rrr ¬∨ ⊃⊃qr ∨r ¬¬r ⊃⊂ ¬rrr
⊃⊂ ¬∨ ⊃⊃qr ∨r ¬¬r ⊃⊂ ¬rrr ∨ ⊃⊃qr ∨r ¬¬r ⊃⊂ ¬rrr ∨ ⊃⊃qr ∨r ¬¬r ⊃⊂ ¬rrr]
?-
∨ ⊃⊃ ∨ ⊃⊃pq ∨q ¬¬q ⊃⊂ ¬qqqr ∨r ¬¬r ⊃⊂ ¬rrr .

[⊃⊃⊂p ⊃⊃⊂⊃qr ∨r ¬¬r ∧q ⊃ ¬¬rr ∨ ⊃⊃⊂⊃qr ∨r ¬¬r ∧ ⊃⊃⊂⊃ ¬ ⊃⊃⊂⊃qr ∨r ¬¬r ∧q
⊃ ¬rr ∧p ⊃ ¬ ⊃⊃⊂⊃qr ∨r ¬¬r ∧q ⊃ ¬rr ⊃⊃⊂⊃qr ∨r ¬¬r ∧q ⊃ ¬rr]
?-
⊃⊃⊂⊃⊃⊂⊃pq ∨q ¬¬q ∧p ⊃ ¬qqr ∨r ¬¬r ∧ ⊃⊃⊂⊃pq ∨q ¬¬q ∧p ⊃ ¬qq ⊃ ¬rr.

[⊃⊃⊂ ¬pp ⊃⊃⊂ ¬qqr ∨r ⊃rq ∨ ⊃⊃⊂ ¬qqr ∨r ⊃rq ⊃⊃⊂⊃ ¬qqr ∨r ⊃rqp]
?-
⊃⊃⊂ ¬ ⊃⊃⊂ ¬ppq ∨q ⊃qp ⊃⊃⊂ ¬ppq ∨q ⊃qpr ∨r ⊃r ⊃⊃⊂ ¬ppq ∨q ⊃qp.

[∧ ⊃⊃⊂p ∧ ⊃⊃⊂qr ∨r ¬¬r ⊃⊂ ¬rrq ∨∧ ⊃⊃⊂qr ∨r ¬¬r ⊃⊂ ¬rrq ¬∧ ⊃⊃⊂qr ∨r ¬¬r ⊃⊂ ¬rrq
⊃⊂ ¬∧ ⊃⊃⊂qr ∨r ¬¬r ⊃⊂ ¬rrq ∧ ⊃⊃⊂qr ∨r ¬¬r ⊃⊂ ¬rrqp]
?-
∧ ⊃⊂ ∧ ⊃⊃⊂pq ∨q ¬¬q ⊃⊂ ¬qqpr ∨r ¬¬r ⊃⊂ ¬rr ∧ ⊃⊃⊂pq ∨q ¬¬q ⊃⊂ ¬qqp.

[∨ ∨ ¬ ∨ ∨¬p ¬¬r ⊃ ¬p ⊃ ¬p ⊃ ¬qq ¬¬r ⊃ ¬¬r ¬ ∨ ∨¬p ¬q ⊃ ¬p ⊃ ¬qq ⊃ ¬rr]
?-
∨ ∨ ¬p ¬r ∨ ∨¬q ¬¬r ⊃ ¬q ⊃ ¬rr ⊃ ¬p ⊃ ¬ ∨ ∨¬q ¬¬r ⊃ ¬q ⊃ ¬rr ∨ ∨ ¬q ¬¬r
⊃ ¬q ⊃ ¬rr.

[⊃ ∨ ⊃p ⊃ ∨ ⊃qr ¬⁻q ⊃ ¬r ⊃ ¬qq ⊃¬p ⊃ ¬ ⊃ ⊂ ∨ ⊃qr ¬⁻q ⊃ ¬r ⊃ ¬qq ⊃ ¬pp]
?-
⊃ ∨ ⊃⊃ ∨ ⊃pq ¬⁻p ⊃ ¬q ⊃ ¬ppr ⊃ ⊃ ¬⁻ ⊃ ∨ ⊃pq ¬⁻p ⊃ ¬q ⊃ ¬pp ⊃ ¬r ⊃ ⊂ ¬ ⊃ ∨ ⊃pq
¬⁻p ⊃ ¬q ⊃ ¬pp ⊃ ∨ ⊃pq ¬⁻p ⊃ ¬q ⊃ ¬pp.

[∨¬¬p ⊃⊃ ¬ ∨ ¬⁻q ⊃⊃ ¬rr ∧rq ∨¬⁻q ⊃⊃ ¬rr ∧rq ∧ ∨ ¬⁻q ⊃⊃ ¬rr ∧rqp]
?-
∨¬¬ ∨ ¬¬p ⊃⊃ ¬qq ∧qp ⊃⊃ ¬rr ∧r ∨¬⁻p ⊃⊃ ¬qq ∧qp.

[∨ ⊃⊃p ∨ ⊃⊃qr ∨r ¬r ⊃⊃ ¬rr ∧rq ∨∨ ⊃⊃qr ∨r ¬r ⊃⊃ ¬rr ∧rq ¬∨ ⊃⊃qr ∨r ¬r
⊃⊃ ¬rr ∧rq ⊃⊃ ¬∨ ⊃⊃qr ∨r ¬r ⊃⊃ ¬rr ∧rq ∨ ⊃⊃qr ∨r ¬r ⊃⊃ ¬rr ∧rq ∧∨ ⊃⊃qr
∨r ¬r ⊃⊃ ¬rr ∧rqp]
?-
∨ ⊃⊃ ∨ ⊃⊃pq ∨q ¬q ⊃⊃ ¬qq ∧qpr ∨r ¬r ⊃⊃ ¬rr ∧r ∨ ⊃⊃pq ∨q ¬q ⊃⊃ ¬qq ∧qp.

[∨ ⊃⊃p ∨ ⊃⊃qrr ⊃⊃ ¬rr ∨rq ∨ ⊃⊃qrr ⊃⊃ ¬rr ∨rq ⊃⊃ ¬∨ ⊃⊃qrr ⊃⊃ ¬rr ∨rq
∨ ⊃⊃qrr ⊃⊃ ¬rr ∨rq ∨∨ ⊃⊃qrr ⊃⊃ ¬rr ∨rqp]
?-
∨ ⊃⊃ ∨ ⊃⊃pqq ⊃⊃ ¬qq ∨qprr ⊃⊃ ¬rr ∨r ∨ ⊃⊃pqq ⊃⊃ ¬qq ∨qp.

[∨ ⊃⊃p ∨ ⊃⊃qr ∨r ¬r ⊃⊃ ¬rr ∨rq ∨∨ ⊃⊃qr ∨r ¬r ⊃⊃ ¬rr ∨rq ¬∨ ⊃⊃qr ∨r ¬r
⊃⊃ ¬rr ∨rq ⊃⊃ ¬∨ ⊃⊃qr ∨r ¬r ⊃⊃ ¬rr ∨rq ∨ ⊃⊃qr ∨r ¬r ⊃⊃ ¬rr ∨rq ∨∨ ⊃⊃qr
∨r ¬r ⊃⊃ ¬rr ∨rqp]
?-
∨ ⊃⊃ ∨ ⊃⊃pq ∨q ¬q ⊃⊃ ¬qq ∨qpr ∨r ¬r ⊃⊃ ¬rr ∨r ∨ ⊃⊃pq ∨q ¬q ⊃⊃ ¬qq ∨qp.

[⊃ ∨ ⊃⊃ ∨ ⊃pq ⊃ ¬pp ⊃⊃qppr ⊃ ¬ ⊃ ∨ ⊃pq ⊃ ¬pp ⊃⊃qpp ⊃ ∨ ⊃pq ⊃ ¬pp
⊃⊃qpp ⊃⊃r ⊃ ∨ ⊃pq ⊃ ¬pp ⊃⊃qpp ⊃ ∨ ⊃pq ⊃ ¬pp ⊃⊃qpp]
?-
⊃ ∨ ⊃p ⊃ ∨ ⊃qr ⊃ ¬qq ⊃⊃rqq ⊃ ¬pp ⊃⊃⊃ ∨ ⊃qr ⊃ ¬qq ⊃⊃rqqpp.

[∨ ⊃⊃p ∨ ⊃⊃qr ∨q ¬q ∧ ⊃rq ⊃ ¬qq ∨p ¬p ∧ ⊃ ∨ ⊃⊃qr ∨q ¬q ∧ ⊃rq ⊃ ¬qqp
⊃ ¬pp]
?-
∨ ⊃⊃ ∨ ⊃⊃pq ∨p ¬p ∧ ⊃qp ⊃ ¬ppr ∨∨ ⊃⊃pq ∨p ¬p ∧ ⊃qp ⊃ ¬pp ¬∨ ⊃⊃pq ∨p
¬p ∧ ⊃qp ⊃ ¬pp ∧ ⊃r ∨ ⊃⊃pq ∨p ¬p ∧ ⊃qp ⊃ ¬pp ⊃ ¬∨ ⊃⊃pq ∨p ¬p ∧ ⊃qp
⊃ ¬pp ∨ ⊃⊃pq ∨p ¬p ∧ ⊃qp ⊃ ¬pp.

[⊃⊃⊃⊃⊃pq ⊃ ¬qq ⊃⊃qppr ⊃ ¬rr ⊃⊃r ⊃⊃⊃pq ⊃ ¬qq ⊃⊃qpp ⊃⊃⊃pq ⊃ ¬qq
⊃⊃qpp]
?-
⊃⊃⊃p ⊃⊃⊃⊃qr ⊃ ¬rr ⊃⊃rqq ⊃ ¬ ⊃⊃⊃qr ⊃ ¬rr ⊃⊃rqq ⊃⊃⊃qr ⊃ ¬rr ⊃⊃rqq
⊃⊃⊃⊃⊃qr ⊃ ¬rr ⊃⊃rqqpp.

[⊃ ∨ ⊃⊃ ∨ ⊃pq ⌐⊦⌐p ⊃⊃qp ⊃ ⌐ppr ⌐⊦ ⊃ ⌐ ⊃ ∨ ⊃pq ⌐⊦⌐p ⊃⊃qp ⊃ ⌐pp ⊃⊃r ⊃ ⌐ ∨ ⊃pq
⌐⊦⌐p ⊃⊃qp ⊃ ⌐pp ⊃ ⌐ ⊃ ∨ ⊃pq ⌐⊦⌐p ⊃⊃qp ⊃ ⌐pp ⊃ ∨ ⊃pq ⌐⊦⌐p ⊃⊃qp ⊃ ⌐pp]
?-
⊃ ∨ ⊃p ⊃ ∨ ⊃qr ⌐⊦⌐q ⊃⊃rq ⊃ ⌐qq ⌐⊦⌐p ⊃⊃ ⊃⊃ ∨ ⊃qr ⌐⊦⌐q ⊃⊃rq ⊃ ⌐qqp ⊃ ⌐pp.

[⊃⊃ ⌐⊦⌐p ∧ ⊃⊃ ⌐⊦⌐q ∧r ⌐q ∨r ⊃rq ⌐p ∨ ⊃⊃ ⌐⊦⌐q ∧r ⌐q ∨r ⊃rq ⊃⊃⊃ ⌐⊦⌐q ∧r ⌐q
∨r ⊃rqp]
?-
⊃⊃ ⌐⊦⌐p ∧q ⌐p ∨q ⊃qp ∧r ⌐ ⊃⊃ ⌐⊦⌐p ∧q ⌐p ∨q ⊃qp ∨r ⊃r ⊃⊃ ⌐⊦⌐p ∧q ⌐p
∨q ⊃qp.

[∧ ⊃⊃p ∧ ⊃⊃qr ∨r ⌐r ∨⌐q ∨q ⌐r ∨∧ ⊃⊃qr ∨r ⌐r ∨⌐q ∨q ⌐r ⌐∧ ⊃⊃qr ∨r ⌐r ∨⌐q
∨q ⌐r ∨⌐p ∨p ⌐∧ ⊃⊃qr ∨r ⌐r ∨⌐q ∨q ⌐r]
?-
∧ ⊃⊃ ∧ ⊃⊃pq ∨q ⌐q ∨⌐p ∨p ⌐qr ∨r ⌐r ∨⌐∧ ⊃⊃pq ∨q ⌐q ∨⌐p ∨p ⌐q ∨∧ ⊃⊃pq
∨q ⌐q ∨⌐p ∨p ⌐q ⌐r.

[∧∨ ⊃ ∧∨ ⊃pq ⌐⊦⌐p ⊃⊃qp ∨q ⌐pr ⌐⊦⌐ ∧ ∨ ⊃pq ⌐⊦⌐p ⊃⊃qp ∨q ⌐p ⊃⊃r ∧∨ ⊃pq ⌐⊦⌐p
⊃⊃qp ∨q ⌐p ∨r ⌐ ∧ ∨ ⊃pq ⌐⊦⌐p ⊃⊃qp ∨q ⌐p]
?-
∧∨ ⊃p ∧∨ ⊃qr ⌐⌐q ⊃⊃rq ∨r ⌐q ⌐⌐p ⊃⊃ ∧∨ ⊃qr ⌐⌐q ⊃⊃rq ∨r ⌐qp ∨ ∧ ∨ ⊃qr
⌐⌐q ⊃⊃rq ∨r ⌐q ⌐p.

[∨ ⊃⊃ ⌐∨ ⊃⊃ ⌐pp ∨pq ⊃⊃qp ∨q ⌐p ∨ ⊃⊃ ⌐pp ∨pq ⊃⊃qp ∨q ⌐p ∨∨ ⊃⊃ ⌐pp ∨pq
⊃⊃qp ∨q ⌐pr ⊃⊃r ∨ ⊃⊃ ⌐pp ∨pq ⊃⊃qp ∨q ⌐p ∨r ⌐∨ ⊃⊃ ⌐pp ∨pq ⊃⊃qp ∨q ⌐p]
?-
∨ ⊃⊃ ⌐pp ∨p ∨ ⊃⊃ ⌐qq ∨qr ⊃⊃rq ∨r ⌐q ⊃⊃ ∨ ⊃⊃ ⌐qq ∨qr ⊃⊃rq ∨r ⌐qp
∨∨ ⊃⊃ ⌐qq ∨qr ⊃⊃rq ∨r ⌐q ⌐p.

[∧ ⊃⊃p ∧ ⊃⊃qr ∨r ⌐r ∨ ⊃rq ⊃q ⌐r ∨∧ ⊃⊃qr ∨r ⌐r ∨ ⊃rq ⊃q ⌐r ⌐∧ ⊃⊃qr ∨r ⌐r
∨ ⊃rq ⊃q ⌐r ∨ ⊃ ∧ ⊃⊃qr ∨r ⌐r ∨ ⊃rq ⊃q ⌐rp ⊃p ⌐∧ ⊃⊃qr ∨r ⌐r ∨ ⊃rq ⊃q ⌐r]
?-
∧ ⊃⊃ ∧ ⊃⊃pq ∨q ⌐q ∨ ⊃qp ⊃p ⌐qr ∨r ⌐r ∨ ⊃r ∧ ⊃⊃pq ∨q ⌐q ∨ ⊃qp ⊃p ⌐q
⊃ ∧ ⊃⊃pq ∨q ⌐q ∨ ⊃qp ⊃p ⌐q ⌐r.[7]

The reader without experience in computational search may not readily appreciate how drastically the proof search space has to be pruned in order to find proofs this quickly for problems this long. The problems consist at the outset of one premiss and one conclusion. On one's first attempt to apply a

---

[7]These 33 problems were the hardest among 50,000 generated by John Slaney testing associativity of various two-place propositional schemata. They were all proved on a Sun4 in an average of less than three quarters of a second by a Prolog proof-finder for minimal logic, based on methods developed below.

rule of inference, one would either choose the premiss, and apply the appropriate elimination rule, or choose the conclusion, and apply the appropriate introduction rule. Which rule is appropriate in these two cases is determined by the dominant operator of the premiss or the conclusion respectively. Now as this method progresses, one generates in general sub-problems with multiple premisses rather than just single ones. Such, for example, could be the case if one were to try ⊃-introduction, and thereby assume the antecedent of the conclusion as a new extra premiss 'for the sake of argument'. Thus in general one has to decide not just between elimination and introduction, but also (when opting for elimination) which of the available premisses at that stage is worth trying as the major premiss.

Each attempted rule application produces further subproblems — those corresponding to the subordinate proofs for the application of the rule in question. Now *if* the search were entirely unconstrained by any knowledge of logical relations, problems such as those above would typically involve traversals of search-trees with more nodes than there are fundamental particles in the universe. So we have to prune the search space.

Some pruning is pretty straightforward — as, for example, when we observe that failure on *any* attempted ∧-elimination entails failure overall. It would be futile to try any alternative rule-applications in the light of such a failure.

The secret behind successful proof search is to incorporate into one's search algorithm as many such constraints as possible. The one just mentioned — regarding failure on an ∧-elimination — is obvious to anyone who appreciates the force of the connective ∧. Other very powerful constraints, however, demand a much more sophisticated understanding of the intricate structure of proofs — of how, if there is any proof at all, then there will be one of such-and-such form. Armed with results like this, one can confine one's search to proofs of that form. This would mean refusing to countenance a great many of the forking paths *prima facie* available to the hunter for proofs. In the chapters that follow we develop such constraints, just a few of which were involved in taming the problems above.

Time, Ockham said, is a garden of forking paths. The computational logician has to agree.

Chapter 4

From Oracles to Rationauts

It is advisable to be clear about ends before choosing means. We have seen in the previous chapter roughly what computational logic could seek to accomplish. But there is still much to be clear about.

A decidable logic is the simplest case of a *decidable theory* based on it. One can 'implement' a decidable theory in a variety of ways, ranging from the evidentially miserly to the evidentially generous.

Take the *decision problem* for a theory T:

> Find correct *Yes/No* answers to problems of the form X?-A, where X is a finite set of premises and A is a conclusion, and the question mark concerns the relation of deducibility within T.

There is a minimal response to the problem.

Bare oracles
One could give a *bare oracle* for the decision problem: a program that computed *Yes/No* answers and gave nothing else as output. This would be a case of extreme evidential miserliness. (It goes without saying that the answers would have to be *correct*. This is true also of the programs involved in the remaining responses.)

Then there are two intermediate responses.

Proof-finders
One can give full reasons for *Yes* answers, in the form of *proofs*. Proofs

are *finite* objects that we can check for correctness[1]. If we know that the proof-finding program is correct, however, we will not have to check them. Instead, we can use them to convince others who may be sceptical about positive answers. I call such a program a *proof-finder*.

A proof-finder for a given theory may be *complete* or *incomplete*. A *complete* proof-finder is one that gives at least one proof for each true statement of deducibility in the theory. An example would be any of the various formulations of classical propositional logic as a system of proofs based on (axioms and) rules of inference. An example, by contrast, of an incomplete proof-finder for a theory would be one which implemented an axiomatic system of arithmetic (such as Peano-Dedekind arithmetic), for the theory consisting of all true sentences of arithmetic[2].

A proof-finder could be complete — insofar as it would eventually, for any given provable problem, find a proof of it — and yet fail, on some unprovable problems, to yield even bare negative decisions. On these problems it would not terminate. A complete *and bounded* proof-finder is one which *will* eventually terminate with a negative verdict on any unprovable problem.

Even with a complete and bounded proof-finder one cannot tell, from its failure to respond by any given time, whether it had not yet had time to find a proof, or whether indeed there was no proof to be had. One simply has to wait. All one knows is that one will not have to wait for ever.

A *hypercomplete* proof-finder would do even better than a merely complete one: it would provide a distinct formal but faithful representation, in the form of a proof, for each of the possibly many different informal arguments that might serve to establish the validity of the transition, in the theory, from premisses X to conclusion A. Hypercompleteness is of necessity an informal notion, like that of computability; but it is important to bear it in mind as an ultimate desideratum. It will turn out, however, that if complete proof-finders written in any version of Prolog based on a depth-first strategy are to have remotely tractable tasks, they must abjure hypercompleteness. Otherwise the proliferation of alternative proofs on backtracking will greatly delay the making of correct negative (and positive) decisions.

Best of all proof-finders would be a hypercomplete and bounded one,

---

[1]It matters not whether we check the correctness of proofs 'by hand' or by means of yet another program — a *proof-checker*. Proof-checkers are not to be confused with proof-finders. The former verify proofhood. The latter find proofs.

[2]as we know from Gödel's incompleteness theorem for arithmetic. See K.Gödel, 'Über formal unentscheidbare Sätze der Principia Mathematica und verwandter Systeme I', *Monatshefte für Mathematik und Physik* 38, 1931, pp.173-198.

which was able to arrange all alternative proofs in some order of ascending complexity. The notion of such order, however, has yet to receive a satisfactory theoretical analysis.

Counterexample-finders

One can give full reasons for *No* answers, in the form of *couterexamples.* *Finite* counterexamples, like proofs, may be checked for correctness. Counterexamples may be used to convince sceptics about negative answers (but see below).

In the case of first-order mathematical reasoning, a counterexample will be a structure — finite or infinite — that forces all the premisses (makes them true), but does not force the conclusion. Some examples:

1. The well-known 'quantifier-switch' fallacy $\forall x \exists y\, Lxy?\text{-}\exists y \forall x\, Lxy$ is finitely counterexemplified in a domain consisting of two individuals who love each other but not themselves.

2. *Axioms for dense linear orderings?-'There is a least element'* can be infinitely counterexemplified in the rational numbers.

3. *Euclid's first four axioms?-Parallels postulate* was infinitely counter-exemplified by Beltrami's construction of a pseudospherical surface within the Euclidean plane (thereby giving a model of Lobachevskian plane geometry, in which there exists more than one line parallel to any given line, and through a point off the latter)[3].

4. *Zermelo-Fraenkel Set Theory, Axiom of Constructibility?-¬(Axiom of Choice)* was infinitely counter-exemplified by Gödel in the constructible universe of sets[4].

There are interesting philosophical problems, however, concerning the status of counterexamples to *X?-A* as supposedly *semantic* objects distinct from *proofs.* One can have philosophical reservations about the epistemic force or persuasive power of an *infinite* counterexample *qua* semantic object. In the case of an infinite counterexample, it could be maintained that what we really have in mind is a well-known *theory*, given by a set of axioms widely

---

[3]See E.Beltrami, 'Saggio di interpretazione della geometria non-euclidea', *Giornale di Matematiche* 6, 1868; also in his *Opere matematiche* Vol.1 (Milano: Napoli, 1902) at p.379.

[4]See K.Gödel, *The consistency of the axiom of choice and of the generalized continuum-hypothesis with the axioms of set theory*, Annals of Mathematics studies, no.3, Princeton 1940.

assumed to be consistent, and enjoying the counterexample as a 'model'[5]; and that the 'counterexemplification' of X?-A consists in the *proof-theoretic* facts that there are proofs of each of the premises in X from those axioms, and a proof that the conclusion A is inconsistent with those axioms. And one can easily contend that a *finite* counterexample is, once again, simply another way of coding *proof-theoretic* facts: facts concerning the existence of proofs of each of the premises in X from (an obviously consistent set of) axioms categorically describing the finite counterexample, and the existence of a proof that the conclusion A is inconsistent with those axioms[6].

Other kinds of counterexample in the *propositional* case may be *logical matrices*. These provide functional interpretations of the connectives over a set of designated and undesignated values. They have to be *sound* for the theory in the sense that every true statement of deducibility in that theory preserves designated value from premises to conclusion under every assignment of values to the propositional variables involved. A matrix counterexample to X?-A is then an assignment of values to the propositional variables involved in X and in A on which each premiss in X takes a designated value and A takes an undesignated value. This is a generalization of the familiar matrix $\{T,F\}$ for classical propositional logic, with T designated and F undesignated, and the usual truth-functional interpretations for the connectives. A class of sound matrices is *complete* for the theory if every false statement of deducibility in that theory has a counterexample using a matrix in that class. A sound and complete class of matrices is said to be *characteristic* for the theory. Another example of a characteristic class of matrices for a theory is the class of Jaskowski matrices for intuitionistic propositional logic[7]. One well-known way of showing that an axiomatisable propositional theory (including a logic) is decidable is to show that it has a characteristic class of *finite* matrices. For then the decision procedure can exploit two enumerations: one of proofs, by virtue of axiomatisability, and

---

[5]Examples: the theory of the natural numbers; the theory of the positive and negative integers; the theory of the rational numbers; the theory of the real numbers; the theories of various kinds of ordering — partial or strict, dense or discrete, bounded or unbounded, etc.

[6]For a fuller development of these revisionist views, see my 'The Withering Away of Formal Semantics?', *Mind and Language*, vol.1, 1986, pp.302-318.

[7]See S.Jaskowski, 'Recherches sur le système de la logique intuitionistique',*Actes du Congrès International de Philosophie Scientifique, VI Philosophie des mathématiques*, Actualités scientifiques et industrielles 393, Paris (Hermann & Cie.) pp.58-61; and G.Rose, *Jaskowski's truth-tables and realizability*, Doctoral dissertation, University of Wisconsin, 1952.

one of the finite sound matrices, testing the latter effectively to see whether they counterexemplify the problem in hand. Eventually either the first enumeration hits on a proof of the problem, or the second enumeration hits on a counterexemplifying finite sound matrix.

A counterexample-finder for a given theory may be *complete* or *incomplete*. A *complete* counterexample-finder is one that gives at least one counterexample for each false statement of deducibility in the theory. Even a sound but incomplete class of matrices can be useful for an algorithm of this third kind. But such a class is usually exploited for the fortuitous benefits it might bestow in attempts by a proof-finder to *prune the search tree in the space of possible proofs*[8].

It is possible for a complete and bounded proof-finder also to be a counterexample-finder (and of finite ones at that) without much further ado. The trace of a terminated and unsuccessful search by such a proof-finder for a proof in response to X?-A is, after all, a finitary object that bears effective scrutiny. It can play the epistemic role of a finite counterexample to X?-A to one who knows how to read it[9].

Finally, we have the full-blown response to the problem, which is to provide programs that I call:

Judicial reasoners
These are both proof-finders and counterexample-finders. That is, they give full *rationes decidendi* for their positive or negative verdicts on deductive problems. The best among these would be the *rationauts*. A rationaut would be able to give the shortest or simplest proof possible as its answer to any *provable* problem, and be hypercompletely ready to give, on request, all alternative proofs, in normal form, in ascending order of length, complexity, roundaboutness or what one will; and would be able to give the shortest or simplest counterexample possible as its answer to any *unprovable* problem.

---

[8] Such, for example, is the happy piecemeal provision made by John Slaney's matrix-generating program *MaGIC* (see reference in chapter 1) at the Automated Reasoning Project in the Australian National University. *MaGIC* will generate small sound matrices for decidable logics such as LR and M, and use them to counterexemplify sequents generated by inductive breakdown of deductive problems in those logics. It is able to speed-up proof search *in the context of the proof-finder of which it is a module* even though the matrices be drawn from a class that is *incomplete* for the logic concerned.

[9] I owe this observation to Seppo Keronen.

The way I propose to set about the task at hand is to aim, modestly, for a complete and bounded proof-finder for a well-chosen decidable propositional logic. It will not be hypercomplete. But its terminated unsuccessful searches could deliver traces playing the role of counterexamples to the unprovable problems concerned. The algorithm for finding proofs will be written in such a way, however, as to allow one to insert various *filters* on the sub-problems generated during the search. We shall have such filters anyway in connection with past recorded successes and/or failures[10]. In just the same way we could incorporate filters exploiting matrices, say, if we so wished. But we shall not actually do so. The only filters we shall employ, apart from those recalling past successes and failures, will concern the various sorts of syntactic relationships that subformulae can bear to containing formulae. That is, we shall try to exploit only the sort of syntactic evidence that it is reasonable to suppose the human reasoner can easily (perhaps often: subconsciously) descry.

One scientific theory can possess the pragmatic virtues of elegance and simplicity to a greater or lesser degree than another. It is a matter of trained taste on the part of practising scientists to decide between them on the basis of such considerations. So too in cognitive science: one can prefer computational models of human logical competence that exploit only what meets the eye syntactically, so to speak, to models that employ, say, nine-element Heyting algebras in their filtrations during search.

Our search heuristics will encode the effect of generally available trans-formations on proofs. It is desirable to get as many of these as possible to be invariant across choice of logical system, so that the proof-finder is more easily adaptable to whatever system one chooses to work in.

A first major challenge will be to *combine aspects of the bottom-up and top-down kinds of search* that human logicians undertake when trying to construct suasive arguments.

A second major challenge is to program a proof-finder that is short enough to admit of an informal *proof of correctness*. We shall be justifying the inclusion of every clause by proof-theoretic considerations concerning the logic in question.

A third major challenge is to *exploit the notion of the relevance of pre-misses to a conclusion* in a manner that I would call *endogeneous* to the proof-finder. One does not want the proof-finder to find proofs indiscrimi-nately, and only thereafter produce one that exhibits genuine relevance in

---

[10]See the discussion in Chapter 6 of *adverting* and *averting* proof-finders.

all its inference steps. One wants rather to use the requirements of relevance to avoid the irrelevant inferential directions and focus on the relevant. Challenges enough. Where, then, do we start?

Chapter 5

Minimal Logic in Perspective

Here are the rules for minimal logic:

$$\overline{A}^{(i)}$$
$$\vdots$$
$$\frac{\bot}{\neg A}{}_{(i)} \qquad \qquad \frac{\neg A \quad A}{\bot}$$

$$\overbrace{\overline{A}^{(i)} \qquad \overline{B}^{(i)}}$$
$$\vdots$$
$$\frac{A \quad B}{A \wedge B} \qquad\qquad \frac{A \wedge B \quad C}{C}{}_{(i)}$$

$$\overline{A}^{(i)} \quad \overline{B}^{(i)}$$
$$\vdots \qquad \vdots$$
$$\frac{A \qquad B}{A \vee B \quad A \vee B} \qquad \frac{A \vee B \quad C \quad C}{C}{}_{(i)}$$

$$\overline{A}^{(i)} \qquad\qquad\qquad \overline{B}^{(i)}$$
$$\vdots \qquad\qquad\qquad \vdots \quad \vdots$$
$$\frac{B}{A \supset B}{}_{(i)} \qquad\qquad \frac{A \supset B \quad A \quad C}{C}{}_{(i)}$$

The perspective will come later.

Our design problem is to program a proof-finder for a given logical system. Actually, the system is not so much 'given', as 'taken'. We choose the system. What criteria, ideally, govern that choice?

1. We should have a philosophical justification of the system's correctness. Its rules should exactly respect the meanings of the logical operators.

2. We should be able to establish its adequacy to demands placed on a logic for applications in science and mathematics; and in technical areas of philosophy, such as truth theory.

3. It should be computationally tractable, at least insofar as one is seeking to emulate and/or improve upon the efficiency of human reasoning.

Now the system M of minimal logic does not quite satisfy the first two of these criteria. Still, we choose it as our starting point: for the simple reason that it will eventually provide smooth access to a system that *does* satisfy those criteria. This is the system IR of *intuitionistic relevant* logic[1]:

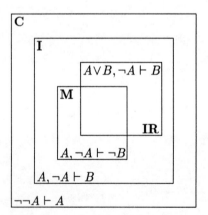

One difference between M and IR has to do with restrictions on applications of rules of inference that involve discharge of assumptions. In M, one can

---

[1]See my *Anti-Realism and Logic, Vol.1: Truth as Eternal*, Oxford University Press, 1987.

blithely apply such rules without having actually *used* the assumptions in question in the subproof(s). Thus each discharge stroke in the rules given above could be construed as labelled with a diamond ($\diamond$) to indicate that discharge is *permissible*, not *obligatory*. In IR, by contrast, one must, in the interests of relevance, have made honest use of certain of these assumptions before being able to apply a rule 'discharging' them. In the following rules for IR, the demand that the assumption should actually have been used is indicated by labelling the discharge stroke with a box ($\Box$). This stricture of *no vacuous discharge* would simply distract the reader with a background in conventional logic, who is concerned to master the *computational* aspects of these investigations. I have therefore chosen, for reasons of gentler exposition and simpler programming at the outset, to defer my computational treatment of IR until that for M is fully accomplished.

For the record, however, here are the rules for IR:

$$\overline{A}^{\,\Box(i)}$$

$$\vdots$$

$$\frac{\bot}{\neg A}_{(i)} \qquad\qquad \frac{\neg A \quad A}{\bot}$$

$$\frac{\overbrace{\overline{A}^{\,\Box(i)} \qquad \overline{B}^{\,\Box(i)}}}{}$$

$$\vdots$$

$$\frac{A \quad B}{A \wedge B} \qquad\qquad \frac{A \wedge B \quad C}{C}_{(i)}$$

(The boxes in $\wedge$-E mean that *at least one* of A, B must have been used.)

$$\overline{A}^{\,\Box(i)} \qquad \overline{B}^{\,\Box(i)}$$

$$\vdots \qquad\qquad \vdots$$

$$\frac{A}{A \vee B} \quad \frac{B}{A \vee B} \qquad\qquad \frac{A \vee B \quad \bot/C \quad \bot/C}{\bot/C}_{(i)}$$

$$\overline{A}^{\,\diamond(i)} \qquad \overline{A}^{\,\Box(i)} \qquad\qquad \overline{B}^{\,\Box(i)}$$

$$\vdots \qquad\quad \vdots \qquad\qquad\qquad \vdots \quad \vdots$$

$$\frac{B}{A \supset B}_{(i)} \quad \frac{\bot}{A \supset B}_{(i)} \qquad\qquad \frac{A \supset B \quad A \quad C}{C}_{(i)}$$

The formulation of ∨-elimination using the $\perp/C$-notation is to be understood as follows: if either of the cases concludes with $\perp$, then one may bring the conclusion of the other case down as the main conclusion.

There is another difference also between M and IR. M does not have the absurdity rule, allowing one to derive anything from a contradiction. IR does not have it either, but, by way of judicious compensation, has the specially devised forms of ⊃-introduction and ∨-introduction given above. These secure the validity of disjunctive syllogism and, most importantly, *the relevantisability of intuitionistic proofs from consistent sets of premisses.*

In IR one can exploit the relaxed rule of ∨-elimination to derive disjunctive syllogism as follows:

$$\cfrac{A\vee B \qquad \cfrac{\neg A \quad \overline{A}^{(1)}}{\perp} \qquad \overline{B}^{(1)}}{B}\,{}^{(1)}$$

One might think that, given the trivial proof of $A\vee B$ from A by ∨-introduction, one could thereby get a proof of B from $\neg A, A$. But in IR this does not go through. The accumulated 'proof' resulting from this naive manoeuvre would have $A\vee B$ standing as conclusion of the introduction rule and as major premiss of the elimination rule. Such an abnormality is not permitted in proofs in the system IR: no application of an introduction rule may be followed immediately by an application of the corresponding elimination rule. This means that the most one could 'glean' from the two little proofs just mentioned — the trivial proof of $A\vee B$ from A, and the proof above of disjunctive syllogism — is the normal form residue of the 'proof' resulting from their accumulation. And this residue is no more than the little proof

$$\cfrac{\neg A \quad A}{\perp}$$

which shows that the newly accumulated premisses from the naive manoeuvre are inconsistent. This indeed is a general feature of IR. Accumulation of proofs, followed by normalizing residuation, produces either a proof of the original conclusion, or a proof that the newly accumulated premisses are inconsistent. We therefore have transitivity of proof only where it matters

— where the newly accumulated premisses are consistent. This means that *if intuitionistic mathematics is consistent, it can be relevantised*[2].

I mention these subtleties of IR by way of further explanation of why we start with the philosophically sub-optimal choice of M as our system for computational treatment. For the specially devised rules of IR just mentioned would simply intrude distracting detail for the reader whose initial concern is to master the basic features of the treatment developed.

The reader familiar with natural deduction will have noticed a difference between the format of my elimination rules and their format in the usual Prawitz-style presentation of systems of natural deduction. In particular, the elimination rules for $\wedge$ and $\supset$ are here given in what I call *parallel* form[3]. The Prawitz-style rules

$$\frac{A \wedge B}{A} \qquad \frac{A \wedge B}{B} \qquad \frac{A \quad A \supset B}{B}$$

are avoided for reasons of computational economy. The reader will see how the parallel version of $\wedge$-elimination, for example, can reduce the number of occurrences of a conjunctive major premiss for elimination within a proof. Instead of having to repeat the premiss *along with its derivation* every time use is made of it, one can simply write it down once and by means of the parallel rule discharge all occurrences of A and of B that have resulted from possibly multiple use of $A \wedge B$.

There is another important feature of our formulation of the rules for M and for IR. Major premisses for elimination 'stand proud' in our proof trees; they never stand as conclusions of any rules. This makes our formulation a *hybrid* between the Prawitz-style natural deduction formulation and the Gentzen-style sequent formulation. It also means, in effect, that we allow *only proofs in normal form*. This is specially advantageous in constraining proof-search.

Such search is often described as *bottom-up* or as *top-down*. In a logical context, as opposed to a logic programming context, what this means is

---

[2] The detailed justification of these proof-theoretic claims can be found in Part II of my *Anti-Realism and Logic, op.cit.*, and in its strongest form (dealing with $\supset$ primitive) in my 'Intuitionistic mathematics does not need *ex falso quodlibet*', typescript. A similar result holds for CR, the relevant version of classical logic. See my 'Perfect Validity, Entailment and Paraconsistency', *Studia Logica* XLIII, 1984, pp.179-198.

[3] The parallel form of $\wedge$-elimination is used by Paulson, but not the parallel form of $\supset$-elimination. See his paper 'A Generic Theorem Prover', *Journal of Automated Reasoning* 5, 1989, at p.378.

the following. A *bottom-up* strategy is one that goes to work on the *conclusion* of the deductive problem posed, and breaks the conclusion up into its constituents, in order to pose further deductive sub-problems with those constituents as *new conclusions*. And a *top-down* strategy is one that goes to work on the *premisses* of the deductive problem posed, breaking them up into their constituents, in order to pose further deductive sub-problems with those constituents featuring as *new premisses*. A *combined* strategy would do both these things, using the rule of *Cut* to 'glue together' the fragments thus created. The conclusions of prooflets obtained by the top-down strategy would be grafted onto the premisses of prooflets obtained by the bottom-up strategy. This indeed reflects the way competent human logicians go about finding proofs. They are guided both by the shape of the conclusion, insofar as it dictates what introduction rule should be applied to yield it; and by the shape of the premisses, insofar as these dictate what elimination rules should be applied in order to unpack the information contained in them.

A nice feature of both sequent and natural deduction systems is that proof-search proceeds by this kind of inductive breakdown of the deductive problem posed. There are, however, important differences between the two systems. In natural deduction, one can break premisses into smaller components *as one descends a branch in the proof tree*. Not so, however, with a sequent proof: here, the sequents get longer and more complicated as one descends any branch in a sequent proof tree. This is because the rules of *elimination* in natural deduction are matched in the sequent system by rules for *introducing the logical operators on the left* of sequents. Thus when working with a sequent system, one's search strategy can be *wholly bottom-up* in the sense that one takes the deductive problem posed (that is, a sequent) and tries to build a sequent proof upwards, which will have that sequent as its conclusion. This will involve not only trying to introduce logical operators on the *right* of sequents (corresponding, in natural deduction, to attempted introductions of logical operators in conclusions), but also trying to introduce logical operators on the *left* of sequents (corresponding, in natural deduction, to attempted eliminations of logical operators in premisses). In the latter case, one has the further fortuitous benefit of achieving, with just one introduction of an operator on the left of the sequent, the effect that in natural deduction would have to be obtained by *repeating the derivation of the major premiss for the corresponding elimination(s)*, devoting a fresh copy of that derivation to every occasion of elimination.

The pro's of *sequent* systems are therefore:

1. The order of bottom-up proof search matches the order of inductive breakdown

2. One can minimize the number of times a premiss is used

The con's of sequent systems, however, are:

1. Each node in the proof-tree is labelled by a whole sequent, which is *not* economical

The pro's of *natural deduction* systems are:

1. They yield insights into the 'lines of reasoning' represented by a proof, *via* the subformula property for branches in normal form proofs

2. Each node in a proof-tree is labelled with only one formula, which *is* economical

The con's of natural deduction systems are:

1. Whenever one uses a sentence as a major premiss for an elimination, one has to repeat its own derivation

In our *hybrid* system we seek to combine the pro's of both the system of natural deduction and the sequent system, and avoid their con's. In our system:

1. Proof-search proceeds by inductive breakdown of the deductive problem posed. Indeed, *bottom-up* proof search in the hybrid system, *all by itself*, can match the order in which human logicians normally effect inductive breakdown of the deductive problem posed. Human logicians, as already remarked, use a combination of bottom-up and top-down methods. They break up premisses and conclusions 'in parallel', so to speak. As in the sequent system, we can reflect this in the hybrid system with a pure bottom-up search strategy.

2. We minimize the number of times a premiss is used.

3. We are able to conserve and exploit the insights into 'lines of reasoning' as given by the subformula property for branches in normal form Prawitz-style proofs.

4. Each node in a proof-tree is labelled with only one formula.

5. Finally, by way of a new advantage, differing discharge requirements can effect the difference between different kinds of connective (e.g. between conjunction and fusion).

These claims would appear to make the hybrid system exceptionally appealing. It promises both logical rigour and computational vigour.

How does the hybrid system preserve those insights into 'lines of reasoning' so nicely represented by the branches within natural deduction proof trees?

The answer is to be had from the notion of the *spine* of any natural deduction in normal form that ends with an elimination[4]. The spine of such a deduction is that sequence of formula occurrences that can be traced up from the conclusion at the very bottom, through the premisses of applications of elimination rules immediately above. It ends on one of the undischarged assumptions of the deduction, standing of course as a major premiss for an elimination. Remember that in a natural deduction in normal form, no major premiss for an elimination can stand as the conclusion of an introduction.

Every major premiss for an elimination in any natural deduction in normal form belongs to a unique maximal spine determining a unique subdeduction. The latter is the subdeduction whose conclusion is the bottommost formula occurrence of the spine.

Suppose we have a spine in such a natural deduction of the conclusion A from premisses among which is B, and that this spine is the sequence $A, C_1, \ldots, C_n, B$, of which none is a disjunction. Then each member of the spine is an immediate (accessible positive) subformula of its immediate successor. And in the hybrid proof Π corresponding to the natural deduction in hand, the spine will be re-located in a series of links between assumptions discharged by elimination rules, and their major premisses. (An example soon to be given will illustrate this situation.) The topmost major premiss of the spine, namely B, will stand bottom-leftmost of the hybrid proof Π. It will be the major premiss of what is now the terminal (elimination) step of Π. That step will discharge C_n in the immediate subproof Π_1 of Π. C_n will be the major premiss of the terminal (elimination) step in Π_1. That step will discharge C_{n-1} in the immediate subproof Π_2 of Π_1. C_{n-1} will be the major premiss of the terminal (elimination) step in Π_2. That step will

---

[4]See my 'Natural deduction and Gentzen sequent systems for intuitionistic relevant logic', *Journal of Symbolic Logic* 52, 1987, pp.665-80.

discharge C_{n-2} in the immediate subproof Π_3 of Π_2. C_{n-2} will be the major premiss of the terminal (elimination) step in Π_3 ... and so on, until we reach A, which will be the (trivial) immediate subproof Π_{n+1} of Π_n.

Now for the promised illustration. In the following natural deduction, the spine is the rightmost branch:

$$B \quad \dfrac{\dfrac{C \land (B \supset (D \land A))}{B \supset (D \land A)}}{\dfrac{D \land A}{A}}$$

We can see how in the following hybrid proof corresponding to this natural deduction, the spine becomes inverted, with its members linked by discharges:

$$\dfrac{C \land (B \supset (D \land A)) \qquad \dfrac{\dfrac{B \supset (D \land A)}{}^{(3)} \qquad B \qquad \dfrac{\dfrac{D \land A}{}^{(2)} \quad \dfrac{}{A}^{(1)}}{A}_{(1)}}{A}_{(3)}}{A}$$

This example shows clearly how reasoning 'down' from premisses in a natural deduction is matched in a hybrid proof by building 'up' from below. This is why I have chosen the term 'hybrid' to describe the new kind of proof: it combines *into upward search alone* both the upward search (from the conclusion) and downward search (from the premisses) that one engages in with natural deductions. Later we shall see how important this is when we formulate algorithms in Prolog for finding proofs. Because of the way Prolog builds up ground terms in the course of a computation, we shall have a great gain in elegance and efficiency by devising proof-terms that can be constructed in a bottom-up fashion.

Finding proofs in minimal logic is strictly more difficult than doing so in classical logic: the decision problem for M is PSPACE-complete, while that for C is NP-complete. Notwithstanding this difference, it is worth pointing out that a proof-finder for minimal logic is *ipso facto* a proof-finder for classical logic:

THEOREM: $\Delta \vdash_C \phi \Leftrightarrow \Delta, \neg\phi \vdash_M \bot$.

THEOREM[5]: $\Delta \vdash_C \bot \Leftrightarrow \Delta \vdash_M \bot$.

Thus a proof-finder for M can be deployed as one for C; one simply looks for a *reductio ad absurdum* of the premisses with the negation of the conclusion, should the latter be other than $\bot$. This 'proof-finder' for C may run more slowly as a result of dealing with an inherently PSPACE-complete problem; but at least it will be complete and correct for C if it is so for M.

We have located M with respect to C, I and IR. We have given the rules of inference of M, and motivated a new 'hybrid' system of proof based on them. We have explained why M is the starting point for our computational investigations. It is time now to embark on them.

---

[5] D.Leivant, 'Syntactic translations and provably recursive functions', *Journal of Symbolic Logic* 50, 1985, pp.682-688; cf. also my 'Truth Table Logic, with a Survey of Embeddability Results', *Notre Dame Journal of Formal Logic* 30, 1989, pp.459-484.

Chapter 6

Exploring the Rules

The move to parallel forms of elimination rule for $\wedge$ and $\supset$ has interesting ramifications. It limits our freedom to re-order the application of rules in a proof in normal form. Recall that a normal proof in Prawitz-style natural deduction has no sentence occurrence standing as the conclusion of an introduction and as the major premiss of the corresponding elimination. Not every Prawitz proof is normal. A proof in the hybrid system (using rules in parallel form), however, is normal *by definition*, in that major premisses for eliminations have to 'stand proud'. They therefore do not stand as conclusions of introductions. *Nor do they stand as conclusions of eliminations.* And this is what limits one's freedom to re-order steps in a hybrid proof. A simple illustration will suffice. We start with a Prawitz-style proof in normal form:

$$
\cfrac{
  \cfrac{A\wedge(B\vee C)}{B\vee C} \qquad
  \cfrac{\overset{\displaystyle -(1)}{B} \quad B\supset(D\wedge E)}{D\wedge E} \qquad
  \cfrac{\overset{\displaystyle -(1)}{C} \quad C\supset(D\wedge E)}{D\wedge E}
}{\cfrac{D\wedge E}{D}}{}_{(1)}
$$

Note that the $\vee$-elimination can be shuffled down past the $\wedge$-elimination that follows it:

$$
\cfrac{
  \cfrac{A\wedge(B\vee C)}{B\vee C} \qquad
  \cfrac{\cfrac{\overset{\displaystyle -(1)}{B} \quad B\supset(D\wedge E)}{D\wedge E}}{D} \qquad
  \cfrac{\cfrac{\overset{\displaystyle -(1)}{C} \quad C\supset(D\wedge E)}{D\wedge E}}{D}
}{D}{}_{(1)}
$$

This freedom in re-ordering the final two eliminations is not to be had in the hybrid system. There is only one hybrid proof of our little problem, and it corresponds in an obvious way to the *second* Prawitz proof above, but not to the first:

$$
\frac{\displaystyle A\wedge(B\vee C)\quad \frac{\displaystyle (6)\underline{\hspace{1cm}}\quad \frac{\displaystyle (5)\underline{\hspace{0.5cm}}\quad B\supset(D\wedge E)\quad \frac{\displaystyle (2)\underline{\hspace{1cm}}\ \ \underline{\hspace{0.3cm}}(1)}{D\wedge E}\quad D_{(1)}}{B}\quad D}{B\vee C}\quad \frac{\displaystyle (5)\underline{\hspace{0.5cm}}\quad C\supset(D\wedge E)\quad \frac{\displaystyle (4)\underline{\hspace{1cm}}\ \ \underline{\hspace{0.3cm}}(3)}{D\wedge E}\quad D_{(3)}}{C}\quad D}{D}}{D}
$$

This illustrates a quite general cautionary note on transforming any Prawitz proof Π (in normal form) into its hybrid counterpart: steps of $\vee$-elimination are *prima donnas* and demand attention first.

As observed in the previous chapter, every major premiss for an elimination in any normal Prawitz proof belongs to a unique maximal spine. Major premisses of $\vee$-eliminations can be shuffled downwards within these spines by means of transformations of the general form

$$
\begin{array}{c}
\underline{\quad}^{(i)}\ \ \underline{\quad}^{(i)} \\
A\quad B \\
\Pi_1\quad \Pi_2\quad \Pi_3 \\
\dfrac{A\vee B\quad C\quad C}{\dfrac{C\qquad\qquad (\Sigma_1)\ (\Sigma_2)}{D}}{}_{(i)}
\end{array}
\quad\longmapsto\quad
\begin{array}{c}
\underline{\quad}^{(i)}\qquad\qquad \underline{\quad}^{(i)} \\
A\qquad\qquad B \\
\Pi_2\qquad\qquad \Pi_3 \\
\dfrac{\Pi_1\ \ \dfrac{C\ (\Sigma_1)\ (\Sigma_2)}{D}\quad \dfrac{C\ (\Sigma_1)\ (\Sigma_2)}{D}}{\dfrac{A\vee B\qquad\qquad D}{D}}{}_{(i)}
\end{array}
$$

Here the conclusion C of the $\vee$-elimination in the preimage is the major premiss of an elimination: precisely *which* elimination determining whether one has no minor subproofs Σ, or just Σ_1, or both Σ_1 and Σ_2. With $\wedge$-elimination there is no minor subproof to worry about. With $\neg$-elimination and $\supset$-elimination there is just one; and with $\vee$-elimination there are two.

After each such transformation there is a new pattern of maximal spines of subproofs of the transform. The major premiss $A\vee B$ now belongs to a spine that does not contain C immediately below $A\vee B$. Instead, it contains D immediately below $A\vee B$. C meanwhile has had two new occurrences created, each of which belongs to a distinct new maximal spine *ending* on an occurrence of D immediately below it.

This process of downward shuffling must eventually terminate, yielding a normal proof in which every major premiss for $\vee$-elimination is the *second* member of the maximal spine that it determines. On this spine there will be no other major premises for ∨-elimination. We call the resulting proof the *shuffled version* of the original proof. It is of course in normal form, and has exactly the same conclusion and undischarged assumptions as the original. Moreover if the original ended with an elimination, then the shuffled version ends with ∨-elimination. And if the original ended with an introduction, so too now does the shuffled version — indeed, with the same one. We refer to this feature as the *preservation of introductory or eliminative character*.

Recipe for hybridising a normal Prawitz proof Π[1]:

Take the shuffled version Σ of Π. If at any stage you encounter a proof ending with an *introduction*, simply mimic it in the hybrid system and proceed to the immediate subproofs. Whenever you encounter a proof ending with an *elimination*, re-cast the topmost elimination on its spine in the appropriate form dictated by the rules for the hybrid system. Repeat this step until you reach the bottom of the spine. As each elimination is thus re-cast, the transforms you require of immediate subproofs will be obtained by recursive application of this recipe.

Ω

There is an easy transformation f in the other direction, taking one from a hybrid proof to a Prawitz proof in normal form. f distributes across introduction rules, and the elimination rules for ∨ and ¬. f applied to a hybrid proof ending with ∧-elimination calls for a copy of a Prawitz-style ∧-elimination step to be grafted over each undischarged assumption occurrence of a conjunct of the major premiss in the f-transform of the subproof for hybrid ∧-elimination. Finally, the f transform of a hybrid proof Ξ of C ending with a ⊃-elimination with major premiss $A ⊃ B$ is obtained as follows. Take the f-transform Π of the minor subproof of A, and the f-transform Σ of the major subproof of C from (among other assumptions) B. Extend Π with one step of Prawitz-style ⊃-elimination, with major premiss $A ⊃ B$ and conclusion B. Call the result Θ. Now graft a copy of Θ over every undischarged assumption occurrence of B in Σ. The result is the sought

---

[1]Cf. proof of Theorem 3, concerning transformation of normal natural deductions into cut-free sequent proofs, in my 'Natural deduction and Gentzen sequent systems for intuitionistic relevant logic', *loc.cit.* It employs essentially the same idea.

f-transform of the hybrid proof Ξ.

THEOREM: The *Cut Rule*

$$\frac{X \vdash A \quad A, Y \vdash B}{X \vdash B}$$

is admissible for the system of hybrid proof (for M).

Proof: Take hybrid proofs Π of A from X, and Σ of B from A,Y. Find their f-transforms, which are Prawitz proofs in normal form. Graft a copy of the f-transform of Π over each undischarged assumption occurrence of A in the f-transform of Σ. Normalize the resulting proof; and then hybridise the result.

Ω

Clearly, if a normal Prawitz proof Π ends with an elimination, so too does its hybridised version. And if Π ends with an introduction, so too does its hybridised version. So both shuffling and hybridising preserve introductory or eliminative character.

A hybrid proof encodes the structural information of a sequent proof, but does so more economically. This is because single sentences, rather than whole sequents, label its nodes. But in creating a hybrid proof from a normal natural deduction we have had to shuffle $\vee$-eliminations downwards. Thus the target hybrid proof may well contain redundant chunks of proof that occur but once in the source natural deduction. A glance at our example above bears this out. The source natural deduction contains only one copy of the elimination step from $D \wedge E$ to E. When the $\vee$-elimination is shuffled downwards, however, two copies of this step are created, one for each of the case-proofs. Final conversion to hybrid form preserves this prolixity. So this will prove to be a redundancy expense in the sought objects of our computations. The normality requirement (corresponding to the absence of cuts in a sequent proof) entails repetition of chunks of proof that could otherwise be avoided by recourse to cuts.

This may well point to an important computational saving by human mathematicians. In their judicious choice of lemmata as deductive half-way houses, they may be effecting computational economies. These economies might be squandered in the attempt to make a *direct* deductive transition from axioms to theorems, unaided by the logical orienteering points provided by their lemmata.

So normality, or freedom from cuts, is bought at the cost of redundancies within proofs. But it is a price worth paying, and one against which we can safely hedge. We shall be pursuing a bottom-up search strategy. For this to work, the proofs sought must be in the sequent or hybrid system. In order to keep the associated redundancy payments to a minimum, we need some good book-keeping. Whenever a deductive sub-problem presents itself we ought to check (against our records of past successes) whether we have indeed already solved the problem in the course of our earlier computation. If we have, then we simply enter a 'pointer' to the earlier solution. Call this the *ditto tack*.

A tree proof yields an *acyclic graph* proof — the kind of object sought by the ditto tack — by means of a straightforward procedure. Identify all redundant chunks of tree proof, bearing in mind that these can be nested. Replace all copies of any most deeply nested redundant chunk with pointers to a master copy of that chunk. Repeat this procedure until there are no more redundancies. Note that master copies, after the first step of the procedure, can have pointers within them.

An algorithm that deploys the ditto tack I shall call an *adverting* algorithm. Adversion modifies the mathematical nature of the objects sought and found. Instead of conceiving of these proofs as trees, with their nodes labelled by sentences, we can conceive of them as acyclic graphs, with no redundancies (apart from trivial proofs, should we wish to avoid the degenerate case of a pointer to A as a proof of A from A).

An algorithm that makes use of past *failures*, I shall call an *averting* algorithm.

By taking the ditto tack, adverters hew to the path of *least computational discovery*. (Here we rule out recall as an act of discovery.) This is not to be confused with the path of least computing time, or least memory space. Recording the results of successful sub-computations, and checking them as often as turns out to be necessary to avoid any redundancies, could well *increase* the time and space overheads in computing solutions to deductive problems. This is because the algorithm may not be able to exploit past successes frequently enough to make the hoarding of inferential laurels worthwhile. Indeed, this turns out to be quite a problem in Prolog, where the use of a dynamic predicate $alreadydone(\_,\_)$ with frequent look-up tends, in the writer's experience, to *increase* run-times, even on large problems with many $\lor$-eliminations.

I take comfort, however, from that experience; for it shows how efficient the algorithm for genuine proof discovery is. I am as happy with earlier delivery of tree proofs with redundancies as with later delivery of acyclic graph proofs with none. But my algorithm can cater for both tastes; it comes in both adverting and averting versions.

There is a logical metatheorem behind the safe pursuit of proof by cases by either kind of algorithm:

THEOREM: $X, A \lor B \vdash C \Leftrightarrow X, A \vdash C$ and $X, B \vdash C$ (where we assume without loss of generality that X does not contain $A \lor B$)

Bearing this in mind, we can state

ALGORITHMIC RULE 1
If there is a disjunction among the premisses, then — subject to whatever priority ranking may apply to disjunctive premisses — look for a hybrid proof ending with $\lor$-elimination

Such *up-front $\lor$-eliminations* gives frequent cause for aversion. For if either of the case-proof searches fails, we can immediately terminate the overall proof search. Greater proof-theoretic sophistication is needed, however, for the priority-ranking of premisses; more on that below. We confine ourselves at this stage to the observation that if either disjunct is in X, then elimination of *that* disjunction would obviously be superfluous. Such a disjunction could be safely 'backgrounded', and never drawn on as a major premiss for elimination.

The theorem above has an obvious companion for conjunction. A conjunctive premiss has exactly the logical power of its two conjuncts:

THEOREM: $X, A \land B \vdash C \Leftrightarrow X, A, B \vdash C$ (where we assume without loss of generality that X does not contain $A \land B$)

Thus we have

ALGORITHMIC RULE 2
If there is a conjunction among the premisses, then — subject to whatever priority ranking may apply to conjunctive premisses — look for a hybrid proof ending with $\land$-elimination

We call this *up-front* ∧-*elimination*. Once again, if the sub-problem admits of no proof, neither does the overall problem. Major premisses for ∧-elimination are superfluous, of course, if both conjuncts are already available as premisses; and accordingly can be backgrounded.

Rule 1 and Rule 2 illustrate very clearly what is meant by the *inductive breakdown* of a deductive problem. Each poses an overall problem, and then directs attention to sub-problems that are essentially *simpler*. Such a sub-problem involves a set of premisses and a conclusion that together are of *lower logical rank*, in a sense that can be precisely defined. One tentative measure is the total number of occurrences of logical operators and propositional variables involved in the premisses and the conclusion. In each sub-problem for ∨-elimination, *the disjunctive major premiss is replaced by a disjunct not already available among the premisses*. In the sub-problem for ∧-elimination, *the conjunctive major premiss is replaced by the conjuncts*, at least one of which is not already available among the premisses. Thus on the tentative measure we have reduced complexity; and any measure we may subsequently adopt would have to agree with the tentative measure on this.

The obvious algorithmic rules associated with the introduction rules for logical operators are easily seen to involve just such inductive breakdown, as do Rule 1 and Rule 2 above, dealing respectively with elimination of ∨ and of ∧.

What about elimination of ¬ and of ⊃? Here we have to proceed more carefully, and tolerate what turns out to be a more gradual inductive breakdown. Let us look at ¬-elimination first.

Our overall problem, let us suppose, is to derive ⊥ from a set X of premisses, among which is ¬B. With major premiss ¬B, the rule of ¬-elimination calls for a so-called *minor proof* of B. *But the premiss set for the minor proof is the same*: namely, X. A moment's reflection on the simple example ¬A, ¬$A ⊃ A$?-⊥ shows that one needs all the premisses for the minor for ¬-elimination.

This means that the breakdown, as measured by logical complexity of premisses and conclusion, is not monotonic. A more refined measure of inductive complexity, however, registers this breakdown as break*down*. It incorporates a record of such minor problems posed; and the algorithm enjoins one to avoid any node of the search tree that involves posing it again. Something like[2] this strategem is *necessary* in order to prevent infinite loop-

---

[2] I say 'something like' with good reason: see the discussion in Chapter 14 of the *Dyckhoff device*, *fettering* and *hobbling*. They all prevent infinite loops in proof search,

ing in the execution of the search algorithm, as the following example of a non-terminating search on the unprovable problem $\neg\neg A?\text{-}\neg A$ shows:

$$
\vdots
$$

$$
\cfrac{\cfrac{\cfrac{\dfrac{\neg\neg A \quad \neg A}{\bot}}{\neg\neg A \quad \neg A}}{\cfrac{\bot}{\neg\neg A \quad \neg A}}}{\cfrac{\bot}{\neg A}}
$$

We need also, however, to show that the strategem in question is *sufficient* to prevent looping. Let the tentative measure of inductive complexity intimated above be $\mu(X; A)$. For a set S of deductive problems, $\mu(S)$ is determined from the values $\mu(d)$, d a member of S, in some straightforward way (by addition, say). The more refined measure could then be as follows. Let the complexity of a deductive problem $X?\text{-}A$ be the ordered pair $(\mu(S), \mu(X; A))$, where S is the set of all possible deductive subproblems that may still be posed. Forbidding another look at a minor is tantamount to striking it from S, thereby reducing complexity in this coordinate of the new measure. When A is $\bot$, this reduces complexity overall. For $(\mu(S-\{Y, \neg B?\text{-}\bot\}), \mu(Y, \neg B; B))$ is lower than $(\mu(S), \mu(Y, \neg B; \bot))$.

The same need for a more refined measure of inductive breakdown arises in the case of $\supset$-elimination. Here the overall problem is to derive C from the set X of premises, among which is $A \supset B$. With major premiss $A \supset B$, the rule of $\supset$-elimination calls for a minor proof of A, once again with X as its set of premises. The same considerations apply as in the case of $\neg$-elimination. But, unlike $\neg$-elimination, $\supset$-elimination has a major sub-proof as well as a minor one. In the major, one seeks the overall conclusion C not from the set X of premises, but from *the set that results from X upon replacing $A \supset B$ by B*. If we fail to prove the major, we fail to find a proof for $X?\text{-}C$.

The method of loop-detection and prevention just discussed is but one of four methods available for dealing with the problem posed by minors for $\supset$-elimination and $\neg$-elimination. In a later chapter we shall discuss some others. They are what I shall call the *Dyckhoff device*, the method of *fettering* and the method of *hobbling*.

---

but by different means.

So far we have discussed inductive breakdown of a deductive problem on the assumption that a decision has already been made to apply, say, an introduction rule, or to apply an elimination rule with a particular major premiss chosen from the available premisses. But we have not yet indicated how *these* strategic decisions are to be made.

We turn to this question in the next chapter.

Chapter 7

How does one search for proofs?

Remember we are building up hybrid proofs from below. After each tentative step the residual problem or problems are ones that are simpler than the preceding one, on the inductive measure explained above. At every stage the micro-problem takes this form:

Have we failed on this one before? If so, fail again.[1]
(Then any other filters that ingenuity may deliver; after which, if the problem is still with us, we ask:)
Is the conclusion already among the premisses?
If so, take it as a proof of itself from itself.[2]
If not, we have to choose some formula to go to work on! That is, either
(I) we settle on the conclusion, and try applying the *introduction* rule for its dominant operator; or
(E) we focus on some premiss, and try applying the *elimination* rule for its dominant operator.

The filters stop wild goose chases. The (non-atomising) triviality condition stops one from taking Humpty Dumpty apart and then putting him back

---

[1] If we use the procedural programming device of *cuts* ('!') in Prolog, this failure filtration will be effected simply by failure, after encountering a cut in the program, to unify the instance in hand of the problem proof predicate with any clause heads involving that predicate.

[2] When this move is restricted to propositional atoms, we shall say that the algorithm follows an *atomising strategy*.

again. Then one goes foraging:

   (I) is the *introduction strategy*; *(E)* is the *elimination strategy*.

And an awful lot depends on how one's algorithm toggles between them.

The above form of the micro-problem is actually that of a pure *depth-first search strategy*, according to which one filters a problem and then forages, taking sub-problems in serial turn. A little breadth could be added to the algorithm's vision by slightly changing the order in which we do things upon breakdown by a rule (such as ∧-introduction or ⊃-elimination) that calls for more than one sub-proof. (For these purposes we do not, in the case of an elimination rule, count its major premiss as a sub-proof.) I shall call such rules *splitting* rules. With splitting rules, one can apply filters first to *all* the sub-problems, before foraging on any of them. Earlier failure on a later sub-problem can thereby pre-empt what would turn out to have been fruitless albeit successful foraging on the earlier sub-problems. Real breadth of vision, of course, would come from *parallellising* the whole process, so that the deductive sub-problems generated by any tentative application of a rule were not taken in turn, but rather simultaneously; with failure on any one of them immediately shutting down work on the others.

Apart from full-blown parallelization, there is another method that enables one to hew as much as possible to the nether regions of the *AND-OR* search tree. It enables one sometimes to avoid putting effort into reaching giddy heights of early (partial) success on the search tree — partial success that will only be dashed later by lower (partial, hence total) failures on related (conjoined) branches. This method is called *iterative deepening*. With iterative deepening, one carries out *depth-limited* depth-first searches, successively increasing the depth limit until one conclusively succeeds or fails. Moreover, one tries to deepen the search *evenly* across the width of the search tree. Iterative deepening is especially useful when there is the danger of *infinite* runaway searches down any one branch. This makes it useful for *first-order* logic, in which the runaway branches can corespond to models with infinite domains. But with our decidable propositional logics we are not forced to resort to this method. Once properly pruned, their search trees (on any deductive problem) are *finite*.

It should be stressed that the choice of a search method *once one's search space has been properly understood, pruned and defined*, is an issue that is *orthogonal* to the deeper issue of *how* one so prunes and defines the search space. All the proof-theoretical results in this book are pressed in the service of *lopping great chunks off the search tree*. How one then chooses to explore the topiary that remains is a matter of individual taste and programming

preferences. If a search method is thought of as a general way of choosing
one's hops from one node to the next, then we might say: *lopping is independent of hopping; but the more lopping, the faster any kind of hopping.*
For the sake of simplicity, I have confined my investigations so far to
depth-first versus breadth-first methods. Interestingly, I have not found
that modest breadth makes for a faster proof-finder. But again this might
have more to do with computational costs incurred by Prolog itself than
with the algorithmic credentials of modest broadening *per se*. Broadening
involves memory costs, because of queuing; and look what happened to the
Polish economy.

There is, however, a logical reason why depth-first proof search might
in general be faster than breadth-first. In a depth-first search on the first
sub-problem at any tentative rule-application, one might record many more
failures on the way to eventually finding the first sub-proof. These failures
are then available for filtration of the second sub-problem (and further sub-
problems it may generate), which accordingly — if it is to fail — could
well fail earlier. The advantages of parallel failure filtration are therefore
offset by the coarseness of the filters, for want of a good history education.
If this is so, then it may be worthwhile trying for modest breadth only
with those filters whose likelihood of success does not thus depend on the
history of the computation. A *relevance* filter would be a good example here:
one that imposed a *necessary* condition for deducibility formulated, say, in
terms of effectively determinable patterns of recurrence of subformulae in
premises and conclusion. But again, the relative efficacy of using such filters
in a broader strategy depends on how close they come to being *sufficient*
conditions for deducibility. If they are necessary but nowhere near sufficient,
all the broad or quasi-parallel effort of filtering before foraging will be to
lesser avail.

The failure filter should be called *dynamic*; the relevance filter, *static*.
Both impose necessary conditions for deducibility. The closer the latter come
to sufficiency, the more *highly charged* they are. Moral: *confine dynamic
filters to a depth-first strategy, and broaden only with those static filters that
are highly charged.*

Filters apply to problems of the form $X?\text{-}A$. Dynamic filters consult a
fluctuating data-base of entries of that form. In the course of a computation,
new entries may be *asserted* into the data-base; and existing entries may be
retracted. Both assertion and retraction involve scanning all existing entries
up to some point that is determined by how they are *ordered* within the data-
base. This is necessary with assertion in order to avoid redundant entries;

and is necessary with retraction in order to avoid an oversight. There is, therefore, a significant saving to be made if the data-base can be *partitioned* according to the form of its entries X?-A. This reduces the extent to which such scanning has to be undertaken; and the savings can be significant.

One obvious partition involves only two classes: entries of the form X ?-$\perp$, and entries of the form X?-A, where A is not $\perp$. The latter class might be partitioned further into two classes: one with A atomic, the other with A compound. Or indeed, we could go further and partition the compound ones also into classes according to their dominant operators.

Filters whose data-bases involve *no* partitioning into non-trivial sub-classes are called *homogeneous*; and those whose data-bases *do* involve such partitioning are called *heterogeneous*.

Further moral: *make filters as heterogeneous as possible*; that is, *divide and rule*.

We turn now to foraging. The average deductive problem poses an *embarras de richesses*. The connoisseur, however, knows whether to go for the single *objet d'art* (the conclusion) or the collection of *bric-à-brac* (the premisses); instinctively knows, too, which of the latter to choose first for closer appraisal. I shall call this the *choice problem*. Its satisfactory solution is the main feature of a good proof-finder.

A proof-finder follows the *elimination strategy* if it chooses premisses before the conclusion, even when the latter is compound. It follows the *introduction strategy* if it chooses the conclusion before any of the premisses, even when one of the latter is compound. It follows a *mixed strategy* if its choices are not thus strictly partitioned, but can alternate between premisses and conclusion, depending on syntactic circumstances.

I shall design a mixed strategy. It will be *non-trivially* mixed. That is, it will toggle between introductions and eliminations in a way that has significant 'blocks' of introduction rules alternating with significant 'blocks' of elimination rules. This goes beyond the *trivial mixture* that would be involved by combining the following *algorithmic rule of trivial proof* with an otherwise pure elimination strategy:

> *RULE OF TRIVIAL PROOF: Given any problem X?-A, check whether A is in X. If so, then take A as a proof of itself. If not, make this further check before proceeding with the search for a non-trivial proof: if A is a disjunction, check whether either disjunct is in X — and if one is, take the obvious one-step proof by $\vee$-introduction as the sought proof; if A is a conditional, check*

whether its consequent is in X — and if it is, take the obvious one-step proof by $\supset$-introduction (with vacuous discharge) as the sought proof.

This rule of trivial proof, with the further check that it recommends for disjunctive and conditional conclusions, ensures that, for example, the problems

$$A \wedge B, C \ ?\text{-} \ A \vee C$$
$$A, A \supset B, C \ ?\text{-} \ B \vee C$$
$$B \wedge C, C \ ?\text{-} \ A \supset C$$
$$B, B \supset C, C \ ?\text{-} \ A \supset C$$

receive their obvious one-step proofs respectively, rather than the two-step proofs that can be constructed by first performing the obvious eliminations before introducing the main operator of the conclusion[3]. With the last of these problems, the more prolix alternative can also be avoided by the method of *premiss reduction:*

get rid of $B \supset C$ as a premiss if you already have C as a premiss,

or, equivalently, the method of *backgrounding redundant premisses:*

never choose as major premiss for an elimination any conditional whose consequent is already available as a premiss; or any disjunction one of whose disjuncts is already available as a premiss; or any conjunction both of whose conjuncts are already available as premisses.

Now let us consider the relative order in which any eliminations should be attempted. Then we shall consider the order, relative to eliminations, in which each kind of introduction should be attempted.

Consider first the relative ordering of $\wedge$-elimination and $\vee$-elimination. Assume we have a problem $X?\text{-}E$ to which both could apply — there is a premiss $A \wedge B$ and there is a premiss $C \vee D$ in X. Now $\vee$-elimination

---

[3]What is meant here by 'first performing ... before ...' is that a *Prawitz proof* would have the elimination higher up and the introduction lower down; while a *sequent proof* or *hybrid proof* would have both steps, of which the elimination could be the final one.

is a splitting rule, while ∧-elimination is not. Thus if one were to try ∨-elimination first, the ∧-elimination would have to be performed *twice* — once within each case-proof. By applying ∧-elimination first, however, one gets into the two case-proofs by means of only *one* application of ∨-elimination.

The two residual sub-problems — deriving E from A, B, C and the remaining premisses, and deriving E from A, B, D and the remaining premisses — are the same, regardless of the order in which we attempt the two eliminations. Thus neither of the two orders brings any special benefit such as faster failure filtration.

Accordingly, we choose to apply ∧-eliminations before ∨-eliminations.

And both these kinds of elimination should precede any attempted ⊃-elimination. This is because failure on *any* sub-problem arising from the former entails overall failure; whereas failure *on a minor* for ⊃-elimination does not. Failure on a minor just means that we might have chosen the wrong ⊃-premiss, with a nasty (unprovable) antecedent. There may be other ⊃-premisses, with different (and *provable*) antecedents, and with the same consequent – or at least, with a consequent that will do insofar as a proof of the major is concerned. Or indeed one may not need to use any ⊃-premisses at all; in which case, all the more reason for trying them last, if at all. For in that case all the work on their minors would have been an expensive waste. Still, there is at least this consolation from failure with a ⊃-elimination: if we are successful *on its minor*, but fail on its major, then the problem fails overall. This is because of the following obvious result that holds because ⊃-introduction may have vacuous discharge:

THEOREM: $X, A \supset B \vdash C \;\Rightarrow\; X, B \vdash C$

That leaves only ¬-elimination among the elimination rules for consideration. Here our choice problem is solved for us by the fact that ¬-elimination has ⊥ as its conclusion. Thus for any deductive problem with some other conclusion, ¬-elimination is not even applicable. When it *is* applicable, however, we give it the first crack of the whip *after* up-front ∧- and ∨-eliminations. This may give rise to some qualms that we might too easily follow a wrong scent in pursuit of a contradiction that is actually more hidden than we might otherwise realise. Take, for example, $\neg B, C, C \supset (A \wedge \neg A)?\text{-}\bot$. The choice is between applying ¬-elimination to $\neg B$ (which will prove futile), or applying ⊃-elimination to $C \supset (A \wedge \neg A)$. It would seem that undertaking ¬-eliminations immediately after up-front ∧- and ∨-eliminations and before any ⊃-eliminations will lead us up a garden path. But I submit in defence of this strategy that the competent human logician's apparent plumping for ⊃-elimination 'first' in our example is best explained in terms of suppressed awareness of actually having scanned the rival possibility of a ¬-elimination at the outset, and having found it wanting.

Bald contradictions are probably better first choices than hidden ones, once dominant occurrences of ∧ and of ∨ have been disposed of by applying their elimination rules up-front.

In like fashion, if one is trying to prove a sentence A, and is considering which of the ⊃-premises to use for an elimination, it pays to try first those of the form $B \supset A$. (This is suggested by the thought that $\perp$ can be conceived of as a special (atomic) sentence, and $\neg B$ as a way of saying $B \supset \perp$.)

Once ¬-eliminations have been tried (after up-front ∧- and ∨-eliminations) on problems with $\perp$ as conclusion, the invocation of remaining possible eliminations will follow the order that would govern attempted proof by elimination of atomic sentences in general.

As far as eliminations are concerned, then, the order of attempts should be:

1. ∧-elimination

2. ∨-elimination

3. ¬-elimination, should the conclusion be $\perp$

4. ⊃-elimination — where for conclusion A, we try major premisses of the form $B \supset A$ first, and also generally try first those conditionals whose antecedents are already available as premisses (or, in the case of an adverting algorithm, already known to be provable from the premisses)

Because the algorithm is recursive, this ordering will ensure that as soon as a hint of formerly 'hidden' contradiction is unearthed — in the sense that its negated horn surfaces, and up-front ∧- and ∨-eliminations have left it in a field littered only with implications and negations — the algorithm will quickly latch on to it as a major for ¬-elimination, and root around for a proof of the minor.

Now the ordering arrived at above is still provisional; for we have thought little thus far about how to choose any particular conjunctive premiss when in stage (1); or how to choose any particular disjunctive premiss when in stage (2); or how to choose any particular negated premiss when in stage (3); or how to choose any conditional premiss when in stage (4). Within each of these stages, there is presumably a more refined ranking to be had. Indeed, one might even be able so to refine them that the borderlines between stages become blurred. One might find that among the conditional premisses, for example, there are candidates for elimination that are so glaringly good that they should take precedence over some of the disjunctive premisses that enjoy lowly status among the disjunctions.

I shall provide such refinements.

In order to motivate them, however, I have to conduct the foreshadowed enquiry into the relative ordering of introductions with respect to the provisional gross ordering of eliminations given above. Note that the following theorems ensure that introductions of $\neg$, $\wedge$ and $\supset$ can be undertaken with complete peace of mind:

THEOREM: $X \vdash \neg A \Leftrightarrow X, A \vdash \bot$

THEOREM: $X \vdash A \wedge B \Leftrightarrow X \vdash A$ and $X \vdash B$

THEOREM: $X \vdash A \supset B \Leftrightarrow X, A \vdash B$

Introductions of $\neg$, $\wedge$ and $\supset$ are therefore called *safe* introductions. An attempt at such an introduction cannot go wrong, unless the overall problem is to fail. The worst that can go 'wrong', should the overall problem admit of proof, is that an untimely application of one of these rules could *delay* the discovery of a proof. This could happen if, for example, the compound conclusion was going to drop out of the premisses whole anyway: that is, was best arrived at by a series of eliminations followed by the trivial step. In such a case, premature attempts at introduction would see one having to undertake yet more eliminations in order to extract the smaller constituents thus brought into play. An example would be $A \wedge (B \wedge C)?\text{-}B \wedge C$. It can be proved by a single step of $\wedge$-elimination. It is unnecessarily roundabout (thinking in the natural deduction mode for a moment) to derive B from the premiss, then derive C, and then (by $\wedge$-introduction) to obtain $B \wedge C$. But this is what we would in effect be doing by building up a hybrid proof from below whose final step is $\wedge$-introduction: that is, by trying $\wedge$-introduction before $\wedge$-elimination in our search strategy.

How best, then, to try $\neg$-, $\wedge$-, and $\supset$-introductions so as not thereby to delay discovery of a proof? We simply need a way of seeing that the conclusion is unlikely to 'drop out' by elimination. This we shall provide in the next chapter: we shall define what it is for a conclusion to be an *accessible positive* subformula of a premiss. When it is one, there is a chance that it can be made to 'drop out' by elimination. When it is not, the introduction of ¬, ∧ and ⊃ is a sensible option.

But what about disjunction? Unfortunately, ∨-introduction is *unsafe* as an early step of a deductive strategy. This is because $X \vdash A \lor B$ does not guarantee that either $X \vdash A$ or $X \vdash B$. The simple example $A \lor B$?-$B \lor A$ makes it clear that ∨-elimination should be tried before ∨-introduction. Associativity problems such as $A \lor (B \lor C)$?-$(A \lor B) \lor C)$ also make this clear. Indeed, if one tries introductions before eliminations with long associativity problems one may as well go out to lunch while the proof-finder runs; with eliminations before introductions, however, the proofs are swiftly found. And it is not just ∨-eliminations that ought to be tried first. Making the premiss of the last problem a conjunct of a conjunctive premiss, or the consequent of a premiss whose antecedent can be proved, shows clearly that elimination of ∧ and of ⊃, too, should be tried *before* the introduction of ∨ in the conclusion.

So with disjunctive conclusions, elimination should be the preferred first move rather than ∨-introduction: provided, that is, that there is a disjunction suitably buried in the premisses to provide the disjunctive purchase that premature ∨-introduction cannot buy. And *this* requires that there be a premiss containing a disjunction as what I call an *accessible positive subformula*. Only then might the disjunction possibly surface to provide the exploration of cases needed to secure the disjunctive conclusion[4].

I shall in due course define what is meant by 'accessible positive subformula', of both a *direct* and an *indirect* variety. This notion will also enable us to refine the rankings within the respective classes of major premisses for elimination of ∧, ∨ and ⊃.

Pending that refinement, the general moral so far is this:

First try all ∧-, ∨-, and ¬-eliminations, in that order (with elimination of ¬ of course being applicable only if the conclusion is ⊥).

Then try introduction; but, in the case of an ∨-introduction, only if there is no accessible positive disjunction among the premisses.

Then, if (and, so it turns out: only if) the conclusion is atomic or disjunctive, try ⊃-eliminations, choosing first premisses of the

---

[4]I shall call this feature of the algorithm *informed elimination for disjunctive conclusions*.

form $B \supset A$ for overall conclusion A, and in general trying first those conditionals whose antecedents are already available as premisses (or, in the case of an adverting algorithm, already known to be provable from the premisses).

Finally, try $\lor$-introduction for a disjunctive conclusion.

What, now, is this notion of accessibility?

Chapter 8

Accessibility and Relevance

8.1 Accessibility

The best way to display the logico-grammatical form of a sentence in propositional logic is by means of an inverted tree, whose nodes are labelled by logical operators, and whose leaves are labelled by propositional variables. For example, the formula $(A \wedge (B \vee C)) \supset ((A \wedge B) \vee C)$ is represented by the tree

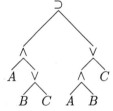

This permits easy tracing of subformula relations. It also enables one to tell at a glance what occurrences of subformulae lie within the scope of what occurrences of operators. The *dominant* operator of a compound formula is at the topmost node. Each subformula occurrence is represented by the subtree determined by its own topmost node within the containing tree.

Take any formula, with topmost node O. Take any subformula of it, as determined by its own topmost node O' identical to or below O. The path leading from O' up to O tells us all we need to know about *what kind of subformula* we are dealing with. This path consists, in the trivial case, of one node. In the non-trivial case, it consists of a sequence of distinct nodes beginning with O' and terminating with O.

When dealing with negations, let us think of them as *binary*, with second argument $\perp$. This allows us to treat $\perp$ as a special kind of atomic formula: one that never occurs as a formula in its own right, but only as the second argument of negations. This ploy helps us to assimilate deductive problems of the form $X?\text{-}\perp$ to ones of the form $X?\text{-}A$, for atomic A; and thereby to unify our strategic thoughts about proof search.

The first kind of subformulae I shall discuss are already well-known in the literature: positive and negative subformulae.

DEFINITIONS

Every formula is a positive subformula of itself.

If $\neg A$ is a positive subformula of B, then $\perp$ is a positive subformula of B, but A is a negative subformula of B. If $A \wedge B$ is a positive subformula of C, then so are A and B; and similarly for disjunction. If $A \supset B$ is a positive subformula of C, then B is a positive subformula of C, but A is a negative subformula of C.

To complete the definition, we repeat the last paragraph with 'positive' and 'negative' interchanged:

If $\neg A$ is a negative subformula of B, then $\perp$ is a negative subformula of B, but A is a positive subformula of B. If $A \wedge B$ is a negative subformula of C, then so are A and B; and similarly for disjunction. If $A \supset B$ is a negative subformula of C, then B is a negative subformula of C, but A is a positive subformula of C.

This can easily be re-interpreted in terms of the paths mentioned above. Take a parity counter capable of two readings: *plus* and *minus*. At O', set your parity counter to *plus*, and note that you have already reached O'! Now trace upwards from O' to O. Conserve parity as you reach any $\wedge$ or $\vee$, and as you reach any $\supset$ or $\neg$ *from the right*[1]. Change parity as you reach any $\supset$ or $\neg$ *from the left*. If your parity counter reads *plus* immediately after reaching O, then (the subformula determined by) O' is a positive one; if it reads *minus*, then it is a negative one.

THEOREM: In a deductive problem $X?\text{-}A$, only positive subformulae of premises in X or negative subformulae of A could ever occur as possible *premises* of sub-problems reached by inductive breakdown. Only negative subformulae of premises in X or positive subformulae of A could ever occur as their *conclusions*.

---

[1] Remember that we are thinking of $\neg$ as binary, with second argument $\perp$.

DEFINITION

O' determines an *accessible positive subformula* just in case (O' is O or, if not,) your parity counter never changed from *plus* as you traced up from O' to O; that is, you never hit ¬ or ⊃ from the left.

Moreover, O' determines a *direct* accessible positive subformula just in case (O' is O or, if not,) you hit *no* occurrence of ∨; and determines an *indirect* one just in case O' is not O and you hit *at least one* occurrence of ∨.

Examples: In the following formulae the asterisks mark the dominant operator occurrences of their *direct* accessible positive subformulae, and daggers mark those of their *indirect* ones:

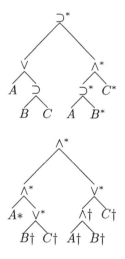

THEOREM: In every minimal proof with *atomic* conclusion A, A is an accessible positive subformula of some undischarged assumption

Proof: By induction on complexity of proofs. The basis is obvious. For the inductive step we consider the proof Π of A by cases according to its last step R — which, since A is atomic, must be an elimination. If R is ¬-elimination, A must be ⊥, which is an accessible positive subformula of the major premiss (a negation), which is an undischarged assumption of Π; and we are done. Now suppose R is one of the other elimination rules. Take any subordinate proof Σ for R of which A is the conclusion. By inductive hypothesis, A is an accessible positive subformula of some undischarged assumption B in Σ. Now inspect the elimination rules and their patterns of discharge. You will see that these rules discharge only such assumptions as are accessible positive subformulae of their major premisses. Now R either discharges B or it does not. If R *does* discharge B, we have that A is an accessible positive subformula of B, which in turn is an accessible positive subformula of the major premiss P of R; whence by transitivity A is an accessible positive subformula of P, which is an undischarged assumption in Π. If, on the other hand, R does *not* discharge B, the result is immediate, since B will be undischarged in Π. Ω

This theorem provides a good filter for proof search. I call it the

ATOMIC ACCESSIBILITY FILTER:

> *Fail any deductive problem X?-A for atomic A if A is not an accessible positive subformula of any premiss.*

And it provides a good heuristic also:

ACCESSIBILITY HEURISTIC

> *In choosing a major premiss for a tentative terminal elimination when seeking a proof for the problem X?-A, give high priority to those that contain A as an accessible positive subformula. Indeed, give even higher priority to those that contain A as a direct accessible positive subformula, especially when no premiss contains a disjunction as a direct accessible positive subformula.*

This is an excellent heuristic, even (perhaps: especially) when confined to atomic A. Whether to apply it to all sentences A depends on how efficient a method one has for 'reading' accessibility. With one's attention narrowed to accessibility of *atoms* one can provide representations of formulae that display facts about accessibility 'on the surface', so to speak, in a way that minimizes computing costs when one wants access to them. With more complex accessible subformulae, however, the representations could become too cumbersome, offsetting the heuristic gains to be had in the non-atomic case.

If this heuristic is implemented only for A *atomic*, we call it the *atomic accessibility heuristic*.

Let us call a proof in Prawitz-style natural deduction and in normal form, a *Prawitz proof*. If it ends with an elimination, let us call it an *E-type* Prawitz proof. If it contains an application of ∨-elimination let us call it *disjunctive*. If it contains no application of ∨-elimination let us call it *non-disjunctive*. (A non-disjunctive proof may still contain an application of ∨-*introduction*.)

THEOREM: For every non-disjunctive E-type Prawitz proof of A, A is a direct accessible positive subformula of some undischarged assumption.

Proof: By induction on the complexity of proofs. The basis is obvious. For the inductive step we consider the proof of A by cases according to the last step R, which by hypothesis is an elimination. If R is ¬-elimination, A must be ⊥, which is a direct accessible positive subformula of the major premiss (a negation). By normality, this negation stands in turn as the conclusion of an elimination step. By inductive hypothesis, the negation is a direct accessible positive subformula of some undischarged assumption. Hence so too is A (= ⊥). When R is ∧-elimination or ⊃-elimination, we have A as a direct accessible positive subformula of the major premiss, which in turn, by normality, stands as the conclusion of an elimination step. By inductive hypothesis, this major premiss is a direct accessible positive subformula of some undischarged assumption. Hence so too is A. Since R by hypothesis cannot be ∨-elimination, we are done. Ω

LEMMA: In every disjunctive E-type Prawitz proof, some major premiss for ∨-elimination is a direct accessible positive subformula of some undischarged assumption.

Proof: Take the shuffled version of the proof. The second member of its spine is a major premiss for ∨-elimination; and on that spine there are no others. This major premiss is therefore a direct accessible positive subformula of some undischarged assumption — namely, the final member of the spine. Ω

THEOREM: If Π is an E-type Prawitz proof of A and no undischarged assumption of Π contains a disjunction as a direct accessible positive subformula, then A is a direct accessible positive subformula of some undischarged assumption of Π.

Proof: By the last lemma, Π is non-disjunctive. By the last theorem we are done. Ω

THEOREM: If Π is a Prawitz proof of A and no undischarged assumption of Π contains a disjunction as a direct accessible positive subformula and A is *not* a direct accessible positive subformula of any undischarged assumption of Π, then Π ends with an introduction.

Proof: Obvious by the previous theorem. Ω

We now have another good heuristic for proof search. I call it the

INTRODUCTION HEURISTIC:

> *With any deductive problem X?-A,*
> *(i) if no member of X contains either A or any disjunction as a direct accessible positive subformula, one need try only proof by introduction;*
> *(ii) if no member of X contains A as an accessible positive subformula, and A has ¬, ∧ or ⊃ dominant, one need try only ¬-, ∧- or ⊃-introduction respectively.*
> *(iii) if A is a disjunction, check at the outset whether either of the disjuncts is available as a premiss in X; if A is a conditional, check at the outset whether its consequent is available as a premiss in X.*

Part (i) is justified by the last theorem above. Part (ii) is justified by the fact, already remarked in the previous chapter, that ¬-, ∧- and ⊃-introduction are *safe* rules anyway. All that part (ii) does is recommend when it would be most timely to apply these introduction rules. And part (iii) coincides with our rule of trivial proof earlier, embodying the common sense in having a quick look to see whether there is a one-step proof staring one in the face.

Note that when A is atomic (and cannot therefore be the conclusion of an introduction) the provision of the introduction heuristic is that of the atomic accessibility filter.

Part (i) of the introduction heuristic can conflict with Algorithmic Rule 1. That is, if there is a conjunctive premiss, but no premiss contains either the conclusion or any disjunction as a direct accessible positive subformula, part (i) enjoins introduction; while Algorithmic Rule 1 enjoins elimination of ∧. In such cases we perform this elimination rather than the introduction. We now have the sought refinement of stages (2), (3) and (4) of the previous chapter: that is, further ranking among themselves of conjunctive premisses; of disjunctive premisses; and of conditional premisses. Suppose we are seeking a proof of A from X. Take the *conjunctive* premisses in X. Try them as major premisses for ∧-elimination in the following more refined order:

First choose conjunctive premisses in which A occurs as a *direct* accessible positive subformula, if there are any

Secondly, choose ones in which A occurs as an *indirect* accessible positive subformula, *but not as a direct one*, if there are any

Finally, try any remaining ones[2]

Likewise, take the *disjunctive* premisses in X. Try them as major premisses for ∨-elimination in the following more refined order:

First choose disjunctive premisses in which A occurs as a (perforce *indirect*) accessible positive subformula, if there are any

Then try any remaining ones

Finally, take the *conditional* premisses in X. Try them as major premisses for ⊃-elimination in the following more refined order:

First choose conditional premisses in which A occurs as a *direct* accessible positive subformula, if there are any

Secondly, choose ones in which A occurs as an *indirect* accessible positive subformula, *but not as a direct one*, if there are any

Finally, try any remaining ones

The terms *direct subclass*, *indirect subclass*[3] and *residual subclass* suggest themselves naturally for these partitions just given.

---

[2] These are lumped together into one class for the time being. We defer the question of how to choose more discriminately *within this class*. A similar remark applies to the 'remainders' mentioned below.

[3] Note that this is the subclass of premisses of the kind in question (conjunctive, disjunctive or conditional) that contain A as an indirect accessible positive subformula *but not as a direct one*. If the latter qualification were omitted, the direct subclass and the indirect subclass would not in general be disjoint, and the algorithm would repeat work unnecessarily. In general, priority classes must form *partitions*.

Having discriminated priority subclasses this finely, we are now in a position to consider some variations of the priority ordering of major premises for elimination. We might wish to try, for example, all the direct subclasses first, then all the indirect ones, and finally all the residual ones. In so doing we would be subordinating the importance of the dominant logical operator to that of whether the contemplated major premiss contains the sought conclusion in a certain way. The ordering given above, however, is the one for which I have settled. This is the one in which we take premises first on the basis of what their dominant operators are, and only thereafter on the basis of whether and how they contain the sought conclusion as a subformula.

The introduction heuristic is justified by the last theorem above and the observation made earlier that the introductory or eliminative character of the final step of a Prawitz proof is preserved under shuffling and hybridisation. Note that our last theorem is about *Prawitz* proofs. Although it legitimates the introduction heuristic guiding search for *hybrid* proofs, one should not too hastily conclude that, in all cases where the preconditions for that heuristic are satisfied, the only *hybrid* proofs will be ones ending with an introduction. All we can say with certainty is that, if there is a hybrid proof, then there is one ending with an introduction. Hence one will not sacrifice logical completeness by confining one's search to proofs ending with an introduction.

For example, as dictated by our last theorem, there is only an introductory *Prawitz* proof for $A \wedge B?\text{-}B \wedge A$:

$$\frac{\dfrac{A \wedge B}{B} \quad \dfrac{A \wedge B}{A}}{B \wedge A}$$

But there are two *hybrid* proofs. One ends with an introduction, showing that the introduction heuristic is correct in this case — one *need* try only proof by introduction. The other ends with an elimination, showing that our last theorem for *Prawitz* proofs does not hold for *hybrid* proofs. The introductory and eliminative hybrid proofs are, respectively,

$$\frac{\dfrac{\overline{A \wedge B} \quad B^{-(1)}}{B} \quad \dfrac{\overline{A \wedge B} \quad A^{-(2)}}{A}}{B \wedge A}_{(1)} \qquad\qquad \frac{A \wedge B \quad \dfrac{\overline{B}^{-(1)} \quad \overline{A}^{-(1)}}{B \wedge A}}{B \wedge A}_{(1)}$$

The question now arises as to where best to locate the introduction heuristic within the algorithm. Since its preconditions render up-front ∨-eliminations inapplicable, it would appear that the choice is between having it immediately before ⊃-eliminations, or having it before any eliminations of any kind. If it were located *after* ⊃-eliminations, it would be otiose. For the algorithm by this stage would be trying proof by introduction anyway. The greater simplicity of proofs by ∧-elimination compared with their introductory rivals speaks in favour of having the introduction heuristic immediately before ⊃-eliminations. Pursuit of proof by introduction (in cases where, if any proof exists, then an introductory one does) yields quicker breakdown of the conclusion to more succinct constituents, on which the accessibility heuristic can then be made to bite. By breaking the conclusion up we can then exploit lines of accessible positive containment to focus our choices of major premises for elimination. This consideration is even more telling if we implement the accessibility heuristic only for problems X?-A with A *atomic*.

By way of illustration of these considerations, take the problem

$C, C \supset (A {\wedge} B), D \supset (B {\wedge} E)$?- $B {\wedge} A$.

The preconditions for the introduction heuristic are satisfied. Suppose, however, that we chose not to follow its advice to seek a proof by introduction. Then we would be looking for a major premiss for ⊃-elimination. The direct and indirect subclasses for such choice turn out, however, to be empty. One is left with the residual subclass, containing the two conditional premisses. In general, with even more distracting premiss sets than that of this example, we could waste a good deal of effort trying major premisses from the residual subclass with no further syntactic guidance. In the present example, we might happen to choose $D \supset (B {\wedge} E)$ before $C \supset (A {\wedge} B)$. But if instead we *do* follow the advice of the introduction heuristic, we find ourselves seeking subproofs (for ∧-introduction) for the following two problems:

$C, C \supset (A {\wedge} B), D \supset (B {\wedge} E)$?- B
$C, C \supset (A {\wedge} B), D \supset (B {\wedge} E)$?- A

and certainly on the second of these the wrong choice of $D \supset (B {\wedge} E)$ as the major premiss for ⊃-elimination will be avoided altogether. For the accessibility heuristic now has a chance to bite, and make us focus on $C \supset (A {\wedge} B)$ as the major premiss for ⊃-elimination in pursuit of the conclusion A.

In the case of disjunctive conclusions, we have seen that elimination is the preferred strategy should there be any premiss containing a disjunction as an accessible positive subformula. This is the same as saying: 'should there be any premiss containing a disjunction as a *direct* accessible positive subformula'. For in such a case there has to be a *topmost* accessible positive ∨-node in the premiss's tree representation, which is to say there has to be a *direct* one.

Recall that a *disjunctive* proof is one that contains an application of ∨-elimination; and an *E-proof* is a (hybrid) proof whose final step is an elimination (*not necessarily of* ∨). We now define a *terminally disjunctive* proof to be an E-proof that has as the major premiss of its final step a formula containing an accessible positive disjunctive subformula.

THEOREM: Suppose Π is an E-proof of a disjunction $A \lor B$ from the set X of undischarged assumptions, and that $A \lor B$ has only E-proofs from X. Then Π can be transformed into a terminally disjunctive proof Π' of $A \lor B$ from X.

Proof: *Basis*: Π is a one-step proof of $A \lor B$ from X. So the final step in Π must be either ∧-elimination or ⊃-elimination. In the former case, $A \lor B$ will be a conjunct of the major premiss; in the latter case $A \lor B$ will be the consequent of the major premiss. Now for the *Inductive Step*: Π ends with ∧-elimination, ⊃-elimination or ∨-elimination. In the latter case we are done. So we need only consider the first two cases.

(i) Π ends with ∧-elimination. Let the subproof for this elimination be Σ. Σ has conclusion $A \lor B$, but it cannot end with ∨-introduction. For if it did, the terminal step of ∧-elimination in Π could be shuffled up past this terminal introductory step of Σ, thereby producing a proof of $A \lor B$ from X whose final step is ∨-introduction, contrary to assumption. So Σ is trivial or ends with an elimination. If it is trivial, we are done. So suppose now that Σ ends with an elimination. By inductive hypothesis applied to Σ, there exists a *terminally disjunctive* Σ' of $A \lor B$ from the undischarged assumptions of Σ. Replace Σ by Σ' within Π to get Θ, say. Remember that Θ, like Π, is here being assumed to end with ∧-elimination. There are three cases to consider for Θ, arising from the three possibilities concerning Σ': that Σ' ends with a step σ of ∨-elimination, ∧-elimination, or ⊃-elimination. Now in each of these three cases the terminal ∧-elimination in Θ can be shuffled upwards past σ to produce the sought proof Π', which will be terminally disjunctive since Σ' is.

(ii) Π ends with ⊃-elimination. Here the reasoning is similar to case (i), with Σ now being the major subproof for the ⊃-elimination.

Ω

So, in the case of disjunctive conclusions, major premises for ⊃-elimination
are to be chosen as follows:

> First try any conditional that contains a direct accessible positive
> disjunction, and whose antecedent is already available among
> the premisses (or, in the case of an adverting algorithm, already
> known to be provable from the premisses).
>
> Then try any remaining conditional *provided that it contains a
> direct accessible positive disjunction.*

By the last theorem, it is unnecessary to try any other available conditional
premisses in X as major premisses for terminal eliminations to obtain disjunctive conclusions.

As we said earlier, an algorithm with this feature will be said to have
informed elimination for disjunctive conclusions.

A sentence is *disjunctive* if it contains a disjunction as a direct accessible
positive subformula. A *set* of sentences is disjunctive if at least one of its
members is.

By our Lemma above, any E-type Prawitz proof with a non-disjunctive
set of undischarged assumptions is non-disjunctive (that is, the proof contains no ∨-eliminations). Its hybrid version will also end with an elimination
and be non-disjunctive.

THEOREM: Suppose Π is a non-disjunctive hybrid proof that ends with an
elimination and whose conclusion A has no introductory proof from the same
undischarged assumptions. Then, obviously, A is atomic or a disjunction;
and Π can moreover be transformed into a non-disjunctive hybrid proof Π′
of A whose final step, which by hypothesis has to be an elimination, has as
its major premiss a formula that contains A as a direct accessible positive
subformula.

Proof: By induction on Π. The basis is obvious, since a one-step Π has one
of the forms

$$\frac{A\wedge B \quad \overline{A}}{A} \qquad \frac{B\wedge A \quad \overline{A}}{A} \qquad \frac{B\supset A \quad B \quad \overline{A}}{A} \qquad \frac{\neg B \quad B}{\bot}$$

For the inductive step, we need only consider Π with one of the forms

$$\pi\dfrac{B\wedge C \quad \dfrac{\dfrac{(i)}{B},\dfrac{(i)}{C}}{\Sigma}\,\sigma\dfrac{}{A}(E)}{A}(i) \qquad\qquad \pi\dfrac{B\supset C \quad \Theta\,B \quad \dfrac{\dfrac{(i)}{C}}{\Sigma}\,\sigma\dfrac{}{A}(E)}{A}(i)$$

Σ is shown as ending with an elimination (called σ). This is because if σ were an introduction, it would have to be a $\vee$-introduction, in which case the terminal elimination step π could be shuffled up past σ, to produce an introductory proof of A, contrary to assumption. By inductive hypothesis, Σ can be transformed into a non-disjunctive hybrid proof Σ' of A whose final step σ is an elimination whose major premiss μ contains A as a direct accessible positive subformula. σ is either $\wedge$-elimination, $\supset$-elimination, or $\neg$-elimination. Replace Σ in Π by Σ' to get Π''. If π discharges μ in Π'', take Π'' as Π'. If π does not discharge μ in Π'', shuffle π up past σ to produce Π'. The transformations involved are straightforward, with the possible exception of the case where both π and σ are $\supset$-eliminations:

$$\dfrac{\Theta\,B\supset C\quad B \quad \dfrac{D\supset E\;D\quad \dfrac{\dfrac{(1)}{C}\;\dfrac{(2)}{C},\dfrac{(2)}{E}}{\Xi\quad\Psi}}{A}2}{A}1 \longrightarrow \dfrac{D\supset E \quad \dfrac{B\supset C\;B\quad \dfrac{(3)}{C}}{\Theta\;\Xi}\;D}{A}3 \quad \dfrac{B\supset C\;B\quad\dfrac{\dfrac{(2)}{C},\dfrac{(1)}{E}}{\Theta\;\Psi}}{A}1$$

This is the only case, also, where Π' may be significantly longer than Π'', by virtue of the extra copy of the minor proof Θ.

Ω

There is another proof of our theorem, as follows. There will be a non-disjunctive Prawitz proof Π^0 corresponding to Π, also ending with an elimination. Given the absence of $\vee$-eliminations, its spine will be a sequence $\mu,\ldots,A$ of major premisses for eliminations, each containing the next one as a direct accessible positive subformula. So A is a direct accessible positive subformula of μ. Recall our recipe for transforming Π^0 into a hybrid proof.

It involves making the topmost elimination on this spine the bottommost step of the hybrid proof. This step has μ as its major premiss, and A as its conclusion.

One might be tempted by the last theorem into making the following *false* conjecture:

> Every hybrid proof of an atomic conclusion A can be transformed into a hybrid proof whose final step is an elimination whose major premiss contains A as an accessible positive subformula.

The misguided thought here is that by dropping the condition that the proof be non-disjunctive, one might be able to compensate by requiring A to be merely accessible positive, and not necessarily *directly* accessible positive, in the final major premiss of the transformed proof. But disjunctive major premisses feature in proofs in ways that dash such a hope. One need only consider the obvious proof for the problem $D,\ B \supset A,\ C \supset A,\ D \supset (B \vee C)$?- A:

$$
\cfrac{D \supset (B \vee C) \quad D}{\quad}
\cfrac{\overset{4}{B \vee C} \quad \cfrac{B \supset A \quad \overline{B}\ ^3}{A} \quad \cfrac{\overline{A}\ ^1}{A}\ ^1 \quad \cfrac{C \supset A \quad \overline{C}\ ^3}{A} \quad \cfrac{\overline{A}\ ^2}{A}\ ^2}{\quad A \quad}\ ^3}{A}\ ^4
$$

The major subproof for its final $\supset$-elimination is already a counterexample to the false conjecture above. And the overall proof shows how the trouble is inherited by a deductive problem all of whose complex premisses are conditionals. Thus upfront $\vee$-elimination cannot be relied on to produce as remaining subproblems ones for which the conjecture would hold.

As it happens, the conjecture is thwarted for M only by the cases where π is $\vee$-elimination, and σ is either $\supset$-elimination or $\neg$-elimination. We have for IR, but not for M, the transformation

$$
\cfrac{\text{B}\vee\text{C} \quad \cfrac{\neg D \quad D}{\bot} \quad \cfrac{\Gamma_2}{\bot}}{\bot}\,{}^{1}
\qquad\longrightarrow\qquad
\cfrac{\neg D \quad \cfrac{\text{B}\vee\text{C} \quad D \quad \cfrac{\Gamma_2}{\bot}}{D}\,{}^{1}}{\bot}
$$

$$
\begin{array}{c}
\overline{B}^{\,1}\\[2pt]
\Gamma_1 \quad \overline{C}^{\,1}\\
\end{array}
\qquad\qquad
\begin{array}{c}
\overline{B}^{\,1}\quad\overline{C}^{\,1}\\[2pt]
\Gamma_1 \quad \Gamma_2\\
\end{array}
$$

which exploits the liberalized form of $\vee$-elimination in IR. But neither IR nor M affords a transformation

$$
\cfrac{\text{B}\vee\text{C} \quad \cfrac{D\supset E \quad D}{A} \quad \cfrac{A \quad \Gamma_3}{A}\,{}^{2}}{A}\,{}^{1}
\;\xrightarrow{\;??\;}\;
\cfrac{D\supset E \quad \cfrac{D \quad \cfrac{\text{B}\vee\text{C} \quad A \quad A}{A}\,{}^{1}}{A}\,{}^{2}}{A}
$$

$$
\begin{array}{c}
{}^{1}\overline{B}\quad {}^{1}\overline{B,E}\;{}^{2}\\[2pt]
\Gamma_1 \quad \Gamma_2 \quad \overline{C}\,{}^{1}\\
\end{array}
\qquad\qquad
\begin{array}{c}
{}^{1}\overline{B,E}\;{}^{2}\quad \overline{C}\,{}^{1}\\[2pt]
B \quad \Gamma_2 \quad \Gamma_3\\
\end{array}
$$

because B could remain undischarged in the minor proof Γ_1.

We must therefore be content for the time being with the strategic advice offered by our theorem concerning *non-disjunctive* proofs. Suppose then that X is a non-disjunctive set of premisses and A is atomic. If there is a proof of A from X, it will be E-type and non-disjunctive. By our theorem, it can be transformed into one whose final step has as its major premiss a formula containing A as a direct accessible positive subformula. *So under these conditions on X and A, one need only ever forage for major premisses in the direct subclass.* The indirect subclass, of course, will be empty, since X is by assumption non-disjunctive. But the residual subclass may be non-empty. We now know, however, that we may ignore the residual class entirely, *provided that X is non-disjunctive.* For *disjunctive* X, however, and even for atomic A, one may (for the time being) have to use a major premiss from any one of the direct, indirect and residual subclasses. Such is the bedevilment by disjunctions.

But when A is a *disjunction*, matters ironically improve. We shall see below that we can then confine our choice of a major premiss to formulae that contain a directly accessible positive disjunction.

In the meantime we pursue conditions on X and A that would render the residual subclass otiose.

THEOREM: In any hybrid proof Π, every major premiss for an elimination is a positive subformula of some undischarged assumption, or is a negative subformula of the conclusion.

Proof: By induction on Π. The basis is obvious. For the inductive step, consider Π by cases according to its terminal step τ. If τ is $\wedge$-introduction or $\vee$-introduction the result is immediate by inductive hypothesis applied to the immediate subproofs(s) of Π. Suppose τ is $\supset$-introduction, so Π has the form

$$\tau\frac{\begin{array}{c} \overline{A} \\ \Sigma \\ B \end{array}}{A \supset B}$$

Any major premiss μ for elimination in Π is in Σ. By inductive hypothesis applied to Σ, μ is positive in some undischarged assumption of Σ, or negative in B. In the latter case, μ is negative also in $A \supset B$, and we are done. In the former case, if μ is positive in some undischarged assumption of Σ other than A, we are also done. If, however, μ is positive in A, then it is negative in $A \supset B$, and we are done. The reasoning when τ is $\neg$-introduction is a reduced version of the foregoing, with $B = \bot$, and the case where μ is negative in B consequently not arising. When τ is an $\wedge$-elimination or $\vee$-elimination the reasoning is easy: if μ is negative in the conclusion of a subproof, it remains so in the conclusion of Π, since the conclusions are identical; and if μ is positive in some undischarged assumption of a subproof, it retains this property whether or not the latter assumption is discharged by τ. If τ is $\neg$-introduction the reasoning is straightforward. If τ is $\supset$-elimination then Π has the form

$$\frac{\begin{array}{ccc} & \overline{B} & \\ & \Theta & \Sigma \\ A \supset B & A & C \end{array}}{C}$$

and we reason as follows. If μ is in Θ, it is positive in some undischarged assumption of Θ, or negative in A; whence it is positive in some undischarged assumption of Π. If μ is in Σ, it is positive in some undischarged assumption of Σ, or negative in C. In the latter case, we are done. In the former case, if μ is positive in some undischarged assumption of Σ other than B, we are also done. If μ is positive in B, however, then it is positive also in $A \supset B$, and we are done.

Ω

This theorem can be used to mitigate somewhat the failure of the conjecture above, for it helps yield the following theorem.

THEOREM: Suppose that X is a set of premisses (possibly disjunctive) *none of which contains a conditional or a negation as a positive subformula*, and that the atomic conclusion A is provable from X. Then obviously any non-trivial proof Π of A from X must be E-type. Moreover, it can be transformed into a proof whose terminal step is an elimination *whose major premiss contains A as an accessible positive subformula*.

Proof: The only elimination rules that can find application in Π are $\wedge$-elimination and $\vee$-elimination. Let either of these occur as the terminal step π of Π, and let either of them be used at step σ immediately above π. If π does not discharge the major premiss for σ, one can shuffle π up past σ. This observation is all that one needs in order to be able to carry out the proof as for our first theorem above.

Ω

The troublesome cases for the process of shuffling π up past σ cannot arise in the proof of the last theorem, since, by the previous theorem, there are no conditional or negated premisses in the proof Π. For IR the mitigation is even better: we need only require that X have no member containing a *conditional* as a positive subformula[4]. Call such X $\supset$-*innocuous*. When in addition X has no member containing a *negation* as a positive subformula, call X $(\supset, \neg)$-*innocuous*.

We now have the following heuristic for IR:

> For $\supset$-innocuous X and atomic A, try only major premisses for elimination that contain A as an accessible positive subformula

Similarly for M:

> For $(\supset, \neg)$-innocuous X and atomic A, try only major premisses for elimination that contain A as an accessible positive subformula

For such X and A, there is no need to forage in the residual subclass for major premisses for elimination.

One cost in so confining our foraging is that the proofs now left within possible purview might contain repetitions of minor subproofs that are occasioned, as we have seen, by the $(\supset, \vee)$- and $(\vee, \vee)$-shuffles. For an averting algorithm, this would not be too much of a problem.

As remarked above, when X is non-disjunctive then the indirect subclass for atomic A is bound to be empty. One looks only at major premisses in the direct subclass, and ignores the residual subclass. For $(\supset, \neg)$-innocuous X, although the indirect subclass may be non-empty, one still ignores the residual subclass. For both conditions on X, the upshot is the same: ignore the residual subclass. One can therefore capture the net strategic effect by allowing a look in the residual subclass, for atomic A, *only when X is both disjunctive and not $(\supset, \neg)$-innocuous*. There is only ever point in trying a major premiss from the residual subclass if X has a member that contains a direct accessible positive disjunction *and* has a member that contains a conditional positively or that contains a negation positively. In IR the restriction is more exacting: to justify a look into the residual subclass, X should have a member that contains a direct accessible positive disjunction *and* a member that contains a conditional positively.

Consider now the effect of this guarantee for an algorithm employing upfront $\wedge$-elimination and upfront $\vee$-elimination, when one comes to forage for

---

[4] The shuffles for the cases where π is $\wedge$-elimination or $\vee$-elimination, and σ is $\neg$-elimination, are easy. We have already seen the $(\vee, \neg)$-shuffle for IR above. The $(\wedge, \neg)$-shuffle is available even in M.

a conditional major premiss. If one is available, then that meets the requirement on X that it have a member that contains a conditional positively. So foraging in the residual subclass is worthwhile only if X is disjunctive : that is, only if one of the available conditional premisses contains a direct accessible positive disjunction.

Remember that the trouble for both M and IR was the unavailability of the transformation

$$
\cfrac{B \lor C \quad \cfrac{\cfrac{\overset{1}{\overline{B}} \quad \overset{1}{\overline{B,E}}^{\,2}}{\cfrac{\Gamma_1 \qquad \Gamma_2 \qquad \overset{\overline{C}^{\,1}}{}}{\cfrac{D \supset E \quad D \qquad A}{A}^{\,2} \quad \Gamma_3}}{A}^{\,1}}{A} \quad \xrightarrow{\ ??\ } \quad \cfrac{\cfrac{D \supset E \quad \cfrac{B \quad \cfrac{\Gamma_1 \quad \cfrac{\overset{1}{\overline{B,E}}^{\,2} \quad \overline{C}^{\,1}}{B \lor C} \quad A}{A}^{\,1}}{D}}{A}^{\,2}}{}
$$

Moreover, as we saw earlier, the $(\lor, \neg)$-shuffle is unavailable for M (although it *is* available for IR). Now for an algorithm that employs up-front $\lor$-elimination, these recalcitrant $\lor$-eliminations with major premiss $B \lor C$ as shown above force recourse to the residual subclass of conditional premisses (with respect to a conclusion A that may be either atomic or a disjunction) *only if such a premiss $B \lor C$ is able to be exposed as a candidate for $\lor$-elimination* by eliminative 'unpacking', beginning lower down with the conditional major premiss chosen from the residual subclass — otherwise $B \lor C$ would have been dealt with by up-front $\lor$-elimination. So we now know that we can confine our search within the residual subclass even further: we need consider only conditional premisses in that subclass that contain a *direct accessible positive disjunction*. It is only such premisses that might yield, upon a series of eliminations, a premiss such as $B \lor C$ in the two schemata given above for abortive $(\lor, \supset)$- and $(\lor, \neg)$-shuffle (in M).

Earlier we had concluded that foraging in the residual subclass of conditional premisses is worthwhile only if one of the available conditional premisses contains a direct accessible positive disjunction. *Now we see that within the residual subclass we need only try premisses of this latter sort.*

8.2 Relevance

There are other filters that we could try besides the accessibility filter. The following one does not weed out invalidities, but rather enables one to collapse premiss sets. For its purposes we take $\perp$ to be an atom occurring in negations.

BASIC RELEVANCE FILTER:

> *If in any deductive problem X?-A no atom (not even $\perp$) is common to both A and some premiss in X, replace it with the deductive problem ?-A*

This filter is justified by the following.

THEOREM: Every minimal proof of A from the set X is such that A has an atom (which may be $\perp$) in common with some undischarged assumption

Proof: Straightforward by induction on the complexity of proof.

As it stands this is a very crude filter, and we should be able to do better with the notion of relevance. The subformula relation is not discriminating enough to give the filter much mesh. It ought to be formulated in a way that pays more attention to the respective *modes of containment* of the shared atoms in the problems that are to be allowed to slip through the net. But the modes in question are precisely what we have been exploring; and reflection on them issues in the next theorem. Before we state and prove it, however, it will be useful to have some special notation for the notions involved.

DEFINITIONS

A *variable* is an atom other than $\perp$.

$\pm(X)$ $=_{df}$ some variable is positive in some member of X and negative in some member of X.

$=(A; X)$ $=_{df}$ some variable has the same parity in A as it has in some member of X.

$\neq(A; X)$ $=_{df}$ some variable has the opposite parity in A from that which it has in some member of X.

(In the above, if ever X is a singleton $\{B\}$, we suppress set brackets and write B. We shall also write X, A for $X \cup \{A\}$.)

Note that it is impossible for $\pm(\bot)$ or $=(\bot; X)$ or $\neq(\bot; X)$ to hold, since $\bot$ is not a variable.

THEOREM: In every minimal proof of A from the set X of undischarged assumptions, one of the following holds:

1. $\pm(X)$

2. $=(A; X)$

3. $\pm(A)$

Proof: By induction on complexity of proof. For the basis, (2) obviously holds. For the inductive step, consider Π by cases, according to the rule applied last in Π.

$\neg$-*introduction*:

$$\Pi \text{ is } \begin{array}{c} X, \overset{-(i)}{A} \\ \Sigma \\ \dfrac{\bot}{\neg A}{\scriptstyle (i)} \end{array}$$

By inductive hypothesis applied to Σ, we have $\pm(X, A)$. It follows immediately that $\pm(X)$ or $=(\neg A; X)$ or $\pm(\neg A)$.

$\neg$-*elimination*:

$$\Pi \text{ is } \begin{array}{c} X \\ \Sigma \\ \dfrac{\neg A \quad A}{\bot} \end{array}$$

We show that (1) holds for Π, that is: $\pm(X, \neg A)$. By inductive hypothesis applied to Σ, we have $\pm(X)$ or $=(A; X)$ or $\pm(A)$. In the first case it follows that $\pm(X, \neg A)$. In the second case it follows also. In the third case as well we have $\pm(\neg A)$, whence $\pm(X, \neg A)$.

For $\wedge$-*introduction*, $\wedge$-*elimination*, $\vee$-*introduction* and $\vee$-*elimination* the result is immediate.

$\supset$-*introduction*:

$$\Pi \text{ is } \begin{array}{c} \overline{X, A}^{-(i)} \\ \Sigma \\ \underline{B}_{(i)} \\ A \supset B \end{array}$$

By inductive hypothesis applied to Σ, we have
(1) $\pm(X, A)$, or
(2) $= (B; X, A)$, or
(3) $\pm(B)$.

In case (1), if $\pm(X)$ we are done. If not $\pm(X)$ then $\neq (A; X)$, whence $= (A \supset B; X)$ and we are done.

In case (2), if $= (B; A)$ then $\pm(A \supset B)$ and we are done. If not $= (B; A)$ then $= (B; X)$, whence $= (A \supset B; X)$ and we are done.

In case (3), we have $\pm(A \supset B)$ and are done.

$\supset$-*elimination*:

$$\Pi \text{ is } \begin{array}{ccc} & & \overline{X_2, B}^{-(i)} \\ X_1 & & \\ \Sigma_1 & & \Sigma_2 \\ \underline{A \supset B \quad A \qquad C}_{(i)} \\ C \end{array}$$

By inductive hypothesis applied to Σ_2, we have
(1) $\pm(X_2, B)$, or
(2) $= (C; X_2, B)$, or
(3) $\pm(C)$.

In case (1), we have $\pm(X_1, X_2, A \supset B)$ and are done.

In case(2), we have $= (C; X_1, X_2, A \supset B)$ and are done.

In case(3), we are done.

Ω

Our theorem for minimal logic can be pictured thus:

M	$A = \bot$	$A \neq \bot$
$X = \emptyset$		$\pm(A)$
$X \neq \emptyset$	$\pm(X)$	$\pm(X)$ or $=(A; X)$ or $\pm(A)$

We now have a filter with a finer mesh.

REFINED RELEVANCE FILTER:

Fail any problem X?-A if it does not satisfy the condition shown in the appropriate box of the diagram above, since that condition is necessary for the existence of a proof. Note that if the condition is satisfied, then it is satisfied for Y?-A if Y includes X. Thus when the respective conditions fail a problem X?-A, they also fail all Z?-A where X includes Z.

The three-fold disjunction in the bottom right-hand corner of the diagram above is the best we can do for minimal logic. The first disjunct is needed because there is a minimal proof of $\neg\neg B$ from the assumption $\neg(A \wedge \neg A)$. The second disjunct is needed because there is a minimal proof of A from $A \wedge B$. The third disjunct is needed because there is a minimal proof of $\neg(A \wedge \neg A)$ from the assumption $\neg\neg B$.

The first and third cases show how the possibility of *vacuous discharge* in minimal logic with $\neg$-introduction (among other rules) allows a degree of irrelevance to creep in. This frustrates the attempt to formulate a really strong relevance filter. In the system IR of *intuitionistic relevant logic* discussed above, we can improve on matters. We digress in the next chapter to do so.

8.3   Proof by cases

We have been discussing filters and heuristics that exploit syntactic relations among formulae. They are designed to prevent fruitless work when
searching for proofs. They do, however, call for a *syntactic module* in one's
proof-finding program, or at the very least for a rather *replete method of representation*[5] of formulae, in order to be implemented. It therefore behoves
us to do as much as we can to avoid fruitless searches without calling on
these extra resources in our program.

Now there are three kinds of fruitless pursuit of *proof by cases*.
The first is where *one of the disjuncts is already available as a premiss.*
We have already taken this possibility into account in our discussion above of
∨-elimination. There we spoke of safely 'backgrounding' such a disjunctive
premiss. We shall call this the *backgrounding strategy*. Another strategy
to much the same effect is that of *premiss set reduction*: simply strike the
redundant disjunction from the premisses, so that it disappears from view
altogether. (Both strategies are available also for *conjunctive* premisses both
of whose *conjuncts* are already available; and for *conditional* premisses whose
consequents are already available.)

The second kind of fruitless pursuit of proof by cases is where *a case-proof
can be obtained without using the case assumption.* This may be because the
case assumption is utterly irrelevant, and could not stand 'used' in *any* proof
of the sought conclusion from the available premisses; or it may be because
there just happens to be a proof of that conclusion that does not make use
of the case assumption. Either way, it would of course be silly (especially if
this turned out to be true of the first case-proof attempted) to pursue 'proof
by cases'; one should simply extract the proof that we already have from the
more meagre assumptions and be well pleased not to have to apply the ∨-
elimination in question. The algorithm can be this clever, however, without
incorporating any highly charged relevance filter. All that one needs is a way
of keeping track of what assumptions have actually been used. Then, when
contemplating the construction of a proof of A with a terminal application
of ∨-elimination, one checks, upon successful formation of each case-proof,
whether the appropriate case-assumption has indeed been used. If not, one
scrubs the tentative 'proof by cases' template and simply takes the 'case-
proof' itself as the overall proof. I shall call this the *briefcase method*.

The third kind of fruitless pursuit of proof by cases using A∨B as major

---

[5]See Chapter 10 for a discussion of replete methods of representation.

premiss is the following. There is a case-proof using A as case assumption (and the algorithm may well find it, even though A might not be *needed*, given the other assumptions). But there is no case-proof *using B* as case assumption. Moreover, this is not because the remaining assumptions, with B, fail to imply the sought conclusion; *but rather because B is utterly irrelevant, in some sense that has yet to be captured by a nice metatheorem.* In such a situation the construction of the first case-proof turns out to be fruitless; ironically, even more so if the availability of the case assumption A was what deflected the algorithm from finding a proof *not* using A! To prevent the search from proceeding in such a case, we ought to apply some sort of relevance filter, or *screen*. And the screen has to be justified by the nice metatheorem not yet to hand. We could make a modest saving of effort with *depth first* application of the screen, which would arrest the search for the *second* case-proof, and make us realise that if any proof of the overall problem is to be had, it will not make use of either the disjunctive premiss contemplated — namely, $A \lor B$ — or the second case assumption B. Alternatively, we could apply the screen *breadth-first* before embarking on the search for either case-proof. This would be a special case, in the event of a contemplated $\lor$-elimination, of precautionary screening that could be done at the outset with any splitting rule.

Note that we have no such screen for minimal logic. M can manage, at best, the briefcase method for avoiding fruitless proof by cases. But we *can* formulate the desired kind of screen for intuitionistic relevance logic.

In the next chapter I shall do what I promised the reader I would *not* do: that is, explore some of the subtleties of IR in comparison with M. We shall establish the nice metatheorem for IR that is needed for effective screening.

Chapter 9

Genetic Screening in IR

The relation $\neq(A;B)$, for formulae A and B, is symmetric, but need not be either transitive or reflexive.

DEFINITIONS

$A_1,\ldots,A_n$ $(n>1)$ is a $\neq$-*chain connecting* A_1 *to* A_n $=_{df}$ for all $i<n$, $\neq(A_i;A_{i+1})$.

A set X of formulae is $\neq$-*connected* $=_{df}$ for all A,B in X, A is connected to B by a $\neq$-chain.

A *genet*[1] of X is a $\neq$-connected subset of X.

Note that the genets of X partition X.

$\mp(X)$ $=_{df}$ (X is a singleton $\{A\}$ and $\pm(A)$) or (X has more than one member and X is a genet).

Note that $\mp(A)$ if and only if $\pm(A)$.

To continue the plant metaphor:
if $=(A;X)$ we say that X *is rooted in* A.

$\nabla(A;X) =_{df}$ every genet of X is rooted in A.

Note that we cannot have $\nabla(\perp;X)$.

---

[1]a term suggested by its use in the population genetics of strawberry plants. A genet is what a graph theorist would call a *component* in a graph whose vertices are formulae and where an edge between vertices A,B represents the symmetric relation $\neq(A;B)$. Moreover, the graph theorist's *paths* in such a graph are what I am calling $\neq$-chains. I am grateful to Brendan MacKay for these terminological observations.

For IR there is a really strong relevance result. It can be pictured as follows:

IR	$A = \bot$	$A \neq \bot$
$X = \emptyset$		$\pm(A)$
$X \neq \emptyset$	$\mp(X)$	$\nabla(A; X)$

THEOREM: In every intuitionistic relevant proof of A from the set X of undischarged assumptions, one of the following holds:

1. $\mp(X)$

2. $\nabla(A; X)$

3. $\pm(A)$

Proof: By induction on complexity of proof. For the basis, (2) obviously holds. For the inductive step, consider Π by cases, according to the rule applied last in Π.

$\neg$-*introduction*:

$$\Pi \text{ is } \begin{array}{c} \overline{X, A}^{(i)} \quad \textit{where this discharge is obligatory} \\ \Sigma \\ \dfrac{\bot}{\neg A}{}^{(i)} \end{array}$$

By inductive hypothesis applied to Σ, we have $\mp(X, A)$. If $X=\emptyset$, we have $\pm(A)$, hence $\pm(\neg A)$ and we are done[2]. Now suppose $X \neq \emptyset$. If $\mp(X)$ then X is rooted in $\neg A$ and we are done. But if on the other hand X partitions into more than one genet[3], then — since $\mp(X, A)$ — each of these must have a member B such that $\neq(B;A)$. Hence each is rooted in $\neg A$, and we are done.

$\neg$-*elimination*:

$$\Pi \text{ is } \quad \begin{array}{c} X \\ \Sigma \\ \hline \neg A \quad A \\ \hline \bot \end{array}$$

We show that $\mp(X, \neg A)$. By inductive hypothesis applied to Σ, we have $(X=\emptyset$ and $\pm(A))$ or $(X \neq \emptyset$ and $\nabla(A;X))$. If $X=\emptyset$ and $\pm(A)$ then $\pm(\neg A)$, whence $\mp(\neg A)$ and we are done. If on the other hand $X \neq \emptyset$ and $\nabla(A;X)$, then, since every genet of X is rooted in A, we have that $X, \neg A$ is a single genet, and we are done.

$\wedge$-*introduction*:

$$\Pi \text{ is } \quad \begin{array}{cc} X_1 & X_2 \\ \Sigma_1 & \Sigma_2 \\ \hline A_1 & A_2 \\ \hline \multicolumn{2}{c}{A_1 \wedge A_2} \end{array}$$

By inductive hypothesis applied to Σ_i, we have (first case) $(\pm(A_i)$ and $X_i=\emptyset)$ or (second case) $(\nabla(A_i;X_i)$ and $X_i \neq \emptyset)$. If the second case holds for $i=1$ or $i=2$, then every genet of $X_1 \cup X_2$, since it includes a genet of X_i, will be rooted, via A_i, in $A_1 \wedge A_2$; and we are done. If, on the other hand, the first case holds for $i=1$ and $i=2$, we have that $\pm(A_1 \wedge A_2)$; and we are done.

---

[2] Note that this is where the reasoning would not go through for minimal logic. For in minimal logic the discharge of A is not obligatory — that is, A need not have been used as an assumption. Thus we cannot conclude that X will be rooted in $\neg A$.

[3] which would mean, in the terminology of graph theory, that A is a *cut-point* of the graph on X, A of the kind described in the previous footnote.

$\wedge$-*elimination*:

$$\Pi \text{ is } \quad \overset{\underline{\quad}(i)}{X,} \overset{\underline{\quad}(i)}{A,} \overset{}{B} \quad \textit{where at least one of these assumptions has been used}$$

$$\Sigma$$

$$\frac{A \wedge B \qquad C}{C}{}_{(i)}$$

By inductive hypothesis applied to Σ we have (first case) ($C=\perp$ and $\mp(X, A, B$
or (second case) ($C \neq \perp$ and $\nabla(C; X, A, B)$). In the first case we have $\mp(X, A \wedge$
and are done. In the second case we have that every genet of $X, A \wedge B$, since
it includes a genet of X, A, B, is rooted in C; so we are done.

$\vee$-*introduction*:

$$\Pi \text{ is } \quad X$$

$$\Sigma$$

$$\frac{B}{A \vee B} \quad \textit{(the case for A in place of B is similar)}$$

By inductive hypothesis applied to Σ, we have (first case) ($X=\emptyset$ and $\pm(B)$)
or (second case) ($X \neq \emptyset$ and $\nabla(B; X)$). In the first case we have $\pm(A \supset B)$
and are done. In the second case we have that every genet of X is rooted in
$A \vee B$ via B, and are done.

$\vee$-*elimination*:

$$\Pi \text{ is } \quad \overset{\underline{\quad}(i)}{X_1, A_1} \quad \overset{\underline{\quad}(i)}{X_2, A_2} \quad \textit{where both these discharges are obligatory}$$

$$\Sigma_1 \qquad \Sigma_2$$

$$\frac{A_1 \vee A_2 \qquad C \qquad C}{C}{}_{(i)}$$

By inductive hypothesis applied to Σ_i, we have (first case) ($C=\perp$ and $\mp(X_i, A$
or (second case) ($C \neq \perp$ and $\nabla(C; X_i, A_i)$). If the first case holds for $i=1$ and
$i=2$ we have $\mp(X_1, X_2, A_1 \vee A_2)$. Suppose now that the second case holds for
$i=1$ or $i=2$. Then every genet of $X_1, X_2, A_1 \vee A_2$, since it includes a genet of
X_i, A_i, is rooted in C, and we are done.

$\supset$-*introduction*:

Case 1:

$$\Pi \text{ is } \begin{array}{l} X, A \quad \underline{}(i) \;\; \text{where } A \text{ has been used} \\ \Sigma \\ \underline{B}(i) \\ A \supset B \end{array}$$

By inductive hypothesis applied to Σ, we have $\nabla(B; X, A)$. If $X=\emptyset$ we have $=(B, A)$, whence $\pm(A \supset B)$ and we are done. Now suppose $X \neq \emptyset$. If $\mp(X)$ then X is rooted in $A \supset B$ and we are done. If on the other hand X partitions into more than one genet, then each of these (since $\mp(X, A)$) must have a member C such that $\neq (C; A)$. Hence each is rooted in $A \supset B$, and we are done.

Case 2:

$$\Pi \text{ is } \begin{array}{l} X \quad \text{where } A \text{ is not in } X \\ \Sigma \\ \underline{B} \\ A \supset B \end{array}$$

The reasoning here is exactly as for $\vee$-introduction above.

Case 3:

$$\Pi \text{ is } \begin{array}{l} X, A \quad \underline{}(i) \;\; \text{where the discharge is obligatory} \\ \Sigma \\ \underline{\perp}(i) \\ A \supset B \end{array}$$

By inductive hypothesis applied to Σ we have $\mp(X, A)$. If $X=\emptyset$ we have $\pm(A)$, whence $\pm(A \supset B)$ and we are done. Now suppose $X \neq \emptyset$. If $\mp(X)$ then X is rooted in $A \supset B$ and we are done. If on the other hand X partitions into more than one genet, then each of these (since $\mp(X, A)$) must have a member C such that $\neq (C; A)$. Hence each is rooted in $A \supset B$, and we are done.

⊃-*elimination*:

$$\begin{array}{ccc} & & \quad\text{—}(i)\ \textit{where the discharge is obligatory} \\ \Pi \text{ is} & X_1 & X_2, B \\ & \Sigma_1 & \Sigma_2 \\ \underline{A \supset B \quad A} & & C \\ & C & \end{array}\ {}_{(i)}$$

By inductive hypothesis applied to Σ_1, we have ($X_1=\emptyset$ and $\pm(A)$) or ($X_1 \neq \emptyset$ and $\nabla(A : X_1)$).

By inductive hypothesis applied to Σ_2, we have ($C=\perp$ and $\mp(X_2, B)$) or ($C \neq \perp$ and $\nabla(C; X_2, B)$).

We first take the case where $C=\perp$ and show that $\mp(X_1, X_2, A \supset B)$. We have $\mp(X_2, B)$.

Suppose $X_1, X_2, A \supset B$ is a singleton. Then $X_1=\emptyset$ and $X_2=\emptyset$. So $\mp(B)$, whence $\pm(B)$, whence $\pm(A \supset B)$, whence $\mp(A \supset B)$ and we are done: that is, $\mp(X_1, X_2, A \supset B)$.

Now suppose $X_1, X_2, A \supset B$ is *not* a singleton. So either $X_1 \neq \emptyset$ or $X_2 \neq \emptyset$. If $X_1 \neq \emptyset$ we have $\nabla(A; X_1)$. Hence $\mp(X_1, A \supset B)$. But we already have $\mp(X_2, B)$. Thus $\mp(X_1, X_2, A \supset B)$. It remains to consider the case where $X_1=\emptyset$ and $X_2 \neq \emptyset$; so we are trying to show that $\mp(X_2, A \supset B)$. But we already have $\mp(X_2, B)$, which yields the desired result immediately.

We now take the case where $C \neq \perp$ and show that $\nabla(C; X_1, X_2, A \supset B)$. We have $\nabla(C; X_2, B)$.

Take any genet Z of $X_1, X_2, A \supset B$.

Suppose $A \supset B$ is in Z. Then Z includes $W \setminus \{B\}$, for some genet W of X_2, B. W is rooted in C. Hence Z is also. But Z was an arbitrary genet of $X_1, X_2, A \supset B$. Hence $\nabla(C; X_1, X_2, A \supset B)$.

Now suppose $A \supset B$ is not in Z. Suppose Z is a subset of X_2. Then again Z is rooted in C. It remains only to consider the case where Z is not a subset of X_2 and does not contain $A \supset B$. Here Z must be a subset of X_1 and accordingly include a genet Y of X_1. X_1 is therefore non-empty. Hence $\nabla(A; X_1)$. Since Y is rooted in A, so is Z. But then Z would include $A \supset B$, contrary to our supposition.

Ω

The question now is: how can one avail oneself of this theorem when devising a proof-finder for intuitionistic relevant logic?

The accessibility heuristic applies to IR as well as to M. It will already ensure that, on problems with atomic conclusions, we prosecute our search for major premises for elimination, *initially*, within the confines of suitable genets. For a genet to be rooted in an *atomic* conclusion, the latter must be a positive subformula of one of the genet's members. And this is certainly secured by the accessibility heuristic, which enjoins us to try first those premisses that contain the atomic conclusion as a *direct accessible* positive subformula, and then those that contain it as an *indirect accessible* positive subformula; and only thereafter to try remaining premisses, if any.

The point to make now is that some of these remaining premisses might prove to be utterly worthless, on grounds of their *irrelevance*, on the basis of the last theorem. The direct and indirect subclasses will, as we have just seen, have all their members in rooted genets. *But the residual subclasses need not.* Now our theorem tells us that only those premisses that are in rooted genets are worth trying. Hence *only those residual premisses that are in rooted genets are worth trying.*

We may state this as the

GENETIC DEFECT SCREEN:

Given any deductive problem $X?$-A, with $A \neq \perp$ and X non-empty, delete all members of X that do not belong to any genet rooted in A[4]

We can think of the screen as helping at all times to focus on the correct choice of premisses for elimination, especially when we are trying premisses in what we have called the residual subclass. We could either screen every problem at the outset, and then rest assured that the residual subclass for any connective will only ever contain premisses that have *survived* such screening; or be mindful of the screen only when we enter the residual subclass, and use it to focus our choices within it.

As a very simple example, consider the following problem for whose solution, via the algorithm framed so far, one will be called upon to explore the residual subclass: $F, F \supset (A \lor B), A \supset C, B \supset C, D \supset E?$-$C$. The algorithm will first explore the possibility that either $A \supset C$ or $B \supset C$ will be the major premiss of the final step of a hybrid proof. This will fail, since neither A nor

---

[4]It is worth noting that there is a very efficient algorithm — linear in the number of $\neq$-links between premisses — for generating genets containing any given premiss (whose rootedness in the conclusion, in turn, can be efficiently determined).

B can be proved for their minors. So the direct subclass will have been to no avail. The indirect subclass happens to be empty. So attention would now have to be turned to the remainder: should we try $F \supset (A \vee B)$ or $D \supset E$? The latter would be pointless, *on the basis of the theorem above*. For $D \supset E$ is not in any genet rooted in C. The algorithm should therefore at this stage be able to ignore it, and proceed to $F \supset (A \vee B)$ as the sole possible major premiss for a terminal $\supset$-elimination. As it happens, it will then succeed.

So the theorem can help even with problems with atomic conclusions.

What now of problems with compound conclusions? Note that our algorithm does up-front $\vee$-eliminations before trying to break down compound conclusions so as to obtain, eventually, atomic conclusions in the sub-problems. And here lurks the danger, for the algorithm in its present form, of *fruitless pursuit of proof by cases. We have to minimise it.*

In the previous chapter we saw how these fruitless pursuits can be of three main kinds. We can now say how the third of them can be avoided by applying the lessons of the theorem for IR above. This third kind of fruitless pursuit of proof by cases was the one where there is a case-proof using one of the case assumptions (say A), but no case-proof using the other case assumption (say B). Moreover, this is not because the remaining assumptions, with B, fail to imply the sought conclusion; *but rather because B is utterly irrelevant. One important sense in which it may be so is now captured by the last theorem.*

I have done what I promised the reader I would *not* do: that is, explore some of the subtleties of IR in comparison with M. I now suspend the discussion of filters, heuristics and screens; and turn to the problem of representation.

Chapter 10

How to represent formulae

We are looking for proofs. So we are rummaging in formulae. We need to know a great deal about their syntactic structure and relations in order to make informed choices. Because formulae are so readily thought of as trees, I shall call this kind of information *arboreal*. Arboreal information is always handy; but how close at hand should it be?

There is a balance to be struck. The first extreme is to take our formulae neat, and use syntactic algorithms. These would extract arboreal information whenever we need it. But then the algorithm would be acquiring arboreal information by 'thinking' a lot. The other extreme is to replace our formulae with some sort of *replete representations*. These would contain as much as possible of the arboreal information 'on the surface', so to speak. Then it could be extracted 'just by looking'. But then the algorithm would also be 'bearing it all in mind'. Given this, how do we make the algorithm as efficient as possible?

The balance to be struck is, crudely, between thinking things out and bearing things in mind. I shall show how things that can be thought out can also be borne in mind. The gross form of the algorithm developed so far will be invariant over decisions about where exactly one finally strikes the required balance. At any branching point in the algorithm where the choice of branch depends on arboreal information, the *neat method* will be to extract it by (re-)computation on the formulae involved; the *replete method* will be to read it off the richer representations of the formulae involved. When these representations are so rich that they contain everything we need 'within themselves' as components, I shall speak of *recursively replete* representations. When they are rich enough to allow one to gain independent access[1] to everything we need *without having to re-compute it*, I shall speak of *partially replete* representations. So one and the same algorithm can come in a neat, or partially replete, or recursively replete version.

Prolog's only data types are *terms*. The logician can think of these as *functional* terms. *Ground terms* are built up from individual constants and n-place function signs in the usual recursive way. In *non-ground*, or *open* terms, individual variables can appear in place of individual constants. There is only one thing to be wary of as a logician, when using Prolog. This is that the logician's formula $F(x_1, \ldots, x_n)$ is rendered in Prolog as $f(X_1, \ldots, X_n)$, swapping upper and lower cases. Moreover, in Prolog there is no *syntactic* distinction between terms that are to denote objects, and terms that are to make statements. This distinction — between the category *Name* and the category *Sentence* — emerges rather as a semantic or pragmatic one. It is only when one *uses* the terms in a program that the *merely referential* and the *truth-bearing* roles of terms can respectively be assigned. Only terms that appear as heads of clauses — that is, as *goal statements* — are of category *Sentence*. They yield (upon appropriate grounding of variables) the *assertions* that the program warrants.

Now formulae can easily be represented as terms in Prolog. Simply take the Polish representation of a formula, and *add the (unnecessary) brackets*. Thus the formula whose tree representation is

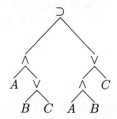

would receive the Prolog representation $\supset (\wedge(a, \vee(b, c)), \vee(\wedge(a, b), c))$. But given the latter, what are we or the machine to do when asked to decide which of the propositional atoms, say, occur as direct accessible positive subformulae? The answer is that we would have to apply the appropriate definitional clauses that characterise such subformulae — which can be stated as clauses in a Prolog program — in order to *derive*, or *work out*, the

---

[1] via pairings, say, of pointers with items of arboreal information pointed to.

answer. For the bracketed Polish representation is *neat*. To be able simply to read the answer off, however, we need the representation to be *replete*. Our problem, then, will be to devise terms that incorporate all the arboreal information we want about formulae in a way that allows us (or the program) to 'read it off' in a much simpler fashion. There are two things we wish to do with formulae when executing the algorithm developed above. We wish to *record problems* of the form X?-A as having admitted of proof or as having failed to admit of proof, and later on possibly *recall* them. We also wish to *detect features*: usually, the presence of subformulae of various kinds.

For the purpose of recording and recalling we shall be using so-called *dynamic predicates* in Prolog. When A is $\bot$, we shall record *consistent(X)* if the problem did not admit of proof; when A is not $\bot$, we shall likewise record *failed(A,X)*. If, on the other hand, the problem *does* admit of proof, we shall record *alreadydone(A,X)*. The resulting positive and negative ledgers built up as computation on a problem proceeds will be consulted at appropriate points in the search algorithm. Before embarking on a search for a proof with a newly generated sub-problem, one will check whether it has been decided already. If so, the result obtained earlier applies again; if not, search proceeds. As soon as a search terminates with a proof, the success is recorded; as soon as it terminates in failure, the failure is recorded. These processes of recording and then recalling turn out to be much faster if one uses, as arguments of the dynamic predicates concerned, not formulae and sets of formulae, but rather *names* of formulae, and *sets of names* of formulae, respectively. Indeed, at the very outset we shall assign, in one-to-one fashion, *numerals* to all subformulae involved in a problem X?-A. These numerals will then serve as their names. They will have to be 'built in' to the representation of each formula. As the search proceeds, new sub-problems will be generated by inductive breakdown. But these sub-problems will of course involve only subformulae of the formulae involved in the original problem[2]. Thus at every stage we shall have a set of numerals for the set of premises, and a numeral for the conclusion of whatever problem we are working on. An algorithm that employs numerals in this way will be called *Gödelian*.

For the purpose of detecting features we shall build in also various sets of formulae as components in the representation of a given formula. The most replete representation would, in addition to being Gödelian, contain

---

[2] or, in the case of Dyckhoff's method, formulae built up from those subformulae — see below.

absolutely every bit of arboreal information we have cared so far to consider:

1. the representations of the immediate constituents of the formula (so that inductive breakdown of representations yields representations!)

2. the set of all positive subformulae

3. the set of all negative subformulae

4. the set of all atoms occurring in the formula

5. the set of all direct accessible positive subformulae

6. the set of all indirect accessible positive subformulae

7. the set of all direct accessible positive atoms occurring in the formula

8. the set of all indirect accessible positive atoms occurring in the formula

9. the set of all logical operators occurring in the formula

10. the depth of the formula

11. the set of all accessible positive disjunctive subformulae

12. any other set of (representations of, or Gödelian numerals for) syntactically related formulae that future ingenuity might reveal to be useful

I reserve for special treatment in a later chapter the ingenuity of a method due to R.Dyckhoff[3]. The method applies to minimal logic and, rather more appropriately, as it happens, to intuitionistic relevant logic. It provides a way of avoiding the computational overheads of loop-detection that are involved in the standard formulation of the elimination rules for ¬ and ⊃. Because the *minor* proofs of these rules might need the major premiss of the elimination for use once more as a premiss, there is a danger of looping when searching for a proof. Dyckhoff's method allows one to avoid that troublesome repeated use of the major premiss within the minor by using instead some suitably 'simpler' formulae constructed from the constituents of the major premiss ($\neg A$ or $A \supset B$) that are revealed once the dominant operator of A is explicitly shown. These constituents are, collectively, and

---

[3]'Contraction-Free Sequent Calculi for Intuitionistic Logic', Research Report CS/91/95, University of St Andrews (forthcoming in *The Journal of Symbolic Logic*).

within the context of the proposed elimination, logicaly tantamount to the major premiss. Bringing them into play in the minor proof as substitutes for the major premiss enables one to achieve inductive breakdown of the deductive problem, albeit not very rapidly; thereby avoiding having to detect loops. Think of a detected and truncated loop as a *hoop*. Dyckhoff's method can be thought of as allowing one to replace hoops with long downward spirals. The suitably 'simpler' formulae that he exploits in connection with ¬- and ⊃-eliminations I shall call *phantom* subformulae of the major premiss in question. Since they are to feature as possible future premisses within the minor proof for the elimination, it is useful to have them as 'constituents' of a replete representation of the major premiss. Hence the provision of item (12) above.

We would effect further economies if (2)-(8), (11) and (12) were included in Gödelian fashion, via their numerals; provided only, of course, that from the numeral one can obtain easy access not only to the formula it stands for, but also to its (partially) replete representation as and when needed. As it happens, the version of Prolog that I have used - NuProlog — provides a method of assigning any ground term t an *address* a. The clause:

$$assert(t, X)$$

instantiates X to the address a. Once an address a has been given, the term in question can be looked up very quickly: the clause

$$clause(X, \_, a)$$

instantiates X to the sought term t.

This encourages one to use addresses rather than Gödelian numerals as the 'pointers' involved in the construction of partially replete representations. Gödelian numerals continue to be used, however, as shorthand for premisses and conclusions for the purpose of recording failures for averting proof-finders, and recording successes for adverting proof-finders. For the numerals are much easier to read in the trace of a computation when one is trying to debug a program that has executed a proof-search incorrectly.

It might be too cumbersome to carry all this arboreal information along in the form of twelve separate components in each formula's representation. First, there is some redundancy anyway in the list above. Feature (11), for example, could be detected by recourse to features (5) and (6) and trawling for disjunctions. Secondly, the benefits of quick feature detection would in some cases be more than offset by the burden of carrying the relevant detail in the representations. This is the problem of striking a balance mentioned earlier.

I propose to make a judicious selection from the list above, building in to the eventual representations only those features that I have found to be generally useful as far as a Prolog program is concerned. This usefulness depends on the frequency with which one needs to detect the feature in question, and on the cost of carrying the information along in the representation.

With a different programming language, offering a different family of data types, the balance might be struck in a different way. It might prove cost effective with such a language to make the representations more replete by including some of the features that I shall be omitting. I dare say also that this could prove to be the case even with variations on the Prolog implementation of the proof-search algorithm developed here. All that is important at this stage is that the reader should be aware of the potential utility of being able to detect various syntactic features; and of the pragmatic nature of the choice of the most useful among these for any particular implementation of the abstract algorithm in a given programming language.

This is one area of research where I believe we stand to benefit by knowing more about the cognitive powers of competent human logicians. How do they manage simply to 'see' some of these features, without undertaking too much recursive computation? It is interesting how, after the proper training and experience, one manages to 'see' certain features very easily with formulae *that are not too long.* Beyond a certain threshold of length, however — which will vary from one human subject to another — one has to resort to recursive computations to detect the features in question. Perhaps the neural network for visual perception of syntactic structure can be trained to be very fast at detecting features in formulae that are not too long; and the brain then has to invoke recursive algorithms for feature detection in the longer ones. No doubt also this threshold constrains in important ways the range of mathematical conjectures that we find interesting, that we are able to entertain with full understanding, and that we can prove or refute. But any investigation of such a line of speculation is to be reserved for a future work.

We noted earlier that the formulae involved in any sub-problem generated by inductive breakdown of an initial problem $X?\text{-}A$ will be subformulae of formulae involved in the latter[4]. Indeed, we can claim something stronger

---

[4] Here we set aside for the moment the kind of inductive breakdown devised by Dyckhoff to avoid looping on minors of ¬- and ⊃-eliminations. The constituents he brings into play

here. Given the possible ways that inductive breakdown can occur, with the rules of inference as standardly formulated, we had this result earlier:

> *THEOREM*: In a deductive problem $X?$-A, only positive subformulae of premisses in X or negative subformulae of A could ever occur as possible premisses of sub-problems reached by inductive breakdown. Only negative subformulae of premisses in X or positive subformulae of A could ever occur as their conclusions.

It will accordingly be useful to distinguish two kinds of representation of formulae involved in a deductive problem. The first kind will be of formulae that could potentially occur as *premisses* in a sub-problem generated by inductive breakdown. The second kind will be of formulae that could occur as a *conclusion* in such a sub-problem. We shall therefore have terms of the form $prem(\_,\ldots,\_)$ and $conc(\_,\ldots,\_)$. And what arboreal components we pack into each will be determined by what we need to know about premisses and conclusions, respectively, for efficient proof-search.

Given that we are working with the system M of minimal logic, we shall not be concerned to include in our representations of formulae the kind of arboreal information involved in our Genetic Defect Screen for the system IR of intuitionistic relevant logic. That is, we shall not be concerned to trace $\neq$-chains within genets, and we shall not be concerned to find members of genets that share a propositional variable (of the same parity) with the conclusion. Indeed, we shall confine ourselves to features (7) and (8): we shall be interested at first[5] only in detecting *atoms* occurring as (direct or indirect) accessible positive subformulae of *premisses*. This will allow us to implement the accessibility filter efficiently; and it will enable us to follow the accessibility heuristic in choosing major premisses for elimination when dealing with a problem $X?$-A with atomic A.

By focusing our attention on only this amount of arboreal information, we are able to make do with a five-place representation $prem(\_,\_,\_,\_,\_)$ and a three-place representation $conc(\_,\_,\_)$. Take any problem $X?$-A. If and only if a formula P occurs as either a positive subformula of some premiss or a negative subformula of A might P occur as a premiss in some sub-problem

---

may turn out *not* to be subformulae of the conclusion or of any premiss of the original problem. Hence my terminology of *phantom* subformulae introduced above.

[5]See the program *MAMBA* discussed in the next chapter. It exploits only arboreal information about *atomic* subformulae (concerning ways they occur in premisses) and involves the standard method of loop-detection in minors of ¬- and ⊃-elimination.

generated from $X?\text{-}A$. Such an occurrence of P will accordingly receive a representation using $prem(\_,\_,\_,\_,\_)$. Likewise if and only if P occurs as either a negative subformula of some premiss or a positive subformula of A might P occur as a conclusion in some such sub-problem. Such an occurrence of P will accordingly receive a representation using $conc(\_,\_,\_)$. Remember that we shall also, at the outset, assign numerals as names to all subformulae involved in $X?\text{-}A$. In doing so we shall specify that $\perp$ is named 0.

Suppose, then, that we have a formula P with numeral N. We shall now describe what one strategy for more (recursively) replete representation might put into each kind of representation of P[6]. $\pi(P)$ will be the *prem* version; $\gamma(P)$ will be the *conc* version. $\rho(P)$ will be ambiguous between the two (meaning 'the contextually appropriate form of representation of P'). Let I be the set of *indirect* accessible positive atoms in P, and J the set of *direct* ones. Then we may define the recursively replete representations $\pi(P)$ and $\gamma(P)$ as follows. For an atom P (other than $\perp$),

$$\pi(P) =_{df} prem(P, N, P, \emptyset, \{P\})$$
$$\gamma(P) =_{df} conc(P, N, P)$$

Note that $\perp$ can only ever occur as a conclusion. We specify

$$\gamma(\perp) =_{df} conc(\perp, 0, \perp)$$

For a compound formula P, suppose the dominant operator is O. Thus P is of the form $O(P_1, \ldots, P_n)$. We further define

$$\pi(P) =_{df} prem(P, N, O(\rho(P_1), \ldots, \rho(P_n)), I, J)$$
$$\gamma(P) =_{df} conc(P, N, O(\rho(P_1), \ldots, \rho(P_n)))$$

The contextually appropriate forms of representation of the immediate subformulae of compound P are easy to specify, as they mimic the definition of positive and negative subformulae. For the various possible forms of compound P the third component of $\pi(P)$ is as follows

---

[6] We make only a modest selection of components, in order to keep the illustration both simple and informative. This strategy has actually proved to be remarkably effective. But it is not claimed to involve the *ideal* amount of information to be carried along in the components of representations.

$\neg(P_1) : \neg(\gamma(P_1))$

$\wedge(P_1, P_2) : \wedge(\pi(P_1), \pi(P_2))$

$\vee(P_1, P_2) : \vee(\pi(P_1), \pi(P_2))$

$\supset (P_1, P_2) : \supset (\gamma(P_1), \pi(P_2))$

Likewise, for the various possible forms of compound P the third component of $\gamma(P)$ is as follows

$\neg(P_1) : \neg(\pi(P_1))$

$\wedge(P_1, P_2) : \wedge(\gamma(P_1), \gamma(P_2))$

$\vee(P_1, P_2) : \vee(\gamma(P_1), \gamma(P_2))$

$\supset (P_1, P_2) : \supset (\pi(P_1), \gamma(P_2))$

We now see why recursively replete representations are potentially cumbersome. Recursively replete representations involve components that are themselves recursively replete representations. By confining ourselves to the sets I, J of *atoms*, we minimise the effects of such recursive repletion. But if we have, say, the phantom subformulae of Dyckhoff's method calling for recursively replete representation as members of a component within a recursively replete representation, then matters might get out of hand, since there are more of these phantom subformulae than there are immediate constituents.

If ever one decides, in such a case, that recursive repletion has become too cumbersome one may wish to adopt the method of *partially replete* representations of premises. In a partially replete representation the sets occurring as components contain only the Gödelian numerals (or addresses) for the formulae, *or for the partially replete representations of the formulae*, that 'are' their members. Thus the 'contained' partial repletions do not actually occur embedded within a containing partial repletion; only pointers to them do. One only needs then a 'master list' of partial repletions with their Gödelian numerals, or an efficient method of recovering partially replete terms from their addresses, in order to be able to access arboreal information 'on the surface' about constituents revealed or otherwise brought into play upon inductive breakdown.

The definition of partially replete representations is like that given above for recursively replete ones, except for the following two important differences. First,

$$\pi(P) =_{df} prem(P, N, O(\alpha(\rho(P_1)), \ldots, \alpha(\rho(P_n))), I, J)$$
$$\gamma(P) =_{df} conc(P, N, O(\alpha(\rho(P_1)), \ldots, \alpha(\rho(P_n))))$$

where $\alpha(t)$ is the *address* of the term t. Secondly, the third components of $\pi(P)$ and of $\gamma(P)$ need not be formula-morphs whose immediate constituents are representations, but can instead be simply the the lists of those 'immediate constituents'. We use quotation marks here because the list method is particularly useful for the partially replete representations that are employed with Dyckhoff's method of effecting ¬- and ⊃-eliminations. Here the various 'phantom' subformulae can be placed as members of the list — their precise position within the list determining the characteristic use that is to be made of them when the Dyckhoff forms of the elimination rules are applied. Thus the partial repletions become now

$$\pi(P) =_{df} prem(P, N, [\alpha(\rho(P_1)), \ldots, \alpha(\rho(P_n))], I, J)$$
$$\gamma(P) =_{df} conc(P, N, [\alpha(\rho(P_1)), \ldots, \alpha(\rho(P_n))])$$

where ρ and n depend on the precise form of P. *We now see clearly that partially replete representations, as terms, have length linear in the length of the formulae represented.*

We shall resort to the method of partial repletion, with its master list of Gödelian baptisms of partial repletions, or a method of addressing the same, only when we adopt the Dyckhoff method of slower inductive breakdown, and its associated invocation of phantom subformulae. Until then, our recursively replete forms will prove to be manageable for even the longest problems we shall encounter. It is the recursively replete, and not the partially replete, method of representation that is employed in the program *MAMBA* discussed in the next chapter.

Our new forms of representation allow us (or Prolog's unification algorithm) to 'read off' the following features:

1. atomicity: via the identity or non-identity of the first and third components of the representation

2. whether a premiss has an accessible positive disjunctive subformula: via the emptiness or otherwise of the fourth component of its representation

3. what the formula actually is!: via the first component of its representation

4. what the direct accessible positive atoms in a premiss are: via the fifth component of its representation

5. what the indirect accessible positive atoms in a premiss are: via the fourth component in its representation

Recording and recalling success or failure is also more economic, via the second components of the representations. For a problem

$$prem(P_1, N_1, P'_1, I_1, J_1), \ldots, prem(P_n, N_n, P'_n, I_n, J_n)?\text{-}conc(A, M, A')$$

the recording and recalling will be done with the pair $\{M, \{N_1, \ldots, N_n\}\}$, at only nominal cost.

So much for our illustration of a more replete method of representing formulae as computationally manageable objects. We turn now to the representation of proofs as computationally accessible ones.

Chapter 11

How to represent proofs

We are looking for proofs. So we need to know when we have found them. Like formulae, proofs in a system of natural deduction, or in our hybrid system[1], have a tree-like structure[2]. The nodes of a proof-tree are labelled by formulae or by rules of inference. We have multiple branching in the proof-trees of our hybrid system when we apply ∧-introduction or any elimination rule. The remaining three rules — ¬-introduction, ∨-introduction, ⊃-introduction — occasion only single branching. Note that a multiply branching rule need not be a splitting rule. Every elimination rule is multiply branching, since its major premiss calls for its own branch, consisting just of itself. (Remember we are dealing here with the hybrid system.) Then there are the branches for its subproofs, of which there will be at least one. Among elimination rules only ∨-elimination and ⊃-elimination involve *more than one* such subproof, and are accordingly splitting rules.

The analogy with formulae suggests a similar method of representation of proofs — as Polish terms, with brackets supplied as a free accessory. Corresponding to logical operators in a formula we have rules of inference in a proof. Corresponding to immediate subformulae we have immediate subproofs. Corresponding to atomic formulae we have trivial proofs — single occurrences of formulae, constituting proofs of themselves from themselves. The schema for a proof of conclusion A that ends with an application of an introduction rule i and has immediate subproofs $\Pi_1, \ldots, \Pi_n$ is $i(A, \Pi_1, \ldots, \Pi_n)$. The schema for a proof of conclusion A that ends with an

---

[1] see Ch.3.

[2] except when they are turned into acyclic directed graphs by the use of pointers to avoid repetition of subproofs: see Ch.4.

111

application of an elimination rule e with major premiss B and immediate subproofs $\Pi_1, \ldots, \Pi_n$ is $e(A, B, \Pi_1, \ldots, \Pi_n)$. O_i will be the introduction rule for an operator O; O_e will be its elimination rule.

Take, for example, the little hybrid proof we used in Ch.3:

$$
\cfrac{
  \cfrac{
    \cfrac{\quad}{B \supset (D \wedge A)}(3) \qquad B \qquad
    \cfrac{\cfrac{\quad}{D \wedge A}(2) \quad \cfrac{\quad}{A}(1)}{A}(1)
  }{A}(2)
}{A}(3)
$$

$$C \wedge (B \supset (D \wedge A))$$

This can be represented by the Prolog term (that is, Polish term with brackets)

$$\wedge\_e(a, \wedge c \supset b \wedge da, \supset\_e(a, \supset b \wedge da, b, \wedge\_e(a, \wedge da, a)))$$

Here I have suppressed the brackets that occur in the Prolog terms for the *formulae* within the proof. This allows us to see more clearly the term structure of the proof itself. There is, however, no analogue within the proof-term of the discharge numerals within the hybrid proof. But these can be supplied. One way to do this is to use the numerals that name formulae. In the proof, replace every occurrence of a formula F with an occurrence of the *pair* $[F, n]$ consisting of the formula F and its numeral n. Now when an assumption is discharged, we can put its numeral into a label λ for the rule application that discharges it. When only one assumption is discharged (as, for example, with ¬-introduction), λ will be the singleton $[n]$ containing its numeral n. When more than one assumption is discharged — that is, when exactly two assumptions are discharged (as, for example, with ∨-elimination) — λ is the pairset $[n_1, n_2]$ of their numerals n_1, n_2. I use square brackets here for perspicuity; and also because that is a Prolog convention for set representation, into which I might as well ease the unfamiliar reader.

λ will be a new final component in the proof-term representing a proof ending with an application of the discharge rule in question. The undischarged assumptions of the proof will now be those whose numerals do not occur in the final component of any schema corresponding to the application of a rule of inference lower down in the proof-tree. (It should be noted that an assumption can be discharged in one subproof but not in another.)

Supposing for the sake of illustration that the numerals 1, 2, 3 displayed in the hybrid proof above were indeed the numerals that named the respective discharged assumptions, and that B has numeral 4 and $C \wedge (B \supset (D \wedge A))$ has numeral 5, the proof-term keeping track of discharges would be

$$\wedge_{-}e(a, [\wedge c \supset b \wedge da, 5], \supset_{-}e(a, [\supset b \wedge da, 3], [b, 4],$$
$$\wedge_{-}e(a, [\wedge da, 2], [a, 1], [1]), [2]), [3])$$

We see here an added benefit of the notation $[F, n]$. It is used only for *assumptions*, not for conclusions. This helps one to keep track of which formula occurrences are assumption occurrences and which are conclusion occurrences. Note too that the numeral n will be available from the representation of the premiss F as $prem(F, n, F', I, J)$ described in the previous chapter.

It is certainly not the intention here to claim that the proof-terms mooted are particularly easy for the reader to grasp. Rather, they are ideal for a machine running a Prolog program for constructing proofs. For proof-terms will be built up as solutions to deductive problems of the form $X?\text{-}A$. A tentative terminal application of an introduction rule i (potentially discharging some assumption) will yield the non-ground proof-term $i(A, \Pi_1, \ldots, \Pi_n, \lambda)$. It is not ground because the subproofs $\Pi_1, \ldots, \Pi_n$ have yet to be determined; as does the precise membership of λ. The same holds in the case of a tentative terminal application of an elimination rule e (potentially discharging assumptions), to get $e(A, [B, m], \Pi_1, \ldots, \Pi_n, \lambda)$. In the case of rules that do not discharge assumptions, λ will not feature in the proof-term; but the problem remains of having to construct ground instances of the subproof variables. On our account of proof-search, then, the proof is produced by constructing a proof-term 'from the outside in', so to speak. One tentatively produces 'proof-templates' (that is, non-ground proof-terms), using rule-applications embodying wanted subproofs, and generates as sub-problems for subsequent search the grounding of the subproof variables involved.

So the Prolog terms for proofs are ideal for computation. They can be much improved upon, however, as objects for human scrutiny, perusal and understanding. One could, of course, write an algorithm that would simply convert a ground Prolog proof-term, once it has been constructed, into the tree-like natural deduction structure with which we are already familiar. Assumptions would then occur at the tops of branches, the conclusion at the root. Numerically annotated discharge strokes would be placed over assumption occurrences that are discharged, and the same numeral would label the inference step lower down that effected the discharge.

That would be ideal for the human logician. But there is a problem associated with it. Such tree-proofs are given to awful *sideways spread*. Any reasonably difficult proof tends to go off the edge of the page, or off the edge of the computer screen. And in the latter case, auto-wrapping produces, if not spaghetti, then woodchip of the proof-tree.

The solution to this problem is to exploit a more Fitch-style representation. It remains isomorphic to the Prolog proof-term, but re-arranges its innards in a perspicuous way. The transformation $f[\Pi]$ that turns a Prolog proof-term Π into the easier-to-read Fitch representation is defined inductively. The basis is simple: on trivial proofs it is the identity transformation. The inductive clause is

$$
f[r(A, \Sigma_1, \ldots, \Sigma_n, \lambda)] \quad =_{df} \quad
\begin{array}{c|l}
 & f[\Sigma_n] \\
 & \vdots \\
 & f[\Sigma_1] \\
\hline
r & \lambda \\
A &
\end{array}
$$

Note here that when the rule r is an elimination rule, Σ_1 will be the major premiss, of the form $[B, m]$. We shall, however, suppress the square brackets in expressions like the last one. We shall also suppress them in the display of λ. If r is not a discharge rule, λ will not appear. We require also that the various $f[\Sigma_i]$ be vertically separated. That is, the topmost part of any one but the topmost should be lower than the bottommost part of the one above it. The f-transform of a Prolog proof-term is designed to minimise sideways spread when displaying the proof. The resulting Fitch-style representation of the proof above will now be

$$\begin{array}{c|c} & \wedge da, 2 \\ & a, 1 \\ \wedge_e & 1 \\ a & \\ & b, 4 \\ & \supset b \wedge da, 5 \\ \supset_e & 2 \\ a & \\ \wedge_e & 3 \\ a & \end{array}$$

This form of display for proofs is almost optimal for computational purposes. Provided the page or screen is wide enough to accomodate each line without wrapping, the Fitch form has this nice feature: each line contains, at a certain indentation, an assumption (discharged or undischarged); or a conclusion; or rule- and discharge-labels for the rule-application that yields the conclusion on the line immediately below those labels.

This form of proof display will become optimal when we take the final step, in due course, of abbreviating the formula occurrences themselves within the proof by means of their Gödelian numerals. This further abbreviation will be effected without any loss of informative structure. Before we do that, however, we shall continue for a while with formulae displayed fully at every one of their occurrences within a proof.

There are some important *disanalogies* between proper Fitch proofs and what I am here calling 'Fitch-style representations' of hybrid proofs. A proper Fitch proof is really a vertical linearization of an acyclic directed graph proof. It involves indentations only with the discharge rules of a Prawitz formulation: ¬-introduction, ⊃-introduction and ∨-elimination. In the latter case, moreover, the major premiss stands *above* the indented case proofs, *at the same indentation* as the conclusion. The Fitch proof proper also allows allows re-iteration of lines at greater indentations below their first occurrences.

Imagine now that all the vertical lines at their various indentations are extended upwards to reach the topmost point of the proof display (or, in general, to reach just below any part of the proof above it that it would otherwise hit):

$$\begin{array}{l}
\qquad\qquad\qquad\quad \wedge da, 2 \\
\qquad\qquad\qquad\quad a, 1 \\
\qquad\qquad \wedge\text{-}e \;\big|\; 1 \\
\qquad\qquad a \\
\qquad\qquad\quad b, 4 \\
\qquad\qquad\quad \supset b \wedge da, 5 \\
\qquad \supset\text{-}e \;\big|\; 2 \\
\qquad a \\
\wedge\text{-}e \;\big|\; 3 \\
a
\end{array}$$

The result is a display that one can easily program the computer to produce line-by-line on the screen, using the vertical bar (or dash) | at appropriate indentations[3]. Each vertical line in the proof above will then become a vertical sequence of these dashes. Indeed, one can place the dashes at a constant space apart. By decreasing this space one can effect significant latitudinal savings in the presentation of longer proofs. 'Longer proofs' tend now to be just that: long in the direction *down* the page (or screen). If in any long proof there is still the need to wrap a line, this is easily seen to be the case, and one's comprehension of the structure of the proof display is not badly disturbed. In this case one will either have a whole line (or more) of vertical dashes, with no formula until the end of the last one — in which case one knows that that formula is formidably indented; and/or have a tail-end piece of wrapped formula not preceded by any vertical dashes to its immediate left — in which case one knows that it belongs to the truncated head piece of formula on the line immediately above.

Here, for example, is the proof display produced by the computer for the formula used for the purposes of illustration in our syntactic discussion in the previous chapter. Aficionados will have recognised it as the axiom of distributivity in R. It is a theorem of M as well. In our computer-generated proof, we have $>$ in place of $\supset$, & in place of $\wedge$, v in place of $\vee$, and $\sim$ in place of $\neg$. The discharge numerals have not been generated in this example; the reader should supply them as an exercise.

---

[3]I am grateful to Seppo Keronen for writing this useful module of the program.

```
NU-Prolog 1.3
1?- Loading m.no.
done
true.
2?-

PROBLEM NUMBER 1:

[] ?- if(and(a, or(b, c)), or(and(a, b), c))

The length of this problem is 11

I take only 0 ms to find the following PROOF,

which has 11 steps of inference:

   |    |    | vi| c
   |    |    | v&abc
   |    |    |    |    | b
   |    |    |    | &i| a
   |    |    | vi| &ab
   |    |    | v&abc
   |    | ve| vbc
   |    | v&abc
   | &e| &avbc
 >i| v&abc
 >&avbcv&abc
```

The final stage, foreshadowed above, in distilling the essentials of a proof's structure depends on having tags, such as Gödelian numerals, for each of the formulae involved in the proof. Suppose the formula $\wedge AB$ has numeral n, and that A and B (which may themselves be complex) have numerals m and k respectively. Then $\wedge AB$ can be rendered as $[\wedge mk, n]$. An *atomic* formula with numeral n would become simply $[n, n]$. Let us call these transforms the *structural labels* of the formulae transformed. If every formula occurrence in a proof is now replaced by an occurrence of its structural label, we obtain a most succinct representation of the proof. Suppose, for example, that the theorem whose proof in minimal logic has just been displayed had Gödelian numerals for its subformulae as follows:

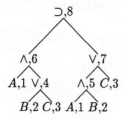

Then the proof just given would become

```
|   |   | vi| 3,3
|   |   | v53,7
|   |   |   |   | 2,2
|   |   |   | &i| 1,1
|   |   | vi| &12,5
|   |   | v53,7
|   | ve| v23,4
|   | v53,7
| &e| &14,6
>i| v53,7
>67,8
```

The saving of representative effort may not be immediately apparent from this one example, to the untutored eye. But the reader should note this laconic feature of any Gödelian display like the one just given, which results in massive abbreviatory savings in proofs involving very long formulae: every 'complex formula occurrence' has one of the forms $[\neg m, n]$, $[\wedge mk, n]$, $[\vee mk, n]$, or $[\supset mk, n]$, *with no more structure to be displayed within the labels* m, n[4]. Let us once more suppress square brackets. The structure of a complex formula such as the conclusion $\supset 67, 8$ of the proof just given can

---

[4]We are of course assuming that a structural label such as $\supset 12$ is read as $\supset (1, 2)$ and not as $\supset$-'*twelve*'!

be recovered hereditarily from the proof itself. 7 is replaced by ∨53 and 6 is replaced by ∧14. In their turn, 5 is replaced by ∧12 and 3 is left alone (being an atom, it is replaced by *itself*!), 1 is left alone and 4 is replaced by ∨23. Finally, in ∧12, 1 is left alone and 2 is left alone; while in ∨23, 2 is left alone and 3 is left alone. *The tree structure of the proof allows one to recover the tree structure of any formula within it.* Moreover, there is now hardly any need for discharge numerals. The Gödelian proof display wears its discharge relations on its sleeve. An occurrence of θ, n is discharged by the first less deeply indented occurrence below it (if any) of combined rule- and structural-labels of any one of the forms

¬i |	⊃i |	∧e |	∧e |	∨e |	∨e |	⊃e |
¬m, n	⊃mk, n	∧np, q	∧pn, q	∨np, q	∨pn, q	⊃pn, q

Chapter 12

How to generate proofs

Proofs, like formulae, can be defined inductively. The basis clause says that an occurrence of a sentence is a proof of that sentence from itself. Then the inductive clauses deal with rules of inference one at a time[1]. I shall detain the reader with only two examples here; and leave as an exercise the provision of the remaining ones.

The first example is of a multiply branching but non-discharging rule: $\wedge$-introduction. Here the inductive clause in the definition of proof reads:

If Π_1 is a proof of A_1 from the set X_1 of undischarged assumptions and if Π_2 is a proof of A_2 from the set X_2 of undischarged assumptions, then

$$\frac{\Pi_1 \quad \Pi_2}{A_1 \wedge A_2}$$

is a proof of $A_1 \wedge A_2$ from the set $X_1 \cup X_2$ of undischarged assumptions.

The second example is of a singly branching discharge rule: $\neg$-introduction. Here the inductive clause in the definition of proof reads:

If Π is a proof of $\perp$ from the set X of undischarged assumptions, then

---

[1]See my *Natural Logic*, Edinburgh University Press, 1978.

$$\frac{\Pi}{\neg A}$$

is a proof of $\neg A$ from the set $X \setminus \{A\}$ of undischarged assumptions.

Note that in this last clause the possible discharge of assumption A is only implicit. There is no requirement that A actually be a member of X, and hence 'available' for discharge. This laxity is characteristic of minimal logic. In intuitionistic relevant logic, as we have already seen, we *would* impose the latter further requirement, in order to prevent 'vacuous' discharge with application of $\neg$-introduction.

When the undischarged assumptions of a proof form a subset of X, we shall say that the proof is *from X*. Note that this does not imply that every member of X occurs in the proof as an undischarged assumption; rather, it means only that every such assumption is in X. Proofs *from X* need not, therefore, *use* all of X. Let us attend now to the first example, namely $\wedge$-introduction. One can re-formulate the clause we have given as a conditional goal statement:

> In order to find a proof Π of $A_1 \wedge A_2$ from X, find a proof Π_1 of A_1 from X and a proof Π_2 of A_2 from X.

Let us introduce now the Prolog predicate $proof(X, A, D)$ to mean 'D is a proof (in minimal logic) of A from X' (in the sense of 'from' just explained). Then the conditional goal statement just given becomes the Prolog clause

$$proof(X, \wedge(A_1, A_2), D) :-$$
$$proof(X, A_1, D_1),$$
$$proof(X, A_2, D_2),$$
$$D = \wedge\_i(\wedge(A_1, A_2), D_1, D_2).$$

or, better,

$$proof(X, \wedge(A_1, A_2), \wedge\_i(\wedge(A_1, A_2), D_1, D_2)) :-$$
$$proof(X, A_1, D_1),$$
$$proof(X, A_2, D_2).$$

We turn now to the second example, namely $\neg$-introduction. One can re-formulate the clause we have given as this conditional goal statement:

In order to find a proof Π of $\neg A$ from X, find a proof Σ of $\bot$ from X, A.

Note that if A is already in X, then X, A is simply X. And even if A is *not* in X, so that X is now *extended* to X, A, it may turn out that the proof Σ does not *use* A — that is, that A is not one of its undischarged assumptions. Our conditional goal statement for $\neg$-introduction becomes the Prolog clause

$$proof(X, \neg A, D) :-$$
$$addElement(A, X, Y),$$
$$proof(Y, \bot, D_1),$$
$$D = \neg\_i(\neg A, D_1).$$

or, better,

$$proof(X, \neg A, \neg\_i(\neg A, D_1)) :-$$
$$addElement(A, X, Y),$$
$$proof(Y, \bot, D_1).$$

Note that we have not bothered here to include mention of any set λ of numerals for discharged assumptions. We are concerned only to bring out the main features of the transition from inductive clauses in the definition of proof to their Prolog counterparts in a proof-finding program.

If one mindlessly transformed all the inductive clauses in the definition of proof into their Prolog counterparts in this way, one would obtain a program that was declaratively correct insofar as the proof predicate was concerned, but procedurally disastrous. It would be hopelessly inefficient. It would have no heuristics for proof search, and would backtrack for aeons on even the simplest of deductive problems. It is actually worth providing some evidence here for this claim.

The Prolog program $SNAIL$[2] consists of just the clauses, such as the two above for $\wedge$-introduction and $\neg$-introduction, that capture the bare essentials of the proof predicate. The only logically intelligent aspects of $SNAIL$ are that we embody Algorithmic Rules 1 and 2 by having the rules of $\wedge$-elimination and $\vee$-elimination first and second, respectively[3]; and that we put all the elimination rules before any introduction rule, thereby making $SNAIL$ follow what we called the *elimination strategy*. Of course, the basis

---

[2] see Appendix.
[3] see Ch.4.

clause has to come first, as it would in any Prolog account of an inductively defined relation.

There are also, of course, some 'bookkeeping' clauses in the program. These keep track of problem length, number of steps in proofs, and time taken to find proofs; and maintain cumulative records of performance. They also take care of the messages that are displayed on the screen when the program deals with a list of problems, and ensure that proofs are displayed in the Fitch form discussed above.

One can use the program in *hand-feeding mode* or in *force-feeding mode*. In *hand-feeding* mode, one will pose a problem of the form $X?\text{-}A$. The program then finds some proof D of A from X, if there is one; otherwise, it reports 'NO DERIVATION'. The program is hypercomplete. It will generate each and every proof, given enough time. After a proof of a hand-fed problem has been given, the program can be prompted to look for another proof of the same problem. It will do so by backtracking. When finally there are no more alternative proofs to be found, it will fail.

In *force-feeding* mode the program can be fed a list of problems of the form $X?\text{-}A$. Each will be posed as $proof(X, A, D)$. As with hand-feeding mode, the program then finds some proof D of A from X, if there is one; otherwise, it reports 'NO DERIVATION'. It then automatically proceeds to the next problem, not bothering to generate any alternative proofs even if they exist.

The first of our programs, called *SNAIL*, is a sound and hypercomplete, non-adverting, non-averting heuristic-, filter-, screen-free proof-finder. The only intelligent features built in to it (by the ordering of its clauses) are, as already remarked, the elimination strategy and Algorithmic Rules 1 and 2. *SNAIL* will be the *only* hypercomplete program in our collection. It is a pristine example of a declaratively correct definition, using Prolog clauses, of *proof* in minimal logic.

SNAIL fares remarkably well on a long list of problems that I have devised for testing and debugging proof-finders[4]. But now and again it runs amok. Here is an example[5]:

---

[4] see Appendix.

[5] Prolog displays the set $[P_1, \ldots, P_n]$ rather perversely as $.(P_1, \ldots, .(P_n, [])\ldots)$. This is because Prolog uses the dot functor to codify ordered sets. The set whose only member is P is $.(P, [])$. The ordered pair $[P, Q]$ is $.(P, .(Q, []))$; and so on.

NU-Prolog 1.3
1?- Loading snail.no.
done
true.
2?-

PROBLEM NUMBER 1:

.(not(p), .(not(and(p, not(q))), .(not(and(not(p), q)),
.(not(and(not(p), not(q))), [])))) ?- #

The length of this problem is 19

I take only 644300 ms to find the following PROOF,

which has 10 steps of inference:


```
|   |   |   |   | q
|   |   |   | &i| ~p
|   |   |   | &~pq
|   |   |  ~e| ~&~pq
|   |  ~i| #
|   |  ~q
| &i| ~p
| &~p~q
~e| ~&~p~q
#
```


Backtracking is the culprit. *SNAIL* will let proofs be *undone* on backtracking. For example, suppose one is trying to prove $A \wedge B$ by $\wedge$-introduction.
Suppose there is a proof of A but no proof of B: so that *SNAIL*, like any
other correct proof-finder, should return the verdict 'NO DERIVATION'.
SNAIL will find a proof of A. But when *SNAIL* fails to find a proof of B, it
will spend more time uselessly trying alternative proofs of A and once more

embarking on the futile search for a proof of B.

One can prevent this futile meandering among the alternative proofs of A by one of two methods.

The *first* method is to modify each $proof(\_, \_, \_)$ subgoal in the body of any clause by the Prolog operator $once(\_)$. This will prevent the search for alternative proofs of A. While we are about it, we might as well also avail ourselves of $once(\_)$ on some of the choices of major premises for elimination. For we know (for conjuctive and disjunctive major premises) that if we fail on any one choice, we shall fail on any other. Thus we should not fruitlessly try alternatives here either.

The *second* method is riskier. This is to place *cuts* (occurrences of '!') immediately after each $proof(\_, \_, \_)$ subgoal. The risk involved is that a problem solved once may turn up again later in the computation; and the cut after its solution the first time round would prevent its solution on the second occasion. The proof-finding program could therefore be logically incomplete.

This risk of logical incompleteness could be averted by making the program into an *adverting* one[6] employing the *ditto tack*. That is, past successes will be recorded, and the second time round a pointer to the proof found earlier would be entered as the solution.

But at this stage we are working with an extremely simple, declaratively correct program. *SNAIL* neither adverts nor averts. So we shall adopt the first method, using $once(\_)$, and allow *SNAIL* to evolve into *SLUG*.

The good thing about *SNAIL* and *SLUG* is that they are so obviously sound and complete proof-finders for minimal logic. 'Program proving' is unnecessary, for they are such direct renderings of the inductive definition of proof in minimal logic. They incorporate no heuristics that would call for proof-theoretic justification, apart from Algorithmic Rules 1 and 2. But even here, it is only *SLUG* that needs the justification that we have already provided for these two rules. For *SNAIL*, the ordering of clauses (with ∧-elimination and ∨-elimination first and second, respectively) might help it find its *first* proof for a given (hand-fed) problem more quickly; but, since it is hypercomplete, further prompting for alternative proofs will eventually produce those in which ∧-eliminations and ∨-eliminations do *not* monopolize the bottom of the proof.

SLUG is a sound and complete, *but not hypercomplete*, non-adverting, non-averting, heuristic-free, filter-free, screen-free proof-finder. By the or-

---

[6] see Ch.4.

dering of its clauses it incorporates the elimination strategy and Algorithmic
Rules 1 and 2.

   SLUG goes about its business much more brusquely; not for it the shiny
meandering paths traced all around the search tree by *SNAIL*. On the problem just given *SLUG* is almost 20,000 times faster:

```
NU-Prolog 1.3
1?- Loading slug.no.
done
true.
2?-
```

PROBLEM NUMBER 1:

```
.(not(p), .(not(and(p, not(q))), .(not(and(not(p), q)),
.(not(and(not(p), not(q))), [])))) ?- #
```

The length of this problem is 19

I take only 33 ms to find the following PROOF,

which has 10 steps of inference:

```
|   |   |   |   | q
|   |   |   | &i| ~p
|   |   |   | &~pq
|   |   | ~e| ~&~pq
|   | ~i| #
|   | ~q
| &i| ~p
| &~p~q
~e| ~&~p~q
#
```

We can use *SNAIL* and/or *SLUG* to generate not only lists of provable
problems, but also lists of *unprovable* problems in minimal logic. These can

then be used to check the correctness of further refinements of *SLUG*. Such refinements may incorporate heuristics justified by the existence of various transformations on proofs; or by metatheorems such as those already proved above, about patterns of occurrence of subformulae in proofs. The most important of these is the accessibility heuristic. We implement it in a later chapter.

To bring this chapter to a close, we take one more step up the evolutionary ladder with *NEWT*. *NEWT* is an *averting SLUG*. That is, *NEWT* records failures, and then avoids searches on previously failed problems. *NEWT* incorporates the algorithm outlined at the beginning of Chapter 7.

NEWT is a sound and complete, but not hypercomplete, non-adverting, averting, heuristic-free, screen-free proof-finder. By the ordering of its clauses it incorporates the elimination strategy and Algorithmic Rules 1 and 2. Its adversion employs a *homogeneous* failure filter (one that does not discriminate among entries $X?\text{-}A$ according to whether A is atomic, or what its dominant operator is).

Note that we have failure recording clauses in *NEWT* immediately after $\wedge$-elimination and immediately after $\vee$-elimination. This is justified by the left-to-right directions of the two theorems[7] behind Algorithmic Rules 1 and 2.

We also provisionally record an overall failure as we enter the major for $\supset$-elimination once the minor has been done. If, however, we *succeed* on the major, this provisional failure is retracted. If we *fail* on the major, then not only will its own failure be independently recorded, but the tentative record of overall failure becomes definite. This is justified by the following obvious results:

THEOREM: $X, A \supset B \vdash A$ and $X, B \vdash C \Rightarrow X, A \supset B \vdash C$

THEOREM: $X, A \supset B \vdash C \Rightarrow X, B \vdash C$

The effect of failure recording is dramatically illustrated by the problem of deciding whether

---

[7] see Ch.4.

$\land \supset \land \supset \land \supset pq \supset qpr \supset r \land \supset pq \supset qp \land \supset p \land \supset qr \supset rq \supset \land \supset qr \supset rqp \supset \land \supset p \land \supset$
$qr \supset rq \supset \land \supset qr \supset rqp \land \supset \land \supset pq \supset qpr \supset r \land \supset pq \supset qp$

is a theorem of minimal logic. *SLUG* is this slow[8]:

```
NU-Prolog 1.3
1?- Loading slug.no.
done
true.
2?-
```

```
PROBLEM NUMBER 1:
```

```
[] ?- and(if(and(if(and(if(p,q),if(q,p)),r),if(r,and(if(p,q),
if(q,p)))),and(if(p,and(if(q,r),if(r,q))),if(and(if(q,r),if(r,
q)),p))),if(and(if(p,and(if(q,r),if(r,q))),if(and(if(q,r),if(r,
q)),p)),and(if(and(if(p,q),if(q,p)),r),if(r,and(if(p,q),if(q,
p))))))
```

```
The length of this problem is 79
```

```
I take only 431750 ms to decide that there is NO DERIVATION
```

By learning from its failures, *NEWT* is 500 times faster than *SLUG*:

```
NU-Prolog 1.3
1?- Loading newt.no.
done
true.
2?-
```

```
PROBLEM NUMBER 1:
```

```
[] ?- and(if(and(if(and(if(p,q),if(q,p)),r),if(r,and(if(p,q),
if(q,p)))),and(if(p,and(if(q,r),if(r,q))),if(and(if(q,r),if(r,
q)),p))),if(and(if(p,and(if(q,r),if(r,q))),if(and(if(q,r),if(r,
q)),p)),and(if(and(if(p,q),if(q,p)),r),if(r,and(if(p,q),if(q,
p))))))
```

---

[8]from now on we display only the most relevant part of a program's output.

The length of this problem is 79

I take only 866 ms to decide that there is NO DERIVATION

Faster than *SLUG* though *NEWT* may be, *NEWT* in turn labours for ages on some problems. Take for example the problem

$[\lor \lor\, a\neg \supset \neg \supset a\neg\neg a\neg \lor b\neg b\neg \supset \neg \supset \lor a\neg \supset \neg \supset a\neg\neg a\neg \lor b\neg b\neg\neg \lor a\neg \supset \neg \supset$
$a\neg\neg a\neg \lor b\neg b\neg \lor c\neg c]$
?-
$\lor a\neg \supset \neg \supset a\neg\neg a\neg \lor \lor b\neg \supset \neg \supset b\neg\neg b\neg \lor c\neg c\neg \lor b\neg \supset \neg \supset b\neg\neg b\neg \lor c\neg c$

which may even exercise the reader somewhat. *NEWT* takes almost seven minutes to find a proof:

```
NU-Prolog 1.3
1?- Loading newt.no.
done
true.
2?-
```

PROBLEM NUMBER 1:

```
.(or(or(a,not(if(not(if(a,not(not(a)))),not(or(b,not(b))))))),
not(if(not(if(or(a,not(if(not(if(a,not(not(a)))),not(or(b,
not(b))))))),not(not(or(a,not(if(not(if(a,not(not(a)))),not(or(b,
not(b)))))))))))),not(or(c,not(c))))))),[]) ?- or(a,not(if(not(if(a
not(not(a)))),not(or(or(b,not(if(not(if(b,not(not(b)))),not(or(c
not(c))))))),not(or(b,not(if(not(if(b,not(not(b)))),not(or(c,
not(c))))))))))))))))
```

I take only 406066 ms to find the following PROOF,

which has 1172 steps of inference:

(Here we suppress the proof display)

```
true.
3?- End of Session
```

We shall eventually evolve a program that will find a proof of this problem 3,500 times faster than *NEWT* (and a much shorter one at that):

```
NU-Prolog 1.3
1?- Loading fetter.no.
done
true.
2?-
```

```
PROBLEM NUMBER 1:

.(or(or(a,not(if(not(if(a,not(not(a)))),not(or(b,not(b)))))),
not(if(not(if(or(a,not(if(not(if(a,not(not(a)))),not(or(b,
not(b)))))),not(not(or(a,not(if(not(if(a,not(not(a)))),not(or(b,
not(b)))))))))),not(or(c,not(c)))))),[]) ?- or(a,not(if(not(if(a
not(not(a)))),not(or(or(b,not(if(not(if(b,not(not(b)))),not(or(c
not(c)))))),not(or(b,not(if(not(if(b,not(not(b)))),not(or(c,
not(c)))))))))))))
```

The length of this problem is 100

I take only 116 ms to find the following PROOF,

which has 104 steps of inference:

(Here we suppress the proof display)

```
true.
3?- End of Session
```

The lesson emerging is that incorporating proof-theoretic considerations into one's proof-finder provides whole orders of magnitude in speed-up on problems of moderate length. We have so far only a modest phylogeny of proof-finding programs. We have shown that each program encounters a problem on which its evolutionary successor is orders of magnitude faster. This is only a worst-case comparison, to be sure, on the evidence given here; but the reader can be assured that it is characteristic of average cases as well.

I shall end this chapter on a mundane book-keeping note. The reader who can mentally trace the computations that would be carried out by *NEWT* (or its predecessors) will have realised that an awful lot of time can be wasted on membership checks called for by *inapplicable* applications of elimination rules. Thus even if the premiss set at a given stage lacks conjunctions, the rule of ∧-elimination will be routinely invoked. That is, the head of the Prolog clause for ∧-elimination will unify with the *proof(_,...,_)* template for the subproblem in hand. Then the search for a conjunctive major premiss will be undertaken — to no avail. The same story of inefficiency can be told for all the other connectives as well.

A considerable saving can be made, therefore, by ensuring that the head of any clause for an elimination fails to unify with a *proof(_,...,_)* template should the latter provide no candidate major premiss for that elimination. This can be done by *partitioning the premisses*. We carry as separate components in the *proof(_,...,_)* predicate the sets of negations, conjunctions, disjunctions and conditionals that partition the compound premisses available. Then, for ∧-elimination, say, we make the head embody the specification of a *non-empty* set of conjunctions among the premisses. In Prolog this is easily done by having the non-ground term [H|T] at the conjunctive component in the *proof(_,...,_)* template. This can be instantiated only by ground terms for *non-empty* sets, since it calls for a *head* in the list of set members, even if the head is followed by the empty *tail*. Similar remarks apply to the components in the *proof(_,...,_)* template corresponding to the other connectives.

Chapter 13

Features of a natural proof-finder

Our theoretical analysis has delivered various possible features of a proof-finding algorithm. Several of these have yet to be incorporated in more highly evolved progeny of *SNAIL, SLUG* and *NEWT*[1]. On the following page is a list of the features we have discussed so far, under natural groupings. They are then re-ordered in the table in the next page so that one can see clearly from the distribution of 0's and 1's (and $\frac{1}{2}$'s) the evolutionary saltations I plan to induce subsequently.

Saltations are called for because the features are varied enough to threaten tedium if one were to follow the incremental pattern of exposition of the last chapter: incorporating one new feature at a time, demonstrating speed-up on some problem over the predecessor program, and then finding a bad case pulling the new program up in its tracks; incorporating another feature, ... , and so on. Moreover, we are in serious danger of running out of zoological labels.

In this chapter a program will be described that incorporates several of the features above. We have already seen it at work before (in Chapter 11), proving the distributivity axiom of R in 0 milliseconds. I call it simply m, for M. In our haphazard journey around the Linnaean hierarchy we can think of having reached *MAMBA*.

---

[1] I owe to Catherine Pickering the observation that any biologically informed reader will detect a jump in phylum here.

SUMMARY OF FEATURES OF PROOF-FINDING ALGORITHMS[2]

Main metalogical feature:
    hypercomplete v. complete but not hypercomplete
    (by virtue of using 'once', or cuts)

Strategies and heuristics:
    up-front ∧-elimination
    up-front ∨-elimination
    depth-first search v. breadth-first search
    elimination strategy
    briefcase method
    accessibility heuristic (atomic conclusions)
    accessibility heuristic (compound conclusions)
    informed elimination for disjunctive conclusions
    premiss partitioning
    backgrounding redundant premisses, or premiss set reduction
    introduction heuristic

Dynamic filters:
    averting (failure filter) — homogeneous v. heterogeneous
    adverting (ditto tack) — homogeneous v. heterogeneous

Static filters:
    basic relevance filter
    refined relevance filter
    atomic accessibility filter
    genetic defect screen (*IR* only)

Economic methods of representation:
    neat method/replete method
    Gödelian (numerals as names of formulae)

---

[2]We are assuming here that the algorithms involve loop-detection in minor proofs for ¬-elimination and ⊃-elimination. We reserve for a later chapter our discussion of Dyckhoff's ingenious (but proof-theoretically impure) device for achieving gradual inductive breakdown by reformulating these two rules by cases according to the form of a complex antecedent.

MENS SAPIENS INTUITIONIS RELEVANTIS

MENS SAPIENS MINIMALIS

m

NEWT

SOME ALGORITHMS AND ...   *SLUG*

SNAIL

... THE DISTRIBUTION OF THEIR FEATURES

complete v. complete but not hypercomplete	0	1	1	1	1	1
up-front ∧-elimination	1	1	1	1	1	1
up-front ∨-elimination	1	1	1	1	1	1
($\frac{1}{2}$ = mixed strategy) elimination strategy	1	1	1	$\frac{1}{2}$	$\frac{1}{2}$	$\frac{1}{2}$
averting (failure filter) — homogeneous v. heterogeneous	0	0	$\frac{1}{2}$	$\frac{1}{2}$	1	1
accessibility heuristic (atomic conclusions)	0	0	0	1	1	1
backgrounding redundant premisses, or premiss reduction	0	0	0	1	1	1
informed elimination for disjunctive conclusions	0	0	0	1	1	1
premiss partitioning	0	0	0	1	1	1
atomic accessibility filter	0	0	0	1	1	1
neat method/replete method	0	0	0	1	1	1
Gödelian (numerals as names of formulae)	0	0	0	1	1	1
depth-first search v. breadth-first search	0	0	0	0	1	1
briefcase method	0	0	0	0	1	1
accessibility heuristic (compound conclusions)	0	0	0	0	1	1
introduction heuristic	0	0	0	0	1	1
adverting (ditto tack) — homogeneous v. heterogeneous	0	0	0	0	1	1
basic relevance filter	0	0	0	0	1	1
refined relevance filter	0	0	0	0	1	1
genetic defect screen (*IR* only)	0	0	0	0	0	1

For the rest of this chapter, I shall be explaining the construction of *MAMBA*. The main burden of explanation has to do with how to incorporate the new features for *MAMBA* that are specially boxed in the preceding figure[3]. The algorithm implemented by the program can be summarised by extraction from earlier discussion.

THE ALGORITHM m

We have a deductive problem $X?$-A posed in minimal logic.

We apply first the

FAILURE FILTER:

> *Have we failed on this one before? If so, fail again.*
>
> (Here we partition problems for the failure filter into classes, according to the form of the conclusion: $\bot$, other atom, negation, conjunction, disjunction, conditional. If $X?$-$\bot$ fails, we record *consistent(X)*; if $X?$-A fails, for $A \neq \bot$, we record *atomicfailed(A,X)*, *notfailed(A,X)*, *andfailed(A,X)*, *orfailed(A,X)*, or *iffailed(A,X)*, as the case may be. *consistent(_)* and the various Ξ*failed(_,_)* are dynamic predicates.)

After applying the failure filter we then apply the

ATOMIC ACCESSIBILITY FILTER:

> *Is A atomic and not an accessible positive subformula of any premiss? If so, fail X?-A. (And record this failure explicitly, if you are not using cuts to prevent this problem ever being looked at again.)*

Then we explore the possibility of

---

[3]Within this chapter this will be the last time I shall use the name *MAMBA*. Reference to *MAMBA* will be implicit throughout what now follows.

TRIVIAL PROOF

> *Is the conclusion already among the premisses? If so, take it as a proof of itself from itself.*

If not, we have to construct a

NON-TRIVIAL PROOF of X?-A, which presents us with the

CHOICE PROBLEM:

Choose some formula to go to work on! That is, either

(I) settle on the conclusion A, and try applying the *introduction* rule for its dominant operator; or

(E) focus on some premiss in X, and try applying the *elimination* rule for its dominant operator.

Generally we prefer *(E)* to *(I)*; but we do not follow a *pure* elimination strategy. We do, to be sure, perform up-front $\land$-eliminations and $\lor$-eliminations. As we shall see, however, $\supset$-elimination cedes priority to *safe introductions* — that is, when the conclusion is a negation, conjunction or implication. So we have the following

ORDERING OF CHOICES:

First try all $\land$-, $\lor$-, and $\neg$-eliminations, in that order (with elimination of $\neg$ of course being applicable only if the conclusion is $\bot$).

(See under 'Atomic accessibility heuristic' for a more refined ranking of choices of major premisses for elimination when the overall conclusion is atomic.)

Then, if the conclusion is a conjunction, a conditional or a negation, try introduction.

Then, if (and, so it turns out: only if) the conclusion is atomic or disjunctive, try $\supset$-eliminations.

Finally, try $\lor$-introduction for a disjunctive conclusion.

With all attempts at ∧-elimination, ∨-elimination and ⊃-elimination, and within each priority subclass[4] when an atomic conclusion A is involved with those rules respectively, follow the

BACKGROUNDING STRATEGY[5], aided by
PARTITIONING OF THE PREMISSES:

> Remember you will have partitioned the compound premisses in X into disjoint classes of negations, conjunctions, disjunctions and conditionals. It is to these components that you will have recourse when seeking major premisses for the corresponding kinds of elimination. If you pick a conjunction from the conjunctive component whose conjuncts are both in X, background it by removing it from the conjunctive component. Likewise, if you pick a disjunction one of whose disjuncts is in X, background it by removing it from the disjunctive component. Finally, if you pick a conditional whose consequent is in X, background it by removing it from the conditional component. In each of these cases, you will never 'see' the backgrounded compound premiss again. (The ones you *do* see will be called *visible*.)

ATOMIC ACCESSIBILITY HEURISTIC

> *In choosing a major premiss for a tentative terminal elimination when seeking a proof for the problem X?-A, with A atomic, give high priority to those that contain A as an accessible positive subformula. Indeed, give even higher priority to those that contain A as a direct accessible positive subformula.*

Suppose you are seeking a proof of atomic A from X. Then here is what the atomic accessibility heuristic combined with the backgrounding strategy bids you do:

---

[4] These priority subclasses will be drawn from this list of three: the subclass of premisses that contain A as a direct accessible positive subformula; the subclass of premisses that contain A as an indirect accessible positive subformula, but not as a direct one; and finally, the subclass of remaining premisses not in either of the first two subclasses (the 'genuinely residual' subclass)

[5] It is not vital, for efficiency, to use backgrounding with conjunctive premisses; and indeed we shall omit it.

Take the *conjunctive* premisses in X. Try them as major premisses for $\land$-elimination in the following more refined order:

First choose conjunctive premisses in which A occurs as a *direct* accessible positive subformula, if there are any.

Background your choice if both its conjuncts are available as premisses.

Secondly, choose ones in which A occurs as an *indirect* accessible positive subformula, *but not as a direct one*, if there are any.

Background your choice if both its conjuncts are available as premisses

Finally, try any remaining ones.

Background your choice if both its conjuncts are available as premisses.

If any attempted $\land$-elimination fails, record failure (according to the form of the overall conclusion A).

Likewise, take the *disjunctive* premisses in X. Try them as major premisses for $\lor$-elimination in the following more refined order:

First choose disjunctive premisses in which A occurs as a (perforce *indirect*) accessible positive subformula, if there are any.

Background your choice if either of its disjuncts is available as a premiss.

Then try any remaining ones.

Background your choice if either of its disjuncts is available as a premiss.

If any attempted $\lor$-elimination fails, record failure (according to the form of the overall conclusion A).

Now, if the conclusion is $\bot$, try $\neg$-elimination with any negated premisses $\neg P$ that may be available, and in the following order: P already available as a premiss; P atomic; P disjunctive; P negated; P conditional; P conjunctive.

Finally, take the *conditional* premisses in X. Try them as major premisses for $\supset$-elimination in the following more refined order:

First, try conditional premisses with A as consequent, if there are any. Among these, go first for ones with antecedents already available as premisses; then for any others.

Secondly, try conditional premisses in which A occurs not as consequent, but as a *direct* accessible positive subformula (and therefore as a direct accessible positive subformula of the consequent), if there are any. Now observe the *obviousness trichotomy* of conditional premisses satisfying this last choice condition: (1) Background your choice if its consequent is already available as a premiss. (2) Then go for ones whose antecedents are already available as premisses. (3) Then go for ones whose antecedents are not already available as premisses, and that therefore call for both a non-trivial minor and a non-trivial major.

Thirdly, try conditional premisses in which A occurs as an *indirect* accessible positive subformula, *but not as a direct one*, if there are any. Observe here too the obviousness trichotomy.

Finally, try any remaining ones — here, too, observing the obviousness trichotomy.

If any attempted ⊃-elimination fails after its minor succeeds, record failure (according to the form of the overall conclusion A).

That ends the advice of the atomic accessibility heuristic.
In the case of *disjunctive conclusions*, major premisses for ⊃-elimination are chosen as follows:

Try conditionals that contain a direct accessible positive disjunction, observing the obviousness trichotomy.

If any attempted ⊃-elimination fails after its minor succeeds, record failure.

Keep the proofs that result on any subproblem $Y?\text{-}B$. If it is the overall problem $X?\text{-}A$, report it as your result. If you have exhausted all the above algorithmic possibilities on any $Y?\text{-}B$ with no success, then you have failed on $Y?\text{-}B$. Record the failure and backtrack. If the failure is on the original problem posed, report it as the result.

END OF THE ALGORITHM m

This account of the algorithm does not go into any of the details of what is involved in applying any of the rules of inference, once one has chosen the conclusion or a particular premiss to go to work on. It also leaves implicit the fact that, for example, the only way to prove a conclusion from the empty set of premisses is by introduction. This will happen anyway on the account above, for want of a premiss to go to work on. But it can be stated as an early clause of the program at the very outset, ensuring that the *proof_by_introduction* predicate is invoked as soon as an empty set of premisses is detected.

There will in fact need to be only two main predicates: *proof*, and *proof_by_introduction*. Proof (via *proof*) will thus be by elimination, with proof by introduction taking place only when *proof_by_introduction* is explicitly called.

What I now need to explain is what components, or arguments, there are to be in these proof predicates. We wish to implement an algorithm that is sensitive to various features of a problem. This enables it to trigger or call various modules at appropriate points. As with Prolog programming in general, this sensitivity is effected by *parametrising the predicates*. That is, we increase the number of components or arguments of the main predicates. These contain information needed in the course of a computation. At each step in a computation this information is relevantly updated or revised, and the resulting information then carried along so that it can be drawn on as and when needed. This happens most importantly when we attempt to apply a rule of inference. For this involves inductive breakdown of the deductive problem — which obliges us to revise the informative features.

We have already indicated what some of these features are.

First, we carry along (and up-date) not only the overall set of premisses for the deductive problem at hand; but also the respective subsets of negated, conjunctive, disjunctive and conditional premisses. This obviates the need for membership checks when testing the applicability of an elimination rule.

Secondly, we carry along, for all the premisses and the conclusion of the problem at hand, those components of what I have called their (more) *replete representations*. For the purposes of the present algorithm, we shall be using exactly the forms of representation discussed in Chapter 10. Note that we are using only the *atomic* accessibility heuristic, not the compound one. It is therefore necessary to carry, in the replete representations, only sets of *atomic* direct accessible positive subformulae, *atomic* indirect accessible positive subformulae, and so on.

The algorithm will therefore need a module to *pre-process* the formulae in an initial problem $X?$-A. It should be stressed here that this shall *not* involve transformation into clausal forms! We do *not* seek to mangle the syntax of the initial problem in order to make it tractable by an unnatural algorithm. Rather, what our pre-processing accomplishes is a species of highly informative embellishment of existing syntactic structure. That pre-existing structure still informs the representation. The latter just adds to it what can be read off from it: facts about accessibility, in the main.

The only exception to this general claim is the attachment of Gödelian numerals as names for formulae. But even then, one can think of this as abbreviation of the second 'appearance' of formulae that 'appear' twice at any one occurrence — once as themselves, and once, autonomously, as names of themselves! Astral formulae, one might call them ... The insight here has indeed been pressed to its limit with the introduction of our Gödelian proof displays in the previous chapter. There, the double 'appearances' of a formula became an occurrence of its numeral, and an occurrence of the appropriate numeralwise representation of the formula in terms of its immediate constituents. In the case of an *atomic* formula, this meant *two* occurrences of its numeral![6]

We summarise now with an account of what goes into each proof predication of the Prolog program. Using letters from regions of the alphabet whose sortal significance we have already been imparting, and various others we have yet to explain, a proof predication has the form

$$proof(S,X,UI,UJ,And,Or,If,Not,conc(A,N,A1),D)$$

where the various arguments are explained in the following inventory[7]:

S is the set of numerals for members of X;
X is the set of (replete representations of) premises;
UI is the *multiset union*[8] of the sets I in those representations;
UJ is the *multiset union* of the sets J in those representations;

---

[6] Even proof theory hereby falls victim to postmodernist conceit.

[7] Recall that in the replete representation $prem(P,M,P1,I,J)$ of a *premiss* P, M is its Gödelian numeral; $P1$ is its repletion; I is the set of its *indirect* accessible positive subformulae; and J is the set of its *direct* accessible positive subformulae. In the replete representation $conc(A,N,A1)$ of a *conclusion* A, N is its Gödelian numeral and $A1$ is its repletion. For a full explanation see Chapter 10. Recall also that *visible* premises are ones that have not been backgrounded.

[8] A multiset may contain more than one 'occurrence' of a 'member'. Their ordering is unimportant; only their multiplicity counts towards the identity condition of the multiset.

And is the set of visible conjunctive premises in X;
Or is the set of visible disjunctive premises in X;
If is the set of visible conditional premises in X;
Not is the set of negated premises in X;
conc(A,N,A1) is as explained in footnote; and
D is the derivation, or proof, being sought.

We have to justify incorporating these components in the proof predicate by the effective use made of them. Let us review their worth.

The first component S is used to record failures by means of the dynamic predicates *consistent(_)* and *failed(_,_)*. The reader should rest assured that the more compact entries that result yield faster look-up and therefore shorter run-times.

The second component X needs no justification except with regard to its being the set of *replete representations* of premises, rather than simply the premises themselves. Again, our experience has been that repletion leads to much quicker determination of syntactic relationships than does a subprogram devoted to their recursive determination, with or without memory for its own past computations. Replete forms also allow quick detection of atomicity: A is the same as $A1$.

The two multiset unions UI and UJ are useful for the following reasons, respectively.

First, UI gives what may be called the *disjunctive character* of the set of premises. UI is empty if and only if no premiss contains a disjunction as an accessible positive formula. So the emptiness of UI is a quickly detectable feature, on unification of the head of a clause, to trigger the atomic accessibility filter. (It would also serve to trigger the *compound* accessibility filter, were we to have that filter as well.) UI is the *multiset union*, rather than simply the set union, so that Frobenian (constituent-wise) updating renders it an accurate record. (Likewise with UJ.)

Secondly, the *non-emptiness* of UJ is also a quickly detectable feature, on unification of the head of a clause, that is required to make it worth even beginning to look for a major premiss in the so-called *direct subclass*. UJ is empty if and only if there are no direct accessible positive atoms in any premiss. So if UJ is empty we should move on to the indirect subclass in our search for a major premiss for elimination. This holds good for $\wedge$-elimination and $\supset$-elimination. The rule of $\vee$-elimination, as already pointed out, involves a premiss that cannot have any direct accessible positive atoms (or any other subformulae, for that matter), since its dominant operator is ∨.

We have already justified partitioning the compound premisses, which entails the use of *And, Or, If* and *Not.*

conc(A,N,A1) is, after all, what we are after from X, and we can tell quickly if it is an atom; if it is, A will be $A1$.

And we are after it via D, the proof term whose construction is what the computation is all about.

Chapter 14

On avoiding loops and blind alleys

14.1 The Dyckhoff Device

So far we have kept our logical rules *pure*. That is, the introduction or elimination of any operator has been accomplished with *fixed furcation* in the proof tree: ∨-elimination calls for a major premiss and two subproofs above the inference stroke; all other eliminations call for a major premiss and just one subproof above the inference stroke; ∧-introduction calls for two subproofs above the inference stroke; all other introduction rules call for just one. The schematic statement of these rules, moreover, has been *singular*: each rule involves just *one* occurrence of the logical operator in question, *and no occurrences of any others*. Take any logical operator ω, and look at its introduction rule. Notice that there is just one occurrence of ω, and that in the conclusion. No other operators appear anywhere in the statement of the introduction rule for ω. Likewise, look at its elimination rule. Notice that there is just one occurrence of ω, and that in the major premiss. No other operators appear anywhere in the statement of the elimination rule for ω.

It is this pure and singular character of our rules — as far as ¬-elimination and ⊃-elimination are concerned — that gives rise to the need for loop-detection in the minor subproofs of those eliminations. All our programs so far have involved loop-detection, a standard feature of proof-finders for a logical system in which the rules are pure and singular. This has been desirable from the point of view of what might be called *logical aesthetics*.

145

But loop-detection is expensive. It requires recording and consulting. In the harsher world of computational logic, where speed in execution enjoys high priority, logical aesthetics may have to be compromised. However reluctant a logician might be to tamper with the lovely scheme of things left by Gentzen and Prawitz, when *computational* considerations hold sway one may have to consider methods based on *impure* and *non-singular* forms of inference rules (which of course would have to generate the same range of deducibilities as the pure and singular ones do). What we call the *Dyckhoff device* is just such a method[1]. It obviates the need for loop-detection. It involves slower but inexorable inductive breakdown of deductive problems, by paying attention to the logical form of P in premisses of the form $\neg P$ and $P \supset Q$.

The (hybrid) Dyckhoff forms of $\neg$-elimination and $\supset$-elimination with major premisses $\neg P$ or $P \supset Q$ depend on the form of P. When P is compound, they are as follows. Note that each has four cases, one for each of the logical operators that may be dominant in P.

Dyckhoff himself does not treat negation separately as a primitive operator. Instead he assimilates it to the conditional, defining $\neg P$ as usual as $P \supset \bot$. I am taking the trouble here to keep negation as a separate primitive because doing so actually leads to an improvement on Dyckhoff's method. The improvement is this: when trying to prove an atom other than $\bot$, one knows one need not try any $\neg$-elimination as the final step. This insight arises naturally when negation is treated separately, and its proof-theoretic justification consists in a completeness proof for a set of Dyckhoff rules in which $\neg$-elimination on negated atoms (see below) is allowed only when the atomic 'antecedent' is already available as a premiss.

Here are the Dyckhoff elimination rules for negations of compound formulae:

---

[1] R.Dyckhoff, 'Contraction-Free Sequent Calculi for Intuitionistic Logic', Research Report CS/91/95, University of St Andrews (forthcoming in *The Journal of Symbolic Logic*). Dyckhoff acknowledges the earlier anticipation of his method by N.N.Vorob'ev, 'A new algorithm for derivability in the constructive propositional calculus', *Trudy Mat. Inst. Steklov* 52, 1958, pp.193-225, English translation in *American Mathematical Society Translations* (2) 94, 1970, pp.37-71.

$$\frac{\neg\neg A \qquad \dfrac{\overline{A}^{(i)} \\ \vdots \\ \bot}{}}{\bot}(i)$$

$$\frac{\neg(A \supset B) \qquad \dfrac{\underbrace{{}^{(i)}\overline{A} \quad , \quad \overline{\neg B}^{(i)}} \\ \vdots \\ B}{}}{\bot}(i)$$

$$\frac{\neg(A \wedge B) \qquad \dfrac{{}^{(i)}\overline{A \supset \neg B} \\ \vdots \\ A}{} \qquad \dfrac{\overline{A \supset \neg B}^{(i)} \\ \vdots \\ B}{}}{\bot}(i)$$

$$\frac{\neg(A \vee B) \qquad \dfrac{\underbrace{{}^{(i)}\overline{\neg A} \quad \overline{\neg B}^{(i)}} \\ \vdots \\ A \vee B}{}}{\bot}(i)$$

And here are the Dyckhoff elimination rules for conditionals with compound antecedents:

$$\frac{(i)\overline{}}{A} \; , \; \overline{B \supset C}^{(i)} \qquad \overline{C}^{(i)}$$

$$\underbrace{\phantom{(i)\overline{A} \; , \; \overline{B \supset C}^{(i)}}}$$

$$\frac{(A \supset B) \supset C \quad B \qquad \qquad D}{D}(i)$$

$$\frac{(i)\overline{}}{A} \; , \; \overline{\bot \supset C}^{(i)} \qquad \overline{C}^{(i)}$$

$$\underbrace{\phantom{(i)\overline{A} \; , \; \overline{\bot \supset C}^{(i)}}}$$

$$\frac{\neg A \supset C \qquad \bot \qquad \qquad D}{D}(i)$$

$$\frac{\overline{A \supset (B \supset C)}^{(i)} \quad \overline{A \supset (B \supset C)}^{(i)} \quad \overline{C}^{(i)}}{}$$

$$\frac{(A \wedge B) \supset C \quad A \qquad \qquad B \qquad \qquad D}{D}(i)$$

$$\frac{\overline{A \supset C}^{(i)} \qquad \overline{B \supset C}^{(i)} \qquad \overline{C}^{(i)}}{}$$

$$\underbrace{\phantom{\overline{A \supset C}^{(i)} \qquad \overline{B \supset C}^{(i)}}}$$

$$\frac{(A \vee B) \supset C \qquad A \vee B \qquad \qquad D}{D}(i)$$

Every subproof in the Dyckhoff rules just given for negation, and every subproof except the rightmost one (of D from C) in the Dyckhoff rules just given for the conditional, is called a *minor* subproof as before. Likewise as before, in $\supset$-elimination the rightmost subproof (of D from C) is called the *major* subproof. There is the following difference, however, between the Dyckhoff rules and the former hybrid rules that were pure and singular: *the premiss set for each minor subproof, like the premiss set for the major subproof, is obtained by* **replacing** *the major premiss in the overall set of premisses by*

the assumption(s) of the form(s) indicated within the subproof in question.
It is no longer necessary, that is, to have the *overall* set of premisses as the
set of premisses for each minor subproof. This *replacement without reten-
tion of the major premiss* is what allows one to do away with loop-detection.
Instead we now conceive of the formulae involved as so ordered in comparative complexity that the replacements represent a strict simplification of
the deductive problem. The new deductive subproblems, that is, *in minor
subproofs as well as in the major one*, will have lower complexity than the
original deductive problem.

The only trouble is of course that the new premisses of the forms displayed in the minor subproofs are not always genuine subformulae of the
major premiss or indeed of any of the other formulae involved in the original
deductive problem. Their sudden appearance on the scene may indeed even
bring operators into play that do not occur in the original problem — as,
for example, with the negation rule above for negated conjuctions. It brings
conditionals into the picture, even though it may be that the conditional
operator does not feature in the original problem.

This trouble is only apparent, however. One can weight the occurrences
of connectives within formulae so that conjunctions and disjunctions are
more complex than conditionals, while still having a well-founded measure
of complexity. Accordingly the replacements arising from the application
of these rules do involve inductive breakdown. The breakdown, however, is
just a little 'slower' than it would be if one were moving always to properly
contained genuine subformulae of formulae at hand. We shall instead call the
new formulae that arise without being genuine subformulae of formulae at
hand, *phantom* subformulae of the major premiss concerned. The relation
'... is a genuine or phantom subformula of ...' is still, by the foregoing
remarks, a well-founded one; thus the rules can be applied without fear of
loops, and without any corresponding need for loop-detection.

We can easily prove the soundness of a Dyckhoff rule by giving a proof
schema built up using the usual (Prawitz or hybrid) rules and embodying
the Dyckhoff minor and major proof schemata in such a way as to show that
the discharges in the Dyckhoff rule in question are justified. For example,
the Dyckhoff rule for conditionals with conditional antecedents:

$$\frac{\overline{A}^{(i)} \quad , \quad \overline{B \supset C}^{(i)}}{\underbrace{\qquad\qquad}_{\Pi}} \qquad \frac{\overline{C}^{(i)}}{\underbrace{\qquad}_{\Sigma}}$$

$$\frac{(A \supset B) \supset C \quad B \qquad\qquad D}{D}\,{}_{(i)}$$

can be derived as follows:

$$\frac{\overline{B}^{(1)}}{\dfrac{A \supset B \quad (A \supset B) \supset C}{C}}$$

$$\frac{\overline{A}^{(2)} \quad , \quad \overline{B \supset C}^{(1)}}{\underbrace{\qquad\qquad}_{\Pi}}$$

$$\dfrac{B}{\dfrac{\dfrac{A \supset B^{(2)} \quad (A \supset B) \supset C}{C}}{\dfrac{\Sigma}{D}}}$$

So that establishes its *soundness*. We establish its *completeness* as follows. We assume the existence of the minor subproof Σ of the usual form of the elimination rule. X will be the set of premisses of Σ other than the major premiss for the elimination in question. (Remember that with the usual form of elimination rule, this major premiss can still occur as an undischarged assumption of the minor subproof Σ.) We assume also (by inductive hypothesis) the existence of such Dyckhoff derivations Π_i as correspond to the usual form of $\supset$-eliminations (Prawitz style, say) with major premisses simpler than and in place of the main one in question. We then show how to construct the Dyckhoff minor proofs from these materials. Thus we show that the Dyckhoff minor exists if the usual one does (Prawitz or Gentzen or hybrid). For the example at hand this is done by exhibiting the composite schema

$$\underbrace{A\ ,\ \overline{A \supset B}}_{\Pi_1}\,{}^{(1)}$$

$$\underbrace{B\ ,\ B \supset C}_{\Pi_2}$$

$$\underbrace{\overline{X,\ (A \supset B) \supset C}}_{\Sigma}\,{}^{(1)}$$

$$\underbrace{A\ ,\ A \supset B}_{\Pi_3}$$

$$B$$

The composite schema here is not, of course, strictly a schema for a hybrid proof. This is because an indicated formula occurrence that stands as conclusion of the sub-schema immediately above it, and as major premiss of the sub-schema immediately below it, will not be featuring in the way required within a hybrid proof. For in hybrid proofs no major premiss for an elimination can have any proof-fragment above it. This difficulty is easily overcome, however: one simply observes that we have, in effect, a normalization theorem for the system of hybrid proof. This is because we have proved above that the cut rule is admissible for the system of hybrid proof. Thus the non-normal proof schema above can be 'normalized' once the particular sub-proofs have been filled in.

For all the other forms of Dyckhoff rules above, the verification of soundness and completeness proceeds along the lines just illustrated. Remember that in order to establish *soundness* of a Dyckhoff rule, one derives it by means of the usual rules (such as the hybrid rules). In order to prove *completeness* of a Dyckhoff rule, note that the displayed assumptions of its minor subproof will imply the major premiss in minimal logic. Hence, if this major premiss is undischarged in the minor subproof of the hybrid rule, the latter subproof will provide passage to the minor conclusion, whence the Dyckhoff minor will easily be constructed.[2]

---

[2]Note that I am applying the main idea of Dyckhoff's approach to the *minors* of ⊃-eliminations. Dyckhoff himself proceeds somewhat differently when the major premisses of such eliminations have conjunctive or disjunctive antecedents. In those cases, he does not split the problem into the minor and major sub-problems. Instead, he simply replaces the major premiss by its simpler counterpart formula(e), and re-poses the deductive question. That is, he performs a premiss-set reduction.

What if the contemplated premiss for a $\supset$-elimination has an atomic antecedent?' One easy option (not, however, the one chosen by Dyckhoff) is to let the Dyckhoff rule in this case be the orthodox one, subject only to this proviso: if the overall conclusion is $\bot$, then the major premiss for $\supset$-elimination should *not* be $\bot$. For otherwise the same deductive problem would be posed in the minor. The resulting set of rules is easily shown to be complete. The proof of completeness is straightforward. One shows how to transform any ordinary proof into a Dyckhoff proof. One does this by induction on the length of the ordinary proof, invoking the completeness schemata above and the normalizability of the Dyckhoff proofs.

I shall call atoms other than $\bot$ *letters*[3].

A second option (not quite the one that Dyckhoff chooses) with regard to $\supset$-eliminations and $\neg$-eliminations with *letter* antecedents is to defer such steps until such time as one reaches a sub-problem in which the antecedent is available as a premiss. But a $\supset$-elimination with antecedent $\bot$ would have the usual form, in which the proof of the minor may use the full set of premisses. It follows, as indicated above, that no deductive power is lost if we restrict applications of the rule in this case by requiring the overall conclusion to be a letter. (For if it were $\bot$, we would simply be re-posing the overall deductive question in the minor.) Thus we have, in effect, a more severely constrained pair of elimination rules for negation and the conditional. Let us call the whole set of rules on this option the *modified Dyckhoff rules*. To prove their completeness we have to proceed a little more ingeniously, by way of a preliminary lemma[4].

Note that the Dyckhoff $\supset$-elimination rule given above for major premisses of the form $\neg A \supset C$ involves the creation, for the minor, of an assumption of the form $\bot \supset C$. It should be borne in mind, therefore, that the lemma will be dealing with a language that is a slight extension of that which we have so far been using. The extended language now allows conditionals with antecedent $\bot$. But this is the *only* sentential context in which $\bot$ is allowed to occur. Note that the lemma does not mention Dyckhoff rules and proofs at this stage. It is concerned only with ordinary proofs according to the hybrid rules with which we have so far been dealing; except, of course, that they now might involve formulae of the form $\bot \supset C$.

---

[3] Elsewhere I have called them *variables*; but I call them *letters* here because of the useful adjective *literal* that will be used in two associated senses below.

[4] The lemma is basically due to Dyckhoff. I have adapted it to take care of negation as a primitive.

Consider any problem $X{:}C$. Suppose that if C is $\bot$ then for no letter A in X does X contain any sentence of the form $A \supset B$ or $\neg A$; and that if C is a letter then for no letter A in X does X contain any sentence of the form $A \supset B$. Such a problem $X{:}C$ will be called *non-literal*.

In sentences of the form $A \supset B$ or $\neg A$, A is called the *antecedent*. Any proof that ends with a step of $\supset$-elimination or $\neg$-elimination, whose major premiss has a letter antecedent, will be called *literal*. Otherwise, it will be called *non-literal*.

LEMMA: Any non-literal problem $X{:}C$ that has an ordinary hybrid proof has a non-literal ordinary hybrid proof.

Proof. The proof is by induction on proofs Π of $X{:}C$. We seek a transform Π' satisfying the conditions of the lemma. If Π is non-literal, we are done. So suppose now that Π is literal: that is, Π ends with a step of $\supset$-elimination or $\neg$-elimination on a major premiss with *letter* antecedent A. We have to show that we can shuffle that step up past the final step of the minor subproof Σ of A. By inductive hypothesis take a non-literal transform Σ' of the minor. Note that none of the undischarged assumptions of Σ' is discharged by the final step of Π. So if Σ' were trivial, $X : C$ would be literal, contrary to assumption. So Σ' is non-trivial. Since the conclusion A of Σ' is a letter, the final step of Σ' is an elimination of $\wedge$, $\vee$ or $\supset$. In the first two cases the upward shuffle is easy. In the third case likewise: and note that since by inductive hypothesis Σ' is non-literal, the major premiss of its final step (a $\supset$-elimination) does not have a letter antecedent. So after the shuffle, when that major premiss Q becomes the major premiss of the terminal step of the transform Π', the requirement of the Lemma is satisfied.

Ω

This Lemma allows an easy proof of completeness of the Dyckhoff rules now in hand for complex and atomic antecedents.

THEOREM: For all ordinary proofs Π of $X:C$ there is a Dyckhoff proof Σ of $X:C$.[5]

Proof. We argue by induction on Π *and* $X:C$. There are four main cases to consider:

1. C is $\bot$, and for some letter A, X has either the form $Y, A, A \supset B$ or the form $Y, A, \neg A$

2. C is not $\bot$, and for some letter A, X has the form $Y, A, A \supset B$

3. C is $\bot$, and for no letter A does X have the form $Y, A, A \supset B$ or the form $Y, A, \neg A$

4. C is not $\bot$, and for no letter A does X have the form $Y, A, A \supset B$

Consider the first case. Suppose that X has the first form indicated. Then there will be an ordinary proof of $\bot$ from Y, A, B. By inductive hypothesis there will be a Dyckhoff proof of the same. Now extend the latter proof with a final step of $\supset$-elimination with available letter antecedent, to obtain the sought Dyckhoff proof of $X:\bot$. Suppose now that X has the second form indicated. Then the sought Dyckhoff is just a single step of $\neg$-elimination.

Consider the second case. The reasoning here is just as in the previous case for the first form for X, with C in place of $\bot$.

Consider the third and fourth cases together. Our Lemma guarantees an ordinary hybrid proof of C from X whose final step is not $\supset$-elimination or $\neg$-elimination with letter antecedent. If this final step is anything other than a $\supset$-elimination or a $\neg$-elimination, the construction of the desired Dyckhoff proof is immediate by inductive hypothesis. But if the final step *is* one of $\supset$-elimination or $\neg$-elimination, we proceed by cases according to its antecedent, which has to be $\bot$ or be compound. If it is $\bot$, the result is immediate by inductive hypothesis. If on the other hand it is compound, then we invoke proof-schemata as discussed above, understood against the background of guaranteed normalizability. The exercise in prooflet arrangement can be left as an exercise for the reader.

Ω

---

[5]Strictly, the theorem should state that there will be a *modified* Dyckhoff proof. I shall suppress the modification from now on.

The reader may have one residual misgiving about allowing the rule of $\supset$-elimination on major premises with antecedent $\bot$ to use in the minor the full set of available assumptions in the overall problem. Is there not a danger here that one's search for a proof might enter a loop? That the danger is only apparent and not real can be seen as follows. The rule in question will be invoked (with, say, major premiss $\bot \supset C$) only when the overall conclusion is not $\bot$. (This is the self-imposed restriction that we justified above.) Thus the deductive problem posed for the minor will be different from the overall one. No looping so far. Now the deductive problem posed in the minor has conclusion $\bot$. Thus we cannot invoke, as the terminal step of the minor proof, another application of $\supset$-elimination with a major premiss of the form $\bot \supset D$ (again, because of our restriction). Whatever other rule *is* invoked for the terminal step of the minor will either yield a one-step solution, in which case the search terminates; or involve further inductive breakdown of the problem. The spectre of looping vanishes.

Equipped as we are now with Dyckhoff elimination rules for $\neg$ and $\supset$ that do not involve loop-detection in their minor subproofs, we can 'plug in' to our program *MAMBA* a Dyckhoff module as an alternative to the present application of $\neg$- and $\supset$-elimination in their usual (hybrid) form. The algorithm remains otherwise exactly as before. This holds in particular for the choice problem insofar as conditional premises are concerned. I call the resulting program *SIDEWINDER*. Its name is a mnemonic for the way it unravels problems inductively in a long spiral, rather than forming hoops (that is, detected loops).

Since *SIDEWINDER* employs the Dyckhoff device, it produces proofs with varying furcation at eliminations of $\neg$ and of $\supset$, depending on the form of P in their major premisses $\neg P$ and $P \supset Q$ respectively. These proofs will therefore tend to be longer than proofs for the same problems produced by *MAMBA* (as measured by the number of steps plus the number of occurrences of topmost formulae). *SIDEWINDER* finds its proofs, however, more quickly.

For any further refinement of *MAMBA* there will now be its corresponding Dyckhoffian *Doppelgänger*. The choice between the two versions rests on the relative importance, to the chooser, of speed versus purity of proof.

14.2   Fettering

Foraging for conditional major premisses is a crucial part of a good proof-finding algorithm. At the point when such foraging becomes appropriate the problem has this form:

> Given $X?\text{-}A$, where X contains one or more conditionals,
> (1) *choose* one such conditional
> (2) find a *minor* subproof
> (3) find a *major* subproof

If the conditional chosen is $P \supset Q$, the minor subproof is a solution to the minor subproblem $X?\text{-}P$; and the major subproof is a solution to the major subproblem $X \setminus \{P \supset Q\}?\text{-}A$. Note that 'major' and 'minor' here are the logical terms used in discussions of conditionals. There is no implied difference in importance or in degree of difficulty.

The main difference between the two subproblems is that, whereas the major involves inductive breakdown, the minor need not — or at least, on a suitable inductive measure such as that discussed earlier, need not involve such *rapid* inductive breakdown. The minor has the same set X of premisses as the original problem; and indeed P may be more complex than A. As we have already noted in earlier discussion, this raises the spectre of looping, or of infinite regress. For, when trying to find a minor subproof one may attempt $\supset$-elimination once again. This, if one's strategy is sufficiently untutored, could involve one in re-posing the minor sub-problem $X?\text{-}P$ within itself. One would thereby embark on an infinite regress. Any method for avoiding such infinite regress, regardless of the new inductive measure it puts at our disposal (with regard to which the minor subproblem can be seen at last to involve inductive breakdown) has the minor subproblem descending the degrees of inductive complexity less rapidly than the major subproblem[6].

There is another difference between the minor and major subproblems. Failure on the major entails failure overall, even if we succeed on the minor. But failure on the minor and success on the major does not entail failure overall. It may be that one need only try a different conditional premiss, or indeed a different approach altogether.

This last difference provides a decisive reason for attempting minor subproofs before major subproofs (for $\supset$-eliminations) on a depth-first strategy.

---

[6]This is true not only of the method of loop-detection discussed in Chapter 6, but also of the methods developed in this chapter: the *Dyckhoff device*, the method of *fettering* and the method of *hobbling*.

Bear in mind that, as just observed, the minor subproblem involves less dramatic inductive breakdown than the major subproblem, regardless of which method we adopt for avoiding loops within minors. On the method of *minors first*, a failed minor prevents us from even looking at the major. Likewise, on the method of *majors first*, a failed major prevents us from even looking at the minor. But, given the different rate of inductive breakdown, one is likely to take longer to reach a negative decision on a failing minor than on a failing major; and take longer to find a proof of a successful minor than a proof of a successful major.

Let us call the minor m and the major M, each with a superscript $+$ or $-$, depending, respectively, on whether it succeeds or fails. A deductive problem attacked by means of an attempted $\supset$-elimination will be called (m,M). Then interpret the symbols m^+, M^+, m^- and M^- as the times taken to reach those respective decisions. (m^i,M^j) represents the nature of the problem (i, $j = 0$ or 1, for failure and success respectively, as the case may be). Let mM be the method of *minors first*, and let Mm be the method of *majors first*. Consider the time taken by each of these methods on each of the four kinds of problem. They are equal on (m^+,M^+). On (m^-,M^+), Mm takes M^+ longer than mM. On (m^+,M^-), mM takes m^+ longer than Mm. Finally, on (m^-,M^-) mM takes m^- and Mm takes M^-. The net result is that we have to compare $m^- + m^+$ for mM with $M^- + M^+$ for Mm. The relative sizes of these quantities should give some indication as to which of the two methods is the faster. Given that inductive breakdown is more rapid for majors than for minors, so that in general m^i would exceed M^i, one would expect Mm to have the edge on mM, on the assumption that the four problem types are evenly distributed. The method Mm of *majors first* should be more efficient than the method mM of *minors first*.

This expectation, however, is empirically refuted. Test runs of programs differing only in this regard (mM versus Mm) reveal that the difference in run-times is characteristically one order of magnitude for problems whose length is two orders of magnitude — with mM faster than Mm, and not, as one might have expected from the foregoing considerations, the other way round.

So what might be the explanation for this unexpected result? It must be that the distribution of problem types is skewed. We can remark first that, since in general a major has a better chance of being provable than the original problem (because in the major subproblem the premiss is replaced by its consequent, which is stronger) we may expect $(m^+,M^+) \cup (m^-,M^+)$ to exceed $(m^+,M^-) \cup (m^-,M^-)$. Moreover, secondly, consequent-wary choice of majors raises the probability of M^+ as opposed to M^-; but we might still give hostage to fortune on m^+ as opposed to m^-. These two considerations explain how there could be a disproportionate swelling of the numbers of attempted (m^-,M^+)-type problems, on which Mm disadvantageously notches up the comparative time deficit of M^+.

Indeed, the *second* consideration in this explanation is borne out by the much greater discrepancy in runtimes between mM and Mm versions that both have consequent-wary choice of conditional premiss *suppressed* (so that there is no prioritizing of choices with an eye to the relation between consequent and overall conclusion). The discrepancy is still, however, in favour of mM over Mm. This in turn points to the residual force of the *first* consideration in our explanation, should it be correct. I conclude tentatively that the method of *minors first*, in the absence of *antecedent-wary* choice of conditional premisses, is to be favoured; and especially so if we exercise *consequent-wary* choice.

As far as (1), (2) and (3) are concerned (assuming we try them in that order — the method of *minors first*) *as soon as (2) is accomplished the overall solution stands or falls with (3)*. Once in possession of a minor subproof, failure to find a major subproof entails failure overall — it would be pointless to try a different choice of conditional major premiss.

This puts pressure on the designer of a good proof-finding algorithm to ensure choices of conditional premisses with easily soluble *minor* subproblems.

There is a possibly countervailing pressure, however, to choose a conditional whose *major* subproblem is easily soluble — one whose *consequent* can be seen to be a promising replacement for the conditional itself within the premiss set, as we seek to derive the conclusion within the major.

Now since antecedents and consequents can be joined willy-nilly to form conditionals, these pressures cannot be expected to agree. They may indeed clash. One is left with an optimization problem.

The problem is to make an optimal choice among what I shall call the *(1,1)-conditionals*, in X, with respect to A. Such a conditional $P \supset Q$ is one whose minor and major both succeed. That is, there is a proof of the minor subproblem $X?\text{-}P$ and a proof of the major subproblem $X \setminus \{P \supset Q\}, Q ?\text{-} A$. Failure of either of these would be registered by 0 in place of 1 in the respective position in the description of the kind of conditional one has, in X, with respect to A. Clearly we want to avoid, on foraging in X, any choice of $(0,0)$-, $(0,1)$- or $(1,0)$-conditionals in X with respect to A. We are looking for a deductive halfway house; and each half of the journey must be negotiable.

We can settle for nothing other than (1,1)-conditionals.

Some of these halfway houses, however, might be better than others. An *optimal* halfway house is one that minimizes the length of the overall journey, and the time taken on it. That is, we want our proof to be as *short* as possible, and we want to find it as *quickly* as possible. So we want to be able to make discriminating choices *among the (1,1)-conditionals in X with respect to A* whenever our algorithm dictates, for X?-A, that the time has come to attempt a $\supset$-elimination.

In any Prawitz-style E-proof whose undischarged assumptions are only conditionals, negations and atoms, different undischarged conditional assumptions are rivals for being the terminal major premises for $\supset$-elimination in a hybrid proof of the same result. Our recipe for hybridisation latched, for the sake of specificity, onto the major premiss of the elimination at the top of the spine; but there is no compelling *need* to make that choice. Other choices can be just as good for the purposes of finding a hybrid counterpart — provided they do not have to be reached by passing up from the conclusion *via* any minor conclusion for $\vee$-elimination. For in such a case the conditional reached is likely to be subservient to the one from whose consequent the major premiss for that $\vee$-elimination had been derived. For example, in the following Prawitz proof of S from P, $P \supset (Q \vee R)$, $Q \supset S$, $R \supset S$ the last two conditionals are subservient to the first one:

$$
\frac{\qquad P \qquad P \supset (Q \vee R)\qquad}{Q \vee R} \qquad \frac{\overset{-1}{Q} \quad Q \supset S}{S} \qquad \frac{\overset{-1}{R} \quad R \supset S}{S}
$$
$$
\frac{\qquad\qquad\qquad\qquad\qquad\qquad\qquad\qquad\qquad\qquad}{S} \ 1
$$

This Prawitz proof, because of the subservience remarked on, can be hybridised only by making the $\supset$-elimination with major premiss $P \supset (Q \vee R)$ terminal. No other conditional can serve as the major premiss of a terminal step in a hybrid version. In general, any conditional premiss (undischarged overall within a Prawitz proof) that occurs in a minor subproof for an application of $\vee$-elimination whose major premiss in turn has been obtained from within the consequent of a conditional major premiss C, is subservient to C. C will be preferred as the major premiss for attempted $\supset$-elimination as we build up a hybrid proof from below.

In the absence of any Prawitz proof in which relations of subservience among undischarged conditional premises can be displayed, how can one tell whether one conditional is subservient to another, when given the bare deductive problem X?-A? I can offer only a tentative answer. To determine whether $C \supset D$ is subservient to $P \supset Q$, try to trace a chain as follows: Start by locating a direct accessible positive disjunction within Q. Take one of the disjuncts R. Then take any conditional $C \supset D$ whose consequent D has an accessible atom in common with A. Now see whether R can be connected to C by a $\neq$-chain in X. If all these conditions obtain, they harbour the prospect that $C \supset D$ might be used as a premiss in the minor subproof for the ∨-elimination arising from the disjunction found in Q — the minor subproof with case assumption R; and that the conclusion of that ∨-elimination will lie on a path in the Prawitz proof leading down to the overall conclusion A. When these conditions obtain, we shall regard *every* conditional in the $\neq$-chain as subservient to $P \supset Q$.

Suppose this investigation is conducted for all pairs of conditionals. In the resulting digraph of subservience among conditionals the best choice of a major premiss for terminal elimination in a hybrid proof would be a *sink*. But in case no sink exists, we are still in the dark as to how to choose a conditional premiss for a terminal elimination.

The quest for easily soluble *minor* subproblems faces the spectre of looping. To avoid looping, one may have to put up with some restrictions on the means of proof-discovery for the minor subproblem. On the other hand, some methods of avoiding looping may circumscribe instead one's choice of conditional premiss with an eye to the role its consequent might play in the *major*.

We have so far considered two responses to the problem of looping. *Both* have managed to keep an informed eye on the consequents of conditional major premisses. These responses have allowed us to use various accessibility tests involving A.

The first response, discussed in Chapter 4, is that of recording the overall problem generating a minor; and avoiding generating that problem again as a minor. This is what we called the method of loop-detection. Its advantage is that it keeps proofs *pure*: applications of $\supset$-elimination have the agreeable singular form

$$
\frac{\begin{array}{ccc} X & X \setminus \{P \supset Q\}, \overline{Q}^{\;i} \\ \Pi & \Sigma \\ P \supset Q \quad P & A \end{array}}{A}\; i
$$

which does not depend on the form of the antecedent P. The disadvantage of loop-detection is that recording and consulting are slow.

The second response, discussed in the preceding section, is that of generating one or more minor subproblems *according to the form of the antecedent P*, in such a way as to achieve inductive breakdown in the minor(s) as well as in the major. This is what we have called Dyckhoff's device. Its advantage is speed. Its disadvantage is that proofs become *impure*, in that they can employ different forms of ⊃-elimination according to the form of the antecedent. The rule of ⊃-elimination becomes *non-singular*. We also find that proofs using the non-singular form of ⊃-elimination may contain formulae that are not subformulae of any premiss, or of the conclusion, of the original problem.

Both the method of loop-detection and Dyckhoff's device, however, allow one to choose conditional premisses $P \supset Q$ for elimination according to a priority ranking *that can depend on how the overall conclusion A is related to the consequent Q*. I shall call this *consequent-wary* choice of major premisses for ⊃-elimination. Both these methods allow *informed foraging*. The one anticipates loops; the other spirals.

There is a third method, however, that anticipates loops, and avoids them, and indeed does so without the cost of recording and consulting, and without the price of impurity of proof. It does, however, involve another kind of disadvantage, which we have not yet encountered: it has to sacrifice informed foraging, at least of the kinds that we have so far employed. I shall call this third method that of *fettered minor proof*. This is because it ties one's hands to a certain extent when attacking minor subproblems, by *not permitting the use of ⊃-elimination (within a minor) until one is sure that the premiss set X has changed*. The method of fettering is justified by the existence of certain transformations on proofs, to be discussed below.

The rules of ⊃-introduction and ¬-introduction (to derive $A \supset B$ and $\neg A$ respectively) are alike in that an application of either allows one to 'throw A upstairs' as a (possibly) new premiss for the subproof involved. Let us therefore call them *attic-rules*.

Let us call ⊃-elimination and ¬-elimination *minor-creating rules*[7].

When contemplating a minor-creating step δ we can, in general, and within carefully definable limits to be explained below, *eschew minor-creators*

---

[7] According to this terminology, V-elimination also creates minors — but we shall reserve the label, for the purposes of our present discussion, just for ⊃-elimination and ¬-elimination.

in the minor subproof for δ that we shall subsequently have to seek. This is
what is meant by *fettering* above. On applying a minor-creating rule, one
can 'register' within the proof predicate on the minor subproblem thus created that *its* proof, if any, is not to use a minor-creator — at least, until
such prohibition is lifted. The registering can be by means of a special argument place of the proof predicate, *Status_for_minor_creator*, with two values,
allow_minor_creator and *prohibit_minor_creator*.

From the previous rider it is clear that there will be special circumstances
allowing one to switch from the value *prohibit_minor_creator* to the value
allow_minor_creator. Just what these special circumstances are, will emerge
below.

We know that we can confine minor proofs to have sets of premises
lacking both disjunctions and conjunctions. We do so by applying up-front
∧-elimination and ∨-eliminations. And we can confine ⊃-eliminations to conclusions that are either atoms or disjunctions. Neither of these constraints in-
duces incompleteness, because ∧-elimination, ∨-elimination, ⊃-introduction,
¬-introduction and ∧-introduction are, as we have observed before, *safe*
rules. Our algorithm exploits these logical facts. For it allows a minor-
creating step δ to be taken only after upfront ∧- and ∨-eliminations have
been done. So there are only conditionals, negations and atoms available as
premises in the resulting minor for δ. And it formulates ⊃-elimination only
for conclusions that are atomic or disjunctive.

Now the minor conclusion for the application of a minor-creating step
cannot be ⊥; so the minor proof, in the presence of the fetter created by our
contemplated step δ, has to be trivial or introductory. ∧-introduction and
∨-introduction do not change the premiss set of the minor; so the danger
of looping still lurks for minor-creators in the minor above either of these
introductions as terminal. These two rules *should*, therefore, preserve fetters
on minor-creators.

We shall show below that ∧-introduction and ∨-introduction *can* preserve fetters on minor-creators within their own subproofs, without loss of
completeness.

The danger of looping would lurk also if, once a minor-creating step had
been taken, we sought to apply within that minor (call it Σ) for A an attic
rule involving the same antecedent as any attic rule that we had applied
earlier in the construction of the proof (that is, *below* the step γ we were
now seeking to make). For the contemplated attic step γ within the minor
Σ — which step would in turn generate the need for a minor Σ′ with the
same conclusion A as Σ — could leave the set X of premises available

for Σ unchanged; or, at least, have available a set of premisses that could lead, upon $\wedge$- and $\vee$-eliminations, to X as the set of available premisses for Σ' in pursuit of A. Attic steps whose antecedents are as described *should*, therefore, preserve fetters on minor-creators within their own subproofs.

We shall show below that attic steps whose antecedents do *not* have the foregoing feature *can* preserve fetters on minor-creators within their own subproofs, without loss of completeness.

It is only attic-rules that can provide reason to *unfetter*, and even then only under the special circumstances now to be explained. Both of the attic-rules, as observed, involve the potential generation of a new premiss in their subproof. I say 'potential' because it may already be available. If, and only if, the sentence A in conclusions of the form $A \supset B$ or $\neg A$ would be a *new* addition to the available premisses, should the proof predicate for the subproblem for the respective attic-rule be unfettered, so as to allow minor-creators as permissible moves (perhaps even terminally) in the subproof.

A simple example showing that we *must* unfetter when A would be a new addition to the available premisses is $B \supset (B \supset A)$, $(B \supset A) \supset A$?-A. The terminal step of any proof of this problem must be $\supset$-elimination. Its major premiss, moreover, has to be $(B \supset A) \supset A$, since the minor B for the other conditional premiss is not derivable (as one can tell by an accessibility test). The terminal step creates the fetter. For the minor above the fetter we have to derive $B \supset A$. To do so we have to use $\supset$-introduction. So we now seek a proof of A from B, $B \supset (B \supset A)$, $(B \supset A) \supset A$. *Any such proof must end with a step of $\supset$-elimination*. Thus for search to be able to proceed successfully, the step of $\supset$-introduction *must unfetter its subproblem*. It may do so, however, only because B is a *new* addition to the premisses.

Now what I mean in general by A being a *new* addition is not only that A should not at present be an available premiss, but also that *it should not have been the antecedent of an earlier attempted application of an attic-rule (lower down in the proof) in pursuit of whose subproof the present problem has been generated.*

THEOREM: Steps of $\wedge$-introduction, $\vee$-introduction and attic steps whose antecedents are shared with earlier attic steps, can preserve fetters on minor-creating steps without loss of completeness.

Proof: Suppose that we have a proof Π with the following properties:

1. Π has an unfettered minor-creating step δ

2. there is a minor-creating step γ in the minor for δ

3. γ is the first minor-creating step on the path ρ leading from δ up to γ that would be *disallowed* by the fetter that is created by δ and preserved up to γ

Then Π can be transformed into a proof Π' in which γ does not occur within the minor of δ, and therefore does not violate the fetter created by δ.

Proof: There are two possibilities each for δ and γ. Moreover, we can without loss of generality assume that the path ρ contains no applications of $\wedge$-elimination or $\vee$-elimination. So there are four possibilities for the terminal step β of that minor: $\wedge$-introduction, $\vee$-introduction, $\supset$-introduction and $\neg$-introduction, where, in the last two cases, we can assume that the antecedent involved is shared with some attic-step lower down in Π (otherwise the fetter created by δ would not have been preserved up to γ).

So there are sixteen possibilities in all for the subproof of Π whose terminal step is δ. Each occurs on the left in the display of transformations below. We show for each such subproof a transform in which γ is re-located so as not to occur in the minor for δ. This means that the forms on the left need never be used. That is, the fetter on minor-creators that is induced by δ can be allowed to rule out the minor-creating step γ, without loss of completeness. Note that ρ runs through Θ in each of the schemata below:

For $\beta = \supset$-elimination; $\neg$-elimination (for which $C=\bot$); $\wedge$-elimination (for which alone Ξ occurs); and $\vee$-introduction:

```
              _                                          _
              B¹                                         B¹
          Γ   Σ                                          Σ
  γ  A⊃B  A   S                                         (S)
     ──────────── 1                                      Θ
          S                                            β C  (Ξ)
          Θ                                 Γ            D
        β C  (Ξ)                       δ   ¬D   ──────────
  δ  ¬D ────────              ─────>    γ  A⊃B  A    ⊥
          D                                ────────────── 1
     ───────────                                  ⊥
          ⊥
```

Note also that in the following if β is $\neg$-introduction then $C=\Theta=\bot$:

```
          Γ
  γ  ¬A   A
     ──────
       ⊥
       Θ
     β C  (Ξ)                            Γ
  δ ¬D ──────                 ─────>  γ ¬A   A      (δ disappears)
       D                                ──────
     ────────                              ⊥
       ⊥
```

```
           Γ
   γ  ¬A   A                                          _
      ──────                                          ⊥²
        ⊥              _                              Θ             _
        Θ              Q¹                           β C  (Ξ)        Q¹
      β C  (Ξ)         Π                     δ  D⊃Q ──────          Π
  δ D⊃Q ──────         R                  Γ          D              R
         D       ────────── 1    ─────> γ ¬A   A ───────────────────── 1
     ──────────────────                   ──────        R
             R                               R                        2
```

These transformations justify the preservation of fetters by $\wedge$-introduction, $\vee$-introduction and attic steps with antecedents shared with earlier attic steps. We are seeking to establish that when the fetter induced by δ formally disallows the step γ above it, the would-be subproof on the left can be transformed into the subproof on the right. The resulting overall proof Π' is of the same conclusion from the same set of undischarged assumptions as Π, but is one in which now the fetter induced by δ is respected — the offending step γ has been re-located so as not to violate the fetter.

The displayed conclusions of the attic steps β in the proof-schemata on the left above are the minor conclusions of the fetter-creating step δ. Above (but not necessarily *immediately* above) each of these conclusions is the conclusion S of the would-be minor-creating step γ. In the intervening section Θ of proof, we are assuming, without loss of generality, that there is no other minor-creating step between γ and β. Now the only possible reason why the transformed proof Π' (containing the transform on the right) should not establish the same overall conclusion as the original proof Π, *and use only assumptions that are undischarged in* Π, is that some step in Θ discharges the major premiss of γ and/or some undischarged assumption of the minor Γ for γ. But this is no cause for concern. For we are assuming, without loss of generality, that there are no applications in Θ of $\wedge$-elimination or $\vee$-elimination. Now we observe that $\wedge$-introduction and $\vee$-introduction do not discharge assumptions — so it is alright for them to find application in Θ. What, finally, about the attic rules? Any attic step on the path leading up from δ to γ by hypothesis failed to lift the fetter created by δ. But this can only be because its antecedent is the antecedent thrown upstairs by some attic-step *below* δ. Thus the same attic-step will be waiting in the transform, below γ, to discharge the same antecedent wherever it may occur as an assumption in the transform. And that disposes of our worry lest some assumption be undischarged in the transform Π' but not in Π.

Ω

Fettering of minor-creators within minors should therefore, and can, be inherited by any subproblems for $\wedge$-introduction, $\vee$-introduction, and attic steps sharing antecedents with earlier attic steps. We shall say that these rules *preserve the fetter*.

Remark 1. Some of the transforms above may seem somewhat quirky, involving as they do an unusual form of $\neg$-elimination:

$$
\frac{\quad \overline{}\,i}{\bot}
$$

$$
\begin{array}{ccc}
 & \Gamma & \Sigma \\
\neg A & A & B \\
\hline
 & B &
\end{array}\, i
$$

which allows $\bot$ to be a premiss for a proof, like an ordinary atom. Provided it behaves only like an ordinary atom, however, this is in order. This form of $\neg$-elimination produces the same system M as does the more usual form.

Having to resort to this unusual inference rule is the price one pays, in M, for refusing to allow ¬-introduction for ¬C to unfetter minor-creating steps when C is the antecedent of an earlier attempted application of an attic rule. That one does indeed *have* to resort to the unusual form of ¬-elimination is established by the unprovability, under a regime of fettering *with the usual form of ¬-elimination*, of the minimally valid ¬$C \supset Q$, ¬A, A?-$C \supset Q$.

In the system I of intuitionistic logic one would not have to pay this price. For in I we would be able to use the absurdity rule to boil down the transform to

$$
\begin{array}{c}
\overset{\displaystyle \overline{\quad\quad}^{1}}{C} \\
\underbrace{\qquad\qquad} \\
\Gamma
\end{array}
$$

$$
\dfrac{\neg A \quad A}{\dfrac{\bot}{R}} \quad absurdity\ rule
$$

$$
\begin{array}{c}
\Theta \\
\dfrac{S}{C \supset S}\ 1
\end{array}
$$

In due course we shall see, however, that a more selective form of fettering will allow us, in M, to use the usual form of ¬-elimination and still keep our stricture on the antecedents of attic-steps that would unfetter.

Remark 2. The reader might wonder at this stage whether fettering could be combined with the Dyckhoff method to produce an even more constrained search for proofs. Unfortunately, the answer appears to be negative; the two constraints seem not to be composable. To see this, observe the transformations given above in the proof of the last theorem, to the effect that fettering does not lead to incompleteness. With the first of these transformations, for example, the major premiss $D \supset Q$ at step δ might lead to the creation of minor proofs in which, at step γ, the major premiss $A \supset B$ happens to be a *phantom* subformula of $D \supset Q$, and not already available among the premisses before the Dyckhoff treatment of ⊃-elimination on $D \supset Q$ at δ. But in the transformed proof, the step γ with major premiss $A \supset B$ is supposed to be performed *before* step δ, as we build up the proof from below. Before $D \supset Q$ has been addressed in Dyckhoff fashion as a possible major premiss for elimination, however, $A \supset B$ might not even be in the picture as an available premiss for elimination.

More generally, phantom formulae of conditional form can result from the Dyckhoff break-up of the major premiss $D \supset Q$ for a step δ of $\supset$-elimination. These phantom subformulae could be undischarged in the Dyckhoff minors for a $\supset$-elimination β with major premiss $A \supset B$ *within* one of the Dyckhoff minors for step δ. In the would-be transform required for tethering[8] to conserve completeness, these phantom subformulae might not in general be available as premisses when building up from below by means of a $\supset$-elimination with $A \supset B$ as its major premiss.

One might try to overcome these difficulties by performing a 'Dyckhoff break-up' in advance of *all* conditionals and negations among the premisses, so that somehow the likes of $A \supset B$ *would* be in the offing at the outset; but it is difficult to see how this could be done without greatly complicating matters.

THEOREM: Fettering does not lead to incompleteness.

Proof: The transformations given above show that any proof can be transformed into one in which, if the fetter is engaged, it can be respected.

Ω

THEOREM: Fettering is sufficient to prevent looping.

Proof: The condition for *unfettering* is an application of an attic-rule whose antecedent has never before been adopted as a premiss after any earlier attempted attic-step. Such antecedents are of course in finite supply within any problem $X?\text{-}A$. As proof search proceeds, every attempted attic-step *reduces* the number of 'new' antecedents for future attic-steps. But only attic-steps can unfetter. In order to embark on an infinite loop, one needs to unfetter. For one needs to get more minors into the picture — otherwise there is just a steady inductive breakdown of the deductive problem, which will eventually terminate. (To guarantee this breakdown we must also ensure that before we embark on a $\supset$-elimination with major premiss $P \supset Q$, the consequent Q is not already available as a premiss.) But every time one tries to create a minor in the prolongation of the attempted loop, one needs

---

[8] see below.

to have *unfettered* since the creation of the previous minor. This unfettering (via an attic-step) uses up one more antecedent for attic-steps. Any loop, if long enough, will eventually have used up all such potentially unfettering antecedents. So unfettering will henceforth be impossible. The next creation of a minor (which will be needed for infinite regress) will therefore induce a fetter that cannot be undone. With fettering thus permanent, the 'loop' will be unable to develop any further.

Ω

The regime of fettering minor-creators within minors enables us to avoid loops without recording whole subproblems for future consultation. All we have to record is a growing index set of attic-step antecedents that have been 'thrown upstairs' as we build up the proof from below. After we have fettered minor-creators in minors, unfettering then takes place via those subsequent attic-steps whose antecedents are not in the index set at that stage.

But we find ourselves in a different predicament now. Observe that before, with Dyckhoff's method or the old method of loop-detection, a consequent-wary choice of conditional premiss might impose the need for unfettered minor proof. The method of fettered minor proof, however, relies on there being transforms with fettered minors. These transforms, however, can have as their terminal steps applications of $\supset$-elimination *whose major premisses might be far removed from the first choice of the consequent-wary on the other two methods.* Repeated application of the transformations just given could make the thread of syntactic connection between T (or $\bot$) and $R \supset S$ too attenuated to guide one to the choice of $R \supset S$. Hence my description of it as *loop-free groping.*

Thus deprived of consequent/conclusion based reasons for choice of conditional major premiss, we would have reason to strive instead for more easily provable minors, comforted at least with the thought that the major, if broached after success on the minor, has at least involved inductive breakdown of the original problem. And to this end — more easily provable minors — it would behove us to *avoid conditionals whose antecedents are atoms not available as premisses.* For such atoms would have to come as conclusions (in the minor) of $\supset$-elimination, contrary to fettering. (Remember that all $\supset$-eliminations take place at a stage when only conditionals, negations and atoms are available as premisses.) With an eye now on the *antecedent* of the conditional premiss, which is to be the conclusion of the minor, we should be paying special heed to *antecedents containing available atomic premisses accessibly*; and to *antecedents containing conditionals or negations accessibly*. The former offer the prospect of quick minor proof by introduction(s); the latter offer the prospect of early unfettering. The best antecedent, of course, is one that is already available as a premiss, and can 'be' the minor proof.

We have the following problem under a regime of fettering minor-creators in minors: we may not be able to be consequent-wary in choice of conditional premisses. This problem is particularly acute if one favours trying to capture, in the proof-finding algorithm, the kind of 'backward-chaining' often involved in the intelligent use of conditional premisses. For example, given the problem P, $P \supset Q$, $Q \supset R$?- R, backward-chaining would involve choosing $Q \supset R$ first, because it has the conclusion R as its consequent; and next, trying to derive the minor conclusion Q. This, in turn, by backward-chaining, involves choosing $P \supset Q$, because it has Q as its consequent. Finally, in trying to derive the minor conclusion P called for by $P \supset Q$ as major premiss, we find the trival proof P. The overall proof, then, would be

$$
\cfrac{Q \supset R \qquad \cfrac{P \supset Q \quad P \quad \overline{Q}^{\,1}}{Q}\ 1 \qquad \overline{R}^{\,2}}{R}\ 2
$$

which, glaringly, has a minor, for its terminal $\supset$-elimination, that ends with $\supset$-elimination! — contrary to fettering of $\supset$-elimination in minors. We know, however, that fettering does not induce incompleteness. The foregoing transformations have ensured that. So there must be a successful fetter-respecting proof search on this problem. Indeed, the following proof can be found under a regime of fettering:

$$
\cfrac{P \supset Q \quad P \qquad \cfrac{Q \supset R \quad \overline{Q}^{\,2} \quad \overline{R}^{\,1}}{R}\ 1}{R}\ 2
$$

Note, however, its terminal major premiss: $P \supset Q$. This bears no direct containment relation to R. There *is* a relation between $P \supset Q$ and R, to be sure, mediated within the overall problem (and the proof) by $Q \supset R$; but this relation is not a 'local' one, determined from $P \supset Q$ and R alone, as would be, say, the relation of *being a (direct) accessible positive subformula*.

Whatever relation may obtain to dictate the choice of $P \supset Q$ as the best choice for bottommost major premiss, it is a *holistic* one, to be determined from the whole premiss set and the conclusion.

Fettering ties our hands. It also blinkers us to obvious and unobjectionable proofs that are the desirable outcome of a natural strategy like backward-chaining. Under a regime of fettering, previous prioritization of conditional premisses could well become *counterproductive*, as those conditional premisses favoured on earlier, consequent-wary methods generate minor subproblems which, even though they are provable, will be thwarted by fettering. *Fettering makes the provability of a subproblem depend on how it has been generated as a subproblem.* Once again, a disagreeable form of holism intrudes.

But surely, one might ask, it should be possible to liberalize the regime of fettering so as to allow fruitful interaction with consequent-wary choice of conditional premisses? What was the danger, after all, in reaching

$$P, \; P \supset Q, \; Q \supset R$$

$$\beta \frac{Q \supset R \quad \alpha \dfrac{\overset{\Pi}{\rule{0pt}{0pt}}}{Q} \qquad \overline{R}^{\,1}}{R}^{1}$$

and wishing to construct Π by means of a terminal step α of $\supset$-elimination, using as its major premiss the *different conditional premiss* $P \supset Q$? Couldn't we fetter at β a little more discerningly, so that when, say, the *conclusion* of the minor for α is different from the conclusion of the minor for β, α won't be precluded by the fettering induced by β? Couldn't we fetter at β, so this suggestion would go, *with respect to* the minor conclusion Q? Then, provided that the contemplated application α of $\supset$-elimination had a minor conclusion distinct from Q, one could permit it.

14.3 Hobbling

The great danger in liberalizing any harsh regime is the anarchy that can arise from the loss of historical consciousness. But the proposal here is not that we allow α to *unfetter* $\supset$-elimination, thereby expunging the memory, induced by β, of fettering with respect to Q. Rather, the proposal is to have α *preserve fettering with respect to Q*, and *not* to have α precluded by fettering *tout court* — by unfettered fettering, as it were. The conditions for creating and preserving the fetter during proof search, and the conditions for unfettering, remain the same as before. It is just that the fettering is to be more selective. One will fetter *only with respect to any minor conclusion encountered since the creation of the present fetter*. So one accumulates prohibited minor conclusions, for the triggering of the prohibitive effect of the fetter, gathering them up in the proof predicate in a special index set at a new argument place. Fettering *with respect to minor conclusions* is really fettered fettering. We shall call it *hobbling*.

THEOREM: *Hobbling does not induce incompleteness*

Proof: Unfettered fettering does not. Ω

THEOREM: *Hobbling*, like fettering, *is sufficient to prevent looping.*

Proof: Any infinite loop requires an infinite succession $Y_1?\text{-}Q_1$, $Y_2?\text{-}Q_2$, $Y_3?\text{-}Q_3$, ... of subproblems generated during proof search. Its infinite extension beyond any stage i requires an attempted minor-creating step to produce a minor $Y_j?\text{-}Q_j$ for some $j > i$. Now there is only a finite supply of possible conclusions Q for minors generated from any problem $X?\text{-}A$, and, as before, a finite supply of antecedents for possible attic-steps that could unhobble minor-creators. As soon as a particular Q has featured as the conclusion of a minor, hobbling prevents it from so featuring again — until unhobbling occurs. So for the loop to progress infinitely, it will, at the next creation of a minor, have to involve a different conclusion for that minor, or be unhobbled before then. Eventually, however, all potential minor conclusions will have been used up, as will all potential 'new' antecedents for attic-steps needed for unhobbling. But the loop will need yet another minor to keep going. The hobbling then occasioned can never be undone, and will prevent further creation of minors. The loop will peter out. Ω

Hobbling is the sought compromise on fettering that we need in order to exercise consequent-wary choice of conditional premises in bottom-up proof search. We have seen how 'backward-chaining' with consequent-wary choices piles up the burden of proof in the minors — where a judicious (terminal) $\supset$-elimination can be a welcome permitted move. *Hobbling allows us to make those judicious $\supset$-eliminations. Unfettered fettering does not.*

For example, a hobbling proof-finder will find this proof:

[] ?- if(if(a,d),if(if(if(b,c),a),if(if(a,c),if(if(b,a),d))))

The length of this problem is 19

I take only 16 ms to find the following PROOF,

which has 18 steps of inference:

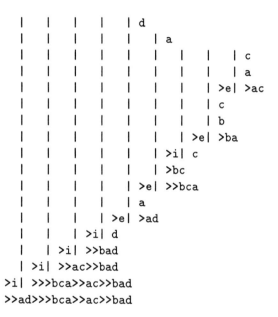

```
|   |   |   |   | d
|   |   |   |   |   | a
|   |   |   |   |   |   |   |   | c
|   |   |   |   |   |   |   |   | a
|   |   |   |   |   |   |   | >e| >ac
|   |   |   |   |   |   |   | c
|   |   |   |   |   |   |   | b
|   |   |   |   |   |   | >e| >ba
|   |   |   |   |   | >i| c
|   |   |   |   |   | >bc
|   |   |   |   | >e| >>bca
|   |   |   |   | a
|   |   |   | >e| >ad
|   |   | >i| d
|   | >i| >>bad
| >i| >>ac>>bad
>i| >>>bca>>ac>>bad
>>ad>>>bca>>ac>>bad
```

in which deductive work has been piled up in the minor. On further prompting, it will also find the next proof (for the same problem) — which, however, is the *only* one that can be found by a fettering program. In the next proof, deductive work is strung out into the majors:

[] ?- if(if(a,d),if(if(if(b,c),a),if(if(a,c),if(if(b,a),d))))

The length of this problem is 19

I take only 16 ms to find the following PROOF,

which has 21 steps of inference:

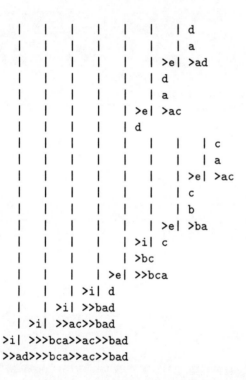

```
|   |   |   |   |   |   | d
|   |   |   |   |   |   | a
|   |   |   |   |   | >e| >ad
|   |   |   |   |   | d
|   |   |   |   |   | a
|   |   |   |   | >e| >ac
|   |   |   |   | d
|   |   |   |   |   |   |   | c
|   |   |   |   |   |   |   | a
|   |   |   |   |   |   | >e| >ac
|   |   |   |   |   |   | c
|   |   |   |   |   |   | b
|   |   |   |   |   | >e| >ba
|   |   |   |   | >i| c
|   |   |   |   | >bc
|   |   |   | >e| >>bca
|   |   | >i| d
|   | >i| >>bad
| >i| >>ac>>bad
>i| >>>bca>>ac>>bad
>>ad>>>bca>>ac>>bad
```

If a minor subproblem is *unprovable*, hobbling will involve exploring many more byways before returning empty-handed. By way of compensation, though, unfettered fettering makes it more difficult to choose the bottommost conditional premiss of a hybrid proof: even if a minor is decided negatively more quickly with unfettered fettering, the way to eventual success on both minor *and major* may be longer than it would be with hobbling.

With hobbling we can retain the usual rule of ¬-elimination in M rather than having to resort to the unusual form remarked on above. Recall the proof-schema which called for the unusual form of ¬-elimination in its transform:

$$
\alpha \; \frac{\overbrace{\quad}^{\displaystyle \overline{C}^{\,1}} \\ \Gamma \\ \neg A \quad A}{}
$$

$$
3 \; \frac{}{C} \qquad \beta \frac{\bot}{\neg C} 1 \quad 2 \; \frac{}{Q} \; , \; \overline{C}^{\,3}
$$

$$
\frac{D \supset Q \qquad \Xi \atop D \qquad \quad \Pi \atop R}{R} \; 2
$$

$$
\Theta
$$

$$
\alpha \; \frac{S / \bot}{C \supset S \; / \; \neg C} \; 3
$$

Recall that the task is to show that, with attic-step α down below, the fetter (or, in this case, the hobble) created by δ on minor-creators in its minor need not be lifted by any step β of ¬-introduction involving the same antecedent as α. Without loss of generality we can assume that A is the first minor conclusion to be nobbled by the hobble as we work up to it from D. Now the *hobble*, as opposed to the *fetter*, comes into effect only if A is identical to D or to the minor conclusion of some minor-creator between A and D that failed to be nobbled by the hobble. Fix on such a conclusion, delete everything above it in the proof tree, and graft over it a copy of Γ. You have thereby got rid of γ, and are done. For in what you have deleted there are no discharging steps whose dirty work cannot be taken over by attic-steps below.

What about hobbling *with no unhobbling*? One might naively think that, since hobbling is not so severe on minor-construction, one might be able to leave a hobble in place, and not provide for unhobbling under such conditions as would lead to unfettering (by attic steps). The following proof, however, shows how even a hobble with respect to A (as opposed to a fetter *tout court*) at δ *must* be lifted by β in order to allow γ, with A as its minor conclusion, to feature as shown:

$$
\cfrac{\cfrac{\cfrac{}{A \supset D}\quad \cfrac{(B \supset C) \supset A \quad \cfrac{\cfrac{A \supset C \quad \cfrac{\cfrac{B \supset A \quad \overline{B}^{\,3} \quad \overline{A}^{\,1}}{A}^{\,1} \quad \overline{C}^{\,2}}{C}}{B \supset C}^{\,3}}{A}^{\,4}}{A}}{A} \quad \overline{A}^{\,4} \quad \cfrac{}{D}^{\,5}}{D}
$$

D has to come by $\supset$-elimination with major premiss $A \supset D$. So we need a minor with conclusion A. We are now obliged to hobble with respect to A. A has to come by $\supset$-elimination. The major premiss now can't be $A \supset C$, because of the hobble we have just created with respect to A. Nor can the major premiss be $B \supset A$, because the minor with conclusion B does not exist (again, by an accessibility test). So the major premiss has to be $(B \supset C) \supset A$. The minor conclusion $B \supset C$ has to come by $\supset$-introduction (step β in the proof above). But C can only come by $\supset$-elimination with major premiss $A \supset C$; for which the minor conclusion A has to be allowed. We *must*, therefore, allow β to lift the hobble *with respect to A* that was created by δ.

Fettering and hobbling are techniques for loop-avoidance. One fetters or hobbles minor-creating rules within minors. The guiding theoretical idea is that in certain proof-contexts we can do without certain applications of rules, without thereby sacrificing completeness. This helps constrain proof search, by limiting the variety of ways in which conclusions may be derived.

Successful fettering, then, reduces the number of possibilities for proofs of outstanding subproblems, constraining proof search to a reduced set of rules for as long as possible. I say 'as long as possible' because of course fettering must sometimes be relaxed as proof search proceeds. We saw earlier, for example, that the supply of a genuinely new premiss from an attempted attic-step can unfetter minor-creation in minors. And cases like the following show that if we do *not* thus unfetter, we will not be able to find a proof when one does in fact exist:

$$
\cfrac{(C \supset A) \supset D \qquad \cfrac{\cfrac{C \supset B \quad \cfrac{}{C}\,3}{A} \quad 3}{C \supset A} \qquad \cfrac{\cfrac{B \supset A \quad \cfrac{}{B}\,2 \quad \cfrac{}{A}\,1}{A}\,1}{}\,2 \quad \cfrac{}{D}\,4}{D}\,4
$$

Had the step of $\supset$-introduction in this proof not been able to unfetter $\supset$-elimination in the special circumstances described above, we would *not* have been able to construct this proof. It is, indeed, the only one available under a regime of fettering. But note that under a regime of *hobbling* as opposed to fettering, one would be able to generate also the proof

$$
\cfrac{(C \supset A) \supset D \qquad \cfrac{\cfrac{B \supset A \quad \cfrac{C \supset B \quad \cfrac{}{C}\,3 \quad \cfrac{}{B}\,1}{B}\,1 \quad \cfrac{}{A}\,2}{A}\,2}{C \supset A}\,3 \qquad \cfrac{}{D}\,4}{D}\,4
$$

Any rule could in principle be fettered, provided only that we had theoretical results to the effect that we do not thereby sacrifice completeness. When the technique is used for purposes other than loop-avoidance, I shall speak not of fettering or hobbling, but rather of *tethering*. The motivation behind these terms is metaphorical. Fettering represents a drastic curtailment of degrees of freedom. Hobbling obliges one to move under some lesser handicap. Tethering, as we shall see, confines one to certain avenues of approach, and prevents one from straying onto the lush pastures between them.

14.4 Tethering

Tethering is especially useful for conclusions $A \lor B$ since these may be obtained not only by $\lor$-introduction but also by $\supset$-elimination. Disjunctions are the only compounds which sometimes can be derived only by elimination, and sometimes can be derived only by introductions. Our algorithm allows $\supset$-elimination, indeed, only for (overall conclusions that are) atoms *or disjunctions*, or where the conclusion is the consequent of the conditional major premiss. This is in recognition of the *need*, as shown by the simple problem $C \supset (A \vee B)?\text{-}C \supset (B \vee A)$, to have ($\supset$-)elimination as well as introduction as a possible route to a disjunction. It would be of great assistance if either or both of these ways of obtaining disjunctions ($\vee$-introduction and $\supset$-elimination) could be tethered.

First let us enquire after the ways in which $\vee$-introduction might be constrained to occur.

THEOREM: Suppose we have a proof

$$
\begin{array}{c}
\overline{}^{\,1} \\
D \\[4pt]
\Sigma \quad \Theta \\[4pt]
\alpha\dfrac{C \supset D \quad C \quad E}{E}\;1 \\[6pt]
\Pi \\[2pt]
G
\end{array}
$$

in which no attic step or step of $\wedge$-elimination or $\vee$-elimination occurs on the path ρ leading up from the conclusion G to α. Suppose also that α is the first step of $\supset$-elimination to be encountered as one moves up the path from G to α. Then the proof can be transformed into a proof of G from the same set of undischarged assumptions, but with α terminal.

Proof: The transform

$$
\begin{array}{c}
\overline{}^{\,1} \\
D \\[4pt]
\Theta \\[2pt]
(E) \\[4pt]
\Sigma \quad \Pi \\[4pt]
\alpha\dfrac{C \supset D \quad C \quad G}{G}\;1
\end{array}
$$

has the same set of undischarged assumptions as the proof given, since ρ does not contain any applications of discharging rules. Ω

The usefulness of this simple theorem lies in what it tells us about any algorithm such as ours, which employs up-front ∧-elimination and ∨-elimination. Suppose we seek to construct a proof of G by means of our search algorithm, once up-front ∧-eliminations and ∨-eliminations have been done. Suppose we seek also to make its terminal step one of ∧-introduction or ∨-introduction. Suppose further that, as we build up the proof from that terminal step we make no attic steps (for the time being). We cannot make any ∧-eliminations or ∨-eliminations either, since no suitable major premises for them could be at hand until a ⊃-elimination with major premiss $P \supset Q$ is performed, possibly releasing a fresh conjunction or disjunction in the form of the new premiss Q for its major subproof. But α is the first ⊃-elimination contemplated. So attempting α would produce a proof schema satisfying the hypotheses of our theorem. This theorem tells us that such a ⊃-elimination α could instead have been undertaken as the terminal step, as in the transform provided for that proof schema. The suggestion is that we should therefore avoid a step like α at that higher point in the proof under construction.

There is an efficiency yield in following this suggestion only when the terminal step for conclusion G is a ∨-introduction. For there is no point in undoing a safe step like ∧-introduction simply because we find that we wish to apply ⊃-elimination above it in circumstances conforming to the hypotheses of our theorem. But with *disjunction* matters stand differently. This is because disjunctions are uniquely privileged (and troublesome!) in being the only compounds allowed, by our algorithm, as conclusions of ⊃-eliminations.

We know now that if we embark on the construction of a proof of a disjunction by taking its terminal step, provisionally, to be one of ∨-introduction, we never *need* to apply above that ∨-introduction any ⊃-elimination for a disjunction[9], *provided that we have attempted no attic step above the terminal step of ∨-introduction.* So on attempted application of ∨-introduction, the proof predicate for the subproblem could have registered within it (again at a special argument place) a temporary prohibition, or *tethering, of attempts to obtain a disjunction by ⊃-elimination.* It is easy to work out, also, that only attic steps need be allowed to *untether* ⊃-elimination for disjunctions. They *ought* moreover to untether; otherwise

---

[9] There is no point in banning steps α of ⊃-elimination (above terminal ∨-introductions) that have *atomic* conclusions. For this would force us to slacken other constraints that we wish to have in place, for consequent-wary choice of conditional major premises for elimination that are to have *disjunctions* as their conclusions.

no proof would be found for the problem $C \supset (A \lor B)$?- $D \lor (C \supset (B \lor A))$.

The proviso in the preceding paragraph — that we should have attempted no attic step above the terminal step of $\lor$-introduction — can actually be strengthened so as to be the same as that for fettering and hobbling. The transform of the last theorem will be to the same net effect as the original proof (involving no more undischarged assumptions) provided that any attic step that *does* occur in Π on the path from G up to α — we now contemplate such a possibility — does not throw upstairs any 'new' assumptions, in the sense already explained above. Thus the tether need only be lifted by such applications of attic rules as involve *new* assumptions being thrown upstairs. We have arrived at a complete account of tethering and untethering of $\supset$-elimination for disjunctions after $\lor$-introduction:

TETHERING OF $\supset$-ELIMINATION FOR DISJUNCTIONS:

The following rule *creates the tether*:
$\lor$-introduction

The following rules *untether*:
$\supset$-introduction
$\neg$-introduction

All other rules *preserve the tether*

What about tethering and untethering $\lor$-introduction, as opposed to $\supset$-elimination for disjunctions? These rules are, after all, the two main ways of deriving disjunctions, as we have already noted. If one can be tethered, what about the other?

THEOREM: Suppose we have a proof Ψ of one of the forms

$$
\beta\frac{\begin{array}{cc}\overline{Q}^{\,1}\ \overline{Q}^{\,1}\\[2pt]\Pi_1\ \ \Pi_2\\[2pt]\alpha\dfrac{A\ \ \ B}{A\land B}\\[4pt]\Sigma\quad \Theta\\[2pt]\dfrac{P\supset Q\ \ P\ \ \ E}{E}\end{array}}{}1
\qquad
\beta\frac{\begin{array}{c}\overline{Q}^{\,1}\\[2pt]\Pi\\[2pt]\alpha\dfrac{A}{A\lor B}\\[4pt]\Sigma\quad \Theta\\[2pt]\dfrac{P\supset Q\ \ P\ \ \ E}{E}\end{array}}{}1
\qquad
\beta\frac{\begin{array}{c}\overline{Q}^{\,1},\overline{A}^{\,2}\\[2pt]\Pi\\[2pt]\alpha\dfrac{B}{A\supset B}2\\[4pt]\Sigma\quad \Theta\\[2pt]\dfrac{P\supset Q\ \ P\ \ \ E}{E}\end{array}}{}1
\qquad
\beta\frac{\begin{array}{c}\overline{Q}^{\,1},\overline{A}^{\,2}\\[2pt]\Pi\\[2pt]\alpha\dfrac{\perp}{\neg A}2\\[4pt]\Sigma\quad \Theta\\[2pt]\dfrac{P\supset Q\ \ P\ \ \ E}{E}\end{array}}{}1
$$

in which the path ρ from β to α does not pass through any minor conclusions; and suppose further that this path contains no $\lor$-elimination. Then

Ψ can be transformed into a proof Ψ' of E from available undischarged assumptions of Ψ, but with β now above α.

Proof: It suffices to establish the desired result under the further restriction that the path ρ contains no step of $\supset$-elimination. That is, we take β to be the topmost step of $\supset$-elimination satisfying the hypothetical conditions for the theorem. Once such β can be moved above α, the argument can be repeated for steps of $\supset$-elimination lower down, as they move up to take over the role of β topmost. On our assumptions now about ρ, ρ can contain applications of only the following rules: $\wedge$-introduction, $\vee$-introduction, $\supset$-introduction, and $\wedge$-elimination. (In the case of $\wedge$-elimination, of course, ρ passes through the conclusion and sub-conclusion, not through the conjunctive major premiss). Note that $\neg$-elimination cannot occur on ρ because of the ban on minor conclusions in ρ. Hence $\neg$-introduction cannot occur on ρ either. For $\neg$-introduction calls for $\perp$ as a conclusion. But the assumption that β is the topmost $\supset$-elimination leaves $\neg$-elimination as the only means of yielding $\perp$ as a conclusion on ρ — which we have seen is impossible.

First shuffle the topmost $\wedge$-elimination on ρ, if any, whose major premiss is discharged in Ψ (hence by some step on ρ) up to just above α; and shuffle the bottommost $\wedge$-elimination on ρ, if any, whose major premiss is not discharged in Ψ down to just below β. Repeat the procedure as often as is necessary, until ρ contains no steps of $\wedge$-elimination. The procedure preserves the order of nesting and pattern of discharges by these $\wedge$-eliminations. Now, as we descend the path ρ from α to β, we can pass through applications of only the following rules: $\wedge$-introduction, $\vee$-introduction, and $\supset$-introduction.

Basis: Θ = conclusion of $\alpha = E$. Apply the 'basis transformations' to obtain, respectively,

$$
\begin{array}{ccccc}
\overline{Q}^1 & \overline{Q}^2 & \overline{Q}^1 & {}^2\overline{A}\ \overline{Q},^1\overline{A}\ ^2 & {}^2\overline{A}\ {}^1\overline{Q},\ \overline{A}^2 \\
\Sigma\ \Pi_1 & \Sigma\ \Pi_2 & \Sigma\ \Pi & \Sigma\ \Pi & \Sigma\ \Pi \\
\cfrac{P{\supset}Q\ P\ A}{\alpha\cfrac{A}{A\wedge B}}{}_1 & \cfrac{P{\supset}Q\ P\ B}{B}{}_2 & \cfrac{P{\supset}Q\ P\ A}{\alpha\cfrac{A}{A\vee B}}{}_1 & \cfrac{P{\supset}Q\ P\ B}{\alpha\cfrac{B}{A{\supset}B}{}^2}{}_1 & \cfrac{P{\supset}Q\ P\ \ \perp}{\alpha\cfrac{\perp}{\neg A}{}^2}{}_1 \\
\end{array}
$$

For Θ non-trivial: E stands as the conclusion of an introduction of $\wedge$, $\vee$ or $\supset$. We now proceed by cases according to the form of E: $C \wedge D$, $C \vee D$ or $C \supset D$ respectively. In each case the transformation now to be applied brings us one step closer to accomplishing our aim; so, inductively, we are done:

$$\beta \cfrac{P \supset Q \quad P \quad \cfrac{\cfrac{\Sigma \quad \overline{Q}^1 \\ \Pi_i \\ \alpha \cfrac{A_i}{B} \; intro \\ \Theta_1 \\ C} \quad \cfrac{\overline{Q}^1 \\ \Theta_2 \\ D}}{C \wedge D}^1}{C \wedge D}
\quad \longrightarrow \quad
\cfrac{\cfrac{P \supset Q \quad P \quad \cfrac{\overline{Q}^1 \\ \Pi_i \\ \alpha \cfrac{A_i}{B} \; intro \\ \Sigma \quad \Theta_1 \\ C}}{C}^1 \quad \cfrac{P \supset Q \quad P \quad \cfrac{\overline{Q}^2 \\ \Sigma \quad \Theta_2 \\ D}}{D}^2}{C \wedge D}$$

$$\beta \cfrac{P \supset Q \quad P \quad \cfrac{\cfrac{^2\overline{C} \; , \; \overline{Q}^1 \\ \Pi_i \\ \alpha \cfrac{A_i}{B} \; intro \\ \Theta \\ \Sigma \quad D}{C \supset D}^2}{C \supset D}^1}{C \supset D}
\quad \longrightarrow \quad
\cfrac{\cfrac{P \supset Q \quad P \quad \cfrac{^2\overline{C} \; , \; \overline{Q}^1 \\ \Pi_i \\ ^2\overline{C} \quad \alpha \cfrac{A_i}{B} \; intro \\ \Sigma \quad \Theta \\ D}}{D}^1}{C \supset D}^2$$

$$\beta \cfrac{P \supset Q \quad P \quad \cfrac{\cfrac{\overline{Q}^1 \\ \Pi_i \\ \alpha \cfrac{A_i}{B} \; intro \\ \Theta \\ \Sigma \quad C}{C \vee D}^1}{C \vee D}}{C \vee D}
\quad \longrightarrow \quad
\cfrac{\cfrac{P \supset Q \quad P \quad \cfrac{\overline{Q}^1 \\ \Pi_i \\ \alpha \cfrac{A_i}{B} \; intro \\ \Sigma \quad \Theta \\ C}}{C}^1}{C \vee D}$$

Ω

Our theorem tells us that if we are forced to use β to get $C \vee D$, then we are *not* forced to use α in the major. So we can tether $\vee$-introduction in majors of $\supset$-eliminations *whose conclusions are disjunctions.*
The theorem is more general than this in its strategic advice. It tells us that we can tether introduction of *any* operator in majors of $\supset$-eliminations. Since, however, disjunctions are the only compounds that can be conclusions of $\supset$-elimination according to our algorithm, we can benefit from the theorem only by means of the tether here proposed. Note also that insofar as the theorem applies to other connectives besides disjunction, *it is by invoking applications of $\supset$-elimination to yield ever simpler conclusions.* This again creates pressure for confining $\supset$-elimination to produce as conclusions only atoms besides disjunctions.

$\vee$-elimination must *untether* $\vee$-introduction (in the minors of the former) within majors of $\supset$-elimination. For if it did not, we would be unable to obtain the only proof that exists of $C, C \supset (A \vee B)?\text{-}B \vee A$:

$$\cfrac{C \supset (A \vee B) \quad C}{B \vee A}\ \scriptstyle 2 \qquad \cfrac{\cfrac{}{A \vee B}\ \scriptstyle 2 \quad \cfrac{\overline{\ \ }^1}{A}\ \ \cfrac{\overline{\ \ }^1}{B}}{\cfrac{B \vee A \qquad B \vee A}{B \vee A}\ \scriptstyle 1}$$

We have arrived at a complete account of tethering and untethering $\vee$-introduction within majors of $\supset$-elimination for disjunctions:

TETHERING OF $\vee$-INTRODUCTION WITHIN MAJORS OF $\supset$-ELIMINATION FOR DISJUNCTIONS:

The following rule *creates the tether within its major*:
$\supset$-elimination (for a disjunction)

The following rules *preserve the tether*:
$\vee$-introduction
$\wedge$-elimination
$\supset$-elimination (within its major — since it creates the tether!)
$\supset$-introduction
$\wedge$-introduction

The following rules *untether*:
∨-elimination
⊃-elimination (within its minor)
¬-elimination

The following rule *does not engage either way*:
¬-introduction

Our two kinds of tethering have concerned the derivation of disjunctions. The first was tethering of ⊃-elimination for disjunctions by an attempted ∨-introduction. The second, conversely, was tethering of ∨-introduction within majors by an attempted ⊃-elimination for a disjunction.

The first kind of tethering (of ⊃-elimination for disjunctions) can actually be achieved without a special parameter in the proof predicate. In our algorithm we seek to derive conclusions that are disjunctions by first trying, after up-front ∧- and ∨-eliminations, steps of ⊃-elimination with any conditional major premiss that contains a disjunction as a direct accessible positive subformula. Thus ∨-introduction does not get a look in until the supply of such conditional major premisses has been exhausted. This has the same effect, therefore, as a tether on ∨-introduction.

Suppose one embarks on one of the two available methods of deriving a disjunction. One bears in mind that, if unsuccessful, one may have to resort eventually to the other one. In the meantime, however, one ensures, via the appropriate tether, that the other method will not have much of a look-in. The transformations justifying the tether on ⊃-elimination for disjunctions produce transforms in which ⊃-eliminations for disjunctions are driven down as far as possible. Conversely, the transformations justifying the tether on ∨-introduction within majors of ⊃-eliminations for disjunctions produce transforms in which ∨-introductions are driven down as far as possible. In each case, the tether on steps of kind κ is justified by transformations that produce transforms in which steps of kind κ are driven down as far as possible.

So the adoption of method κ_1 at the outset lets κ_1 monopolize the search as much as possible, by tethering the alternative method κ_2. The tether is a constraint on proof search. It is justified by the fact that κ_2, if it might be useful subsequently, should have been adopted at the outset! The two fetters on κ_1 and κ_2 respectively polarise our choices. They induce a sort of piecemeal purity of schizophrenic method. It is as though we are to explore two axes, but not the area of the plane between them.

Chapter 15

Proof Theory and Proof Search

15.1 Vindication of a proof-theoretic approach

The reader who has come this far will by now appreciate the resources of a proof-theoretic approach to computational logic. We have studied the fine structure of proofs, and how to constrain them to certain forms. We can then design proof-finders that search for proofs only in those forms. The constraints are tantamount to lopping great chunks off the AND-OR search tree. That search tree arises from the repertoire of rules of inference for the system at hand. Throughout this book I have concentrated on the system of minimal logic. But we have seen *en route* how the methods will transfer, often with greater bite, to the system of intuitionistic relevant logic.

We have seen many features of proof-finders based on proof-theoretic insights: filters, ordering of rules, fettering, etc. There is a bewildering range of possible proof-finders to be had by sampling from these features. In the course of my research on this topic I have devised and tested scores of proof-finders. The experience gained has convinced me that *the most spectacular speed-ups are to be had from good normal-form and filtering theorems*.

It has also taught me that computational logic is at a hazy borderline between the *a priori* and the empirical. Embarrassingly often a proof-finder has failed on a problem, thereby revealing not just a bug[1] but an awful oversight in the proof of some 'metatheorem' on which the programmed constraints were based. One of my reasons for venturing the metatheorems

---

[1] always infuriating, but somehow seldom *embarrassing*!

that I have is that they have passed not only as severe a test of *a priori* reflection as I have been able to bring to bear; they have also passed the test of being programmed as constraints, and not found wanting![2]

It is of course ill-advised to generalize about proof-finders and their relative merits on the basis of just those problems on which one has tested them. The 'worst-case' problems of less than a given length will no doubt vary from one proof-finder to another. But one general rule of thumb can be recommended to beginners: *in sub-classical logics you will find ⊃-eliminations a troublesome source of complexity.*

15.2 Testing proof-finders

I have gathered together many problems (153, to be precise) that have proved useful in debugging proof-finders[3]. These problems are to be found in the Appendix. They range from the utterly trivial to the reasonably complex. Included among them are the minimally provable ones among the seventeen propositional problems in Pelletier's well-known paper[4]. (These are also listed separately.) Pelletier notes that each of them has been responsible for the demise of one or another author's natural-deduction based automated theorem prover. I cut my teeth on these problems when the ideas presented here were in their infancy. All seventeen can now be despatched in around one fifth of a second. (For those interested, only four of them are provable in minimal logic.)

I hope this list of debugging problems will be useful for other researchers. I would say that nearly every defective proof-finder for minimal logic will fail on at least one of these problems.

Pelletier's problems have now receded into relative triviality for the more mature proof-finders that incorporate enough of the proof-theoretic insights provided above. So too have the problems known as Asset, which bedevilled Thistlethwaite *et al.* in their attempts to devise a proof-finder for *LR*, the decidable (non-distributive) fragment of Anderson and Belnap's system *R*. These thirty-two problems arise from sixteen schemata $F(p, q)$ in two propositional variables. They pose for each such schema F the problem of whether $F(a, F(b, c))$ is interdeducible with $F(F(a, b), c)$. Although originally devised

---

[2]at least, with respect to problems on whose solutions other workers agree, by using quite different methods from mine.

[3]These are the problems referred to in Dyckhoff's paper.

[4]J.Pelletier, 'Seventy-Five Problems for Testing Automatic Theorem Provers', *Journal of Automated Reasoning* 2, 1986, pp.191-216.

for *LR*, and for particular metatheoretical purposes in connection with the (then open) decidability problem for *R*, these problems were useful in testing my proof-finders for *M*. Each of them is either 100 or 107 symbols long. (I count as symbols the occurrences, in any premiss or the conclusion, of propositional variables and of logical operators. Parentheses don't count, even in Prolog; indeed, in pure Polish notation there aren't any!)

All thirty-two of these problems are now despatched in about ten seconds. All but one are provable in minimal logic.

Looking for more testing problems, my proof-finder has spent less than three quarters of a second (on average) on each of the thirty-three most difficult problems that John Slaney generously supplied from among 50,000 generated from associativity tests of two-place schemata. These were listed in the Introduction, so they will not be repeated in the Appendix.

These progressions — from Pelletier's problems, to Asset, and then to Slaney's problems — have often illustrated a characteristic feature of improving algorithms. This is that an algorithm *A* that achieves speed-up over another algorithm *A'* on longer problems might very well do so at the cost of some slow-down on the shorter ones. It is therefore very important, when testing proof-finders, to make sure that the problems do not come from below that critical threshold of length where comparison with a previous proof-finder might well be misleading.

For the longer problems (between 100 and 200 symbols long) the proofs can be satisfyingly long — often several hundred steps. I found that the briefcase method (that is, avoiding vacuous discharge of assumptions) could cut the length of these proofs by about two thirds, even though no speed-up was achieved.

This raises another interesting point about efficiency: shouldn't one try to produce proofs that are *as short as possible*, in addition to trying to find them *as quickly as possible*?

15.3   Looking ahead to IR

When a deductive problem *X?-A* is posed, one can read it in different ways:

1. Look for a proof whose conclusion is *A*, and whose undischarged assumptions form exactly the set *X*

2. Look for a proof whose conclusion is *A*, and whose undischarged assumptions, if any, are drawn from the set *X*

3. Look for a proof whose conclusion is *either A or* $\perp$, and whose undischarged assumptions form exactly the set X

4. Look for a proof whose conclusion is *either A or* $\perp$, and whose undischarged assumptions, if any, are drawn from the set X

Let us call (1) the attempt to find an *full exact* solution; (2) the attempt to find a *full proper* solution; (3) the attempt to find a *partial exact* solution; and (4) the attempt to find a *partial proper* solution.

Our proof-finders for minimal logic seek full proper solutions. That is, they look for a proof *of the given conclusion*, but they count as success in their search any proof whose undischarged assumptions are among those stated in the problem. They do *not* require that every one of the stated assumptions actually be used within the proof found.

In (non-relevant) intuitionistic logic and any of its supersystems (such as classical logic) the distinction between a *full* and a *partial* solution is neither here nor there. This is because these systems have the absurdity rule (*ex falso quodlibet*), which makes any proof of $\perp$ *ipso facto* a proof of A.

By contrast, intuitionistic relevant logic can sometimes allow a proof of $\perp$ without allowing a proof of A; and a proof-finder for intuitionistic relevant logic can accordingly be allowed to seek merely *partial proper* solutions at every stage. This is because of the following lovely preservation property of success-in-search:

THEOREM: Let any deductive problem $X?$-A be decomposed into subproblems by means of attempted application of any of the rules of *IR*. If those sub-problems admit of partial proper solution then so too does the original problem.

Proof: Easy by induction, given the forms of the rules of inference for *IR*. Ω

This preservation theorem is of vital significance in reducing the complexity of search[5]. By contrast with the Anderson-Belnap systems R, LR etc., the system *IR* does not sacrifice completeness merely by sacrificing hypercompleteness. With the former systems, where one is intent on *full* solutions (whether exact or proper), it can really make a difference if certain possible solutions to a sub-problem are not available. (This of course can happen

---

[5]or, at least, not *increasing* it! — see below.

with a proof-finder that is not hypercomplete.) It may be precisely the *un-available* would-be sub-proof that is needed to supply the right number of occurrences of undischarged assumptions for discharge by later applications of rules of inference. These rules will in general require *non-vacuous* discharge. Thus it becomes crucial for their attempted applications to have access to all possible 'constellations of use' of the assumptions to hand. It could happen, as we have already said, that some such constellation cannot be delivered by a proof-finder that is not hypercomplete; and that, for want of the assumptions so arranged, later steps cannot be taken; whence the search for a proof fails, even though there really *is* one to be had. It would take hypercompleteness, however, to guarantee its discovery.

Now our methods of constraining proof-search generally involve the loss of hypercompleteness. For minimal logic, this is no problem, because *minimal logic allows vacuous discharge of assumptions*. And for intuitionistic relevant logic, this is no problem either! For, although *IR requires non-vacuous discharge of assumptions*[6], nevertheless *the whole spirit of 'epistemic gain' in IR enjoins one to seek partial proper solutions of deductive problems*. And this is precisely where our last preservation theorem is so valuable. A proof-finder for *IR* can be non-hypercompletely complete.

One final theoretical point about *IR* cannot be overemphasized. It is made by the following theorem. Here we have to understand the decision problem on $X?\text{-}A$ as being positively settled by a proof of any subsequent of $X?\text{-}A$. This includes proper subsequents, and in particular any subsequent of the form $Y?\text{-}\bot$, for any subset Y of X.

THEOREM: The decision problem for propositional *IR* is PSPACE-complete.

Proof: The decision problem for propositional intuitionistic logic is PSPACE-complete[7]. Take any (finite) sequent $X?\text{-}A$ and consider the question whether there is a proof of (any subsequent of) it in *IR*. First decide whether there is a proof of $X?\text{-}A$ in ordinary intuitionistic logic I. If not, then there is no proof in *IR* of any subsequent of $X?\text{-}A$. If, on the other hand, there *is* a proof Π in I of A from (some subset Y of) X, then we can transform Π into

---

[6]except, crucially, in one half of the rule of $\supset$-introduction!

[7]See R.Statman, 'Intuitionistic Propositional Logic is Polynomial Space Complete', *Theoretical Computer Science*, 9, 1979, pp.67-72.

a proof Π' in IR of A or $\perp$ from (some subset of) Y by simply *extracting*[8] any application within Π of the absurdity rule and any rule-application within Π that does not meet the discharge requirements laid down in IR. The modifications in IR to the rules of $\supset$-introduction and $\lor$-elimination ensure that extraction proceeds straightforwardly and inductively on the structure of Π. Note that checking at any stage whether the discharge requirements of IR are satisfied involves at most a search through the set of undischarged assumptions on which the conclusion at that stage depends. The length of this search cannot exceed that of the proof in question. Moreover, the number of times such a search has to be undertaken in the course of constructing Π' from Π is bounded above by the number of steps in Π, hence by the length of Π itself. It follows that the length of search to produce Π' from Π is no worse than quadratic[9] in the length of Π.

Ω

Thus even if we take the high road via I to proofs in IR we stay in the same complexity class as I (and M). But it would be silly to take the high road when our proof-theoretic analysis of relevance affords so many short cuts.

A sequel will investigate the low roads further.

---

[8] The first such proof of an extraction theorem was implicit in my paper 'Entailment and Proofs', *Proceedings of the Aristotelian Society* LXXIX, 1979, pp.167-189. It was explicit as Theorem 2 for a classical system without a primitive conditional, in my paper 'A Proof-Theoretic Approach to Entailment', *Journal of Philosophical Logic* 9, 1980, pp.185-209. The extraction theorem for (first-order) intuitionistic logic with the conditional primitive is proved in detail in my paper 'Intuitionistic Mathematics Does Not Need *Ex Falso Quodlibet*' (unpublished). For (propositional) IR it is in effect the previous 'preservation' theorem.

[9] Mike Wilson helped make this clear to me.

Summary of proof-theoretic results

Chapter 2

THEOREM: Any proof in I of A from X can be transformed into a proof in IR of either A or $\bot$ (absurdity) from (some subset of) X

THEOREM: Any proof in C of A from X can be transformed into a proof in CR of either A or $\bot$ (absurdity) from (some subset of) X

Chapter 5

THEOREM: $\Delta \vdash_C \phi \Leftrightarrow \Delta, \neg\phi \vdash_M \bot$.

THEOREM: $\Delta \vdash_C \bot \Leftrightarrow \Delta \vdash_M \bot$.

Chapter 6

THEOREM: The *Cut Rule*
$$\frac{X \vdash A \quad A, Y \vdash B}{X \vdash B}$$
is admissible for the system of hybrid proof (for M).

THEOREM: $X, A \vee B \vdash C \Leftrightarrow X, A \vdash C$ and $X, B \vdash C$ (where we assume without loss of generality that X does not contain $A \vee B$)

Chapter 7

THEOREM: $X, A \supset B \vdash C \Rightarrow X, B \vdash C$

THEOREM: $X \vdash \neg A \Leftrightarrow X, A \vdash \bot$

THEOREM: $X \vdash A \land B \Leftrightarrow X \vdash A$ and $X \vdash B$

THEOREM: $X \vdash A \supset B \Leftrightarrow X, A \vdash B$

Chapter 8

THEOREM: In a deductive problem $X?\text{-}A$, only positive subformulae of premisses in X or negative subformulae of A could ever occur as possible *premisses* of sub-problems reached by inductive breakdown. Only negative subformulae of premisses in X or positive subformulae of A could ever occur as their *conclusions*.

THEOREM: In every minimal proof with *atomic* conclusion A, A is an accessible positive subformula of some undischarged assumption.

THEOREM: For every non-disjunctive E-type Prawitz proof of A, A is a direct accessible positive subformula of some undischarged assumption.

LEMMA: In every disjunctive E-type Prawitz proof, some major premiss for ∨-elimination is a direct accessible positive subformula of some undischarged assumption.

THEOREM: If Π is an E-type Prawitz proof of A and no undischarged assumption of Π contains a disjunction as a direct accessible positive subformula, then A is a direct accessible positive subformula of some undischarged assumption of Π.

THEOREM: If Π is a Prawitz proof of A and no undischarged assumption of Π contains a disjunction as a direct accessible positive subformula and A is *not* a direct accessible positive subformula of any undischarged assumption of Π, then Π ends with an introduction.

THEOREM: Suppose Π is an E-proof of a disjunction $A \vee B$ from the set X of undischarged assumptions, and that $A \vee B$ has only E-proofs from X. Then Π can be transformed into a terminally disjunctive proof Π' of $A \vee B$ from X.

THEOREM: Suppose Π is a non-disjunctive hybrid proof that ends with an elimination and whose conclusion A has no introductory proof from the same undischarged assumptions. Then, obviously, A is atomic or a disjunction; and Π can moreover be transformed into a non-disjunctive hybrid proof Π' of A whose final step, which by hypothesis has to be an elimination, has as its major premiss a formula that contains A as a direct accessible positive subformula.

THEOREM: In any hybrid proof Π, every major premiss for an elimination is a positive subformula of some undischarged assumption, or is a negative subformula of the conclusion.

THEOREM: Suppose that X is a set of premisses (possibly disjunctive) *none of which contains a conditional or a negation as a positive subformula*, and that the atomic conclusion A is provable from X. Then obviously any non-trivial proof Π of A from X must be E-type. Moreover, it can be transformed into a proof whose terminal step is an elimination *whose major premiss contains A as an accessible positive subformula*.

THEOREM: Every minimal proof of A from the set X is such that A has an atom (which may be $\perp$) in common with some undischarged assumption.

THEOREM: In every minimal proof of A from the set X of undischarged assumptions, one of the following holds:

1. $\pm(X)$

2. $= (A; X)$

3. $\pm(A)$

which can be pictured thus:

M	$A = \perp$	$A \neq \perp$
$X = \emptyset$		$\pm(A)$
$X \neq \emptyset$	$\pm(X)$	$\pm(X)$ or $= (A; X)$ or $\pm(A)$

Chapter 9

THEOREM: In every intuitionistic relevant proof of A from the set X of undischarged assumptions, one of the following holds:

1. $\mp(X)$

2. $\nabla(A; X)$

3. $\pm(A)$

which can be pictured thus:

IR	$A = \perp$	$A \neq \perp$
$X = \emptyset$		$\pm(A)$
$X \neq \emptyset$	$\mp(X)$	$\nabla(A; X)$

Chapter 12

THEOREM: $X, A \supset B \vdash A$ and $X, B \vdash C \Rightarrow X, A \supset B \vdash C$

THEOREM: $X, A \supset B \vdash C \Rightarrow X, B \vdash C$

Chapter 14

LEMMA: Any non-literal problem $X{:}C$ that has an ordinary hybrid proof has a non-literal ordinary hybrid proof.

THEOREM: For all ordinary proofs Π of $X{:}C$ there is a Dyckhoff proof Σ of $X{:}C$.

THEOREM: Steps of $\wedge$-introduction, $\vee$-introduction and attic steps whose antecedents are shared with earlier attic steps, can preserve fetters on minor-creating steps without loss of completeness.

THEOREM: Fettering does not lead to incompleteness.

THEOREM: Fettering is sufficient to prevent looping.

THEOREM: Hobbling does not induce incompleteness.

THEOREM: Hobbling, like fettering, is sufficient to prevent looping.

THEOREM: Suppose we have a proof

$$\alpha \frac{\overset{\displaystyle \overline{}^{\,1}}{D} \quad \begin{array}{cc} \Sigma & \Theta \\ C \supset D \quad C & E \end{array}}{E} \, 1$$

$$\Pi$$

$$G$$

in which no attic step or step of ∧-elimination or ∨-elimination occurs on the path ρ leading up from the conclusion G to α. Suppose also that α is the first step of ⊃-elimination to be encountered as one moves up the path from G to α. Then the proof can be transformed into a proof of G from the same set of undischarged assumptions, but with α terminal.

THEOREM: Suppose we have a proof Ψ of one of the forms

$$\beta \frac{\alpha \dfrac{\overset{\overline{}^{\,1}}{\Pi_1}\ \overset{\overline{}^{\,1}}{\Pi_2}}{A \land B}\ \ \begin{array}{cc}\Sigma & \Theta\\ P\supset Q\ P & E\end{array}}{E}\,1$$

$$\beta \frac{\alpha \dfrac{\overset{\overline{}^{\,1}}{\Pi}}{A \lor B}\ \ \begin{array}{cc}\Sigma & \Theta\\ P\supset Q\ P & E\end{array}}{E}\,1$$

$$\beta \frac{\alpha \dfrac{\overset{\overline{}^{\,1}\ \overline{}^{\,2}}{\Pi}}{A \supset B}\,2\ \ \begin{array}{cc}\Sigma & \Theta\\ P\supset Q\ P & E\end{array}}{E}\,1$$

$$\beta \frac{\alpha \dfrac{\overset{\overline{}^{\,1}\ ,\ \overline{}^{\,2}}{\Pi}}{\neg A}\,2\ \ \begin{array}{cc}\Sigma & \Theta\\ P\supset Q\ P & E\end{array}}{E}\,1$$

in which the path ρ from β to α does not pass through any minor conclusions; and suppose further that this path contains no ∨-elimination. Then Ψ can be transformed into a proof Ψ' of E from available undischarged assumptions of Ψ, but with β now above α.

Chapter 15

THEOREM: Let any deductive problem $X?\text{-}A$ be decomposed into sub-problems by means of attempted application of any of the rules of IR. If those sub-problems admit of partial proper solution then so too does the original problem.

THEOREM: The decision problem for propositional IR is PSPACE-complete.

Appendix: Problems and Proof-Finders

Deductive Debuggers for Minimal Logic

TRIVIAL
[a] ?- a.
[a,b] ?- a.
[not(a)] ?- not(a).
[and(a,b)] ?- and(a,b).
[if(a,b)] ?- if(a,b).
[or(a,b)] ?- or(a,b).

SIMPLE INTRODUCTIONS
[a] ?- not(not(a)).
[a,b] ?- and(a,b).
[b] ?- if(a,b).
[a] ?- or(a,b).
[b] ?- or(a,b).

SIMPLE ELIMINATIONS
[a,not(a)] ?- ⊥.
[and(a,b)] ?- a.
[and(a,b)] ?- b.
[if(a,b),a] ?- b.

SINGLE OPERATORS

IF
[] ?- if(a,a).
[] ?- if(a,if(a,a)).
[] ?- if(a,if(if(a,a),a)).
[] ?- if(a,if(if(a,b),a)).
[if(a,b),if(b,c)] ?- if(a,c).
[] ?- if(if(a,if(a,b)),if(a,b)).
[] ?- if(if(a,b),if(if(a,b),if(a,b))).
[] ?- if(if(a,b),if(if(b,c),if(a,c))).
[] ?- if(if(a,b),if(if(c,a),if(c,b))).
[] ?- if(if(a,b),if(if(if(a,b),c),c)).
[] ?- if(if(b,if(b,a)),if(if(if(b,a),a),a)).
[if(a,if(b,c)),if(a,if(c,d))] ?- if(a,if(b,d)).
[] ?- if(if(a,if(b,c)),if(if(d,b),if(a,if(d,c)))) .
[] ?- if(if(a,d),if(if(if(b,c),a),if(if(a,c),if(if(b,a),d)))) .

NOT
[not(not(not(a)))] ?- not(a).

AND
[and(a,b),and(b,c)] ?- and(a,c).
[and(a,b)] ?- and(b,a).
[and(and(a,b),c)] ?- and(a,and(b,c)).
[and(and(and(a,b),c),d)] ?- and(a,and(b,and(c,d))).
[and(and(and(and(a,b),c),d),e)] ?- and(a,and(b,and(c,and(d,e)))).
[and(and(and(and(and(a,b),c),d),e),f)] ?-
    and(a,and(b,and(c,and(d,and(e,f))))).
[and(and(and(and(and(and(a,b),c),d),e),f),g)] ?-
    and(a,and(b,and(c,and(d,and(e,and(f,g)))))).

OR

[or(a,b)] ?- or(b,a).
[or(or(a,b),c)] ?- or(a,or(b,c)).
[or(or(or(a,b),c),d)] ?- or(a,or(b,or(c,d))).
[or(or(or(or(a,b),c),d),e)] ?- or(a,or(b,or(c,or(d,e)))).
[or(or(or(or(or(a,b),c),d),e),f)] ?- or(a,or(b,or(c,or(d,or(e,f))))).
[or(or(or(or(or(or(a,b),c),d),e),f),g)] ?- or(a,or(b,or(c,or(d,or(e,or(f,g)))))).

TWO OPERATORS

IF-AND

[] ?- if(and(a,b),a).
[] ?- if(and(a,b),b).
[if(a,b), and(a,c)] ?- b.
[] ?- and(if(p,p),if(p,p)).
[] ?- if(and(a,b),and(b,a)).
[if(a,b)] ?- if(and(a,c),b).
[if(a,b)] ?- if(and(c,a),b).
[if(q,r),if(r,and(p,q))] ?- if(q,p).
[if(a,b),if(a,c)] ?- if(a,and(b,c)).
[] ?- if(and(if(a,b),if(a,c)),if(a,and(b,c))).
[] ?- if(and(if(a,c),if(a,if(c,d))),if(a,if(a,d))).
[if(d,and(if(a,b),if(a,c)))] ?- if(if(c,e),if(and(a,d),e)).

IF-OR

[] ?- if(a,or(a,b)).
[] ?- if(b,or(a,b)).
[or(a,b),if(a,b)] ?- b.
[] ?- if(or(a,b),or(b,a)).
[] ?- or(if(p,p),if(p,p)).
[a,if(a,or(b,c))] ?- or(c,b).
[or(a,b),if(a,c),if(b,c)] ?- c.
[if(a,c),if(b,c),or(a,b)] ?- c.
[if(a,c),if(b,c)] ?- if(or(a,b),c).
[b, if(a,if(b,c)), if(b,or(a,c))] ?- c.
[] ?- if(if(a,c),if(if(b,c),if(or(a,b),c))).

IF-NOT

[if(⊥,a),b,not(b)] ?- a.
[if(a,not(a))] ?- not(a).
[] ?- if(if(a,not(a)),not(a)).
[if(not(a),a)] ?- not(not(a)).
[if(a,b)] ?- if(not(b),not(a)).
[not(a)] ?- if(if(b,a),not(b)).
[not(c),if(if(a,b),c)] ?- not(b).
[] ?- if(if(a,b),if(not(b),not(a))).
[if(a,b),if(not(a),b)] ?- not(not(b)).
[if(a,b),if(b,c)] ?- if(not(c),not(a)).
[] ?- if(not(not(a)),not(if(a,not(a)))).
[a, if(a,not(b)), if(a,not(not(b)))] ?- ⊥.
[a, if(a,not(b))] ?- not(if(a,not(not(b)))).
[if(if(a,b),c),if(not(b),d)] ?- if(not(c),d).
[if(a,not(b)),if(not(c),b)] ?- if(not(c),not(a)).
[a, if(a,not(b)), not(not(if(a,not(not(b)))))] ?- ⊥.
[a, not(not(if(a,not(not(b)))))] ?- not(if(a,not(b))).
[not(not(if(a,not(not(b))))), not(not(if(a,not(b)))), a] ?- ⊥.

OR-NOT

[not(or(a,b))] ?- not(a).
[not(or(a,b))] ?- not(b).
[or(a,b),not(a),not(b)] ?- ⊥.
[not(a),or(a,b)] ?- not(not(b)).
[not(b),or(a,b)] ?- not(not(a)).
[or(not(a),b), a] ?- not(not(b)).
[or(a,not(b)), b] ?- not(not(a)).
[or(not(a),not(b)), a] ?- not(b).
[p, q] ?- not(or(not(p),not(q))).
[or(not(a),not(b)), b] ?- not(a).
[p, q, not(q)] ?- not(or(not(p),not(q))).
[or(not(a),not(b)), not(not(a))] ?- not(b).
[or(not(a),not(b)), not(not(b))] ?- not(a).
[q, or(p,not(q))] ?- not(or(not(p),not(q))).
[p, q, or(p,not(q)), or(not(p),not(q))] ?- ⊥.

[p, q, or(p,not(q))] ?- not(or(not(p),not(q))).
[q, not(p), or(p,not(q))] ?- not(or(not(p),not(q))).
[p, not(p), or(p,not(q))] ?- not(or(not(p),not(q))).
[q, not(p), or(p,not(q))] ?- not(or(not(p),not(q))).
[p, or(not(p),q), or(p,not(q))] ?- not(or(not(p),not(q))).
[q, or(not(p),q), or(p,not(q))] ?- not(or(not(p),not(q))).
[or(p,q), or(not(p),q), or(p,not(q))] ?- not(or(not(p),not(q))).

OR-AND
[or(a,and(b,c))] ?- or(a,b).
[or(a,and(b,c))] ?- or(a,c).
[and(a,or(b,c))] ?- or(and(a,b),c).
[and(a,or(b,c))] ?- or(and(a,b),and(a,c)).
[or(a,and(b,c))] ?- and(or(a,b),or(a,c)).

AND-NOT
[and(a,not(a))] ?- ⊥.
[and(a,b),not(a)] ?- ⊥.
[and(a,not(a))] ?- not(b).
[and(b,c),not(and(a,b))] ?- not(a).
[] ?- not(and(not(p),not(not(not(not(p)))))).
[q, not(and(p,q)), not(and(p,not(q))), not(and(not(p),q))] ?- ⊥.
[not(p), not(and(not(p),not(q))), not(and(p,not(q))),
    not(and(not(p),q))] ?- ⊥.
[not(b), not(and(not(a),not(b))),not(and(not(a),not(not(b)))),
    not(and(not(not(a)),not(b)))] ?- ⊥.
[not(and(not(p),not(q))),not(and(not(not(p)),not(q))),not(and(not(p),
    not(not(q))))] ?- not(not(p)).
[not(and(not(p),not(q))),not(and(not(not(p)),not(q))),not(and(not(p),
    not(not(q))))] ?- not(not(and(not(not(p)),not(not(q))))).
[not(a), not(and(not(a),not(b))),not(and(not(a),not(not(b)))),
    not(and(not(not(a)),not(b)))] ?- ⊥.

THREE OPERATORS

IF-OR-AND

[and(if(a,c),if(b,c)),a] ?- c.
[and(if(a,c),if(b,c)),b] ?- c.
[and(if(a,c),if(b,c)),or(a,b)] ?- c.
[if(or(a,b),c)] ?- and(if(a,c),if(b,c)).
[and(if(a,c),if(b,c))] ?- if(or(a,b),c).
[] ?- if(and(a,or(b,c)),or(and(a,b),c)).
[and(if(a,c),if(b,c))] ?- if(or(a,b),c).
[if(p,or(q,r)),if(r,and(p,q))] ?- if(p,q).
[b, and(if(a,if(b,c)),if(b,or(a,c)))] ?- c.
[a,e,if(a,and(b,if(e,or(c,d))))] ?- or(d,c).
[] ?- if(and(if(a,c),if(b,c)),if(or(a,b),c)).
[and(if(a,if(b,c)),if(b,or(a,c)))] ?- if(b,c).
[and(if(a,c),if(b,c)), if(d,or(a,b))] ?- if(d,c).
[] ?- if(and(if(a,if(b,c)),if(b,or(a,c))),if(b,c)).
[if(q,r),if(r,and(p,q)),if(p,or(q,r))] ?- and(if(p,q),if(q,p)).
[] ?- if(and(and(or(p,q),or(not(p),q)),or(p,not(q))),not(or(not(p),not(q)))).
[] ?- and(if(or(p,and(q,r)),and(or(p,q),or(p,r))),if(and(or(p,q),or(p,r)),
    or(p,and(q,r)))).

IF-AND-NOT

[and(not(a),not(b)), if(d,or(a,b))] ?- not(d).
[] ?- if(and(a,b),not(not(and(not(not(a)),not(not(b)))))).
[] ?- and(if(if(p,q),if(not(q),not(p))),if(if(not(q),not(p)),if(p,not(not(q))))).
[] ?- and(if(if(not(p),q),if(not(q),not(not(p)))),if(if(not(q),p),if(not(p),
    not(not(q))))).
[] ?- if(and(and(not(and(not(p),not(q))),not(and(not(not(p)),not(q)))),
    not(and(not(p),not(not(q))))),not(not(and(not(not(p)),not(not(q)))))).
[] ?- if(and(and(not(and(not(p),not(q))),not(and(not(not(p)),not(q)))),
    not(and(not(p),not(not(q))))),not(not(p))).
[if(q,r),if(r,and(p,q)),if(p,not(and(not(q),not(r))))] ?-
    and(if(p,not(not(q))),if(q,p)).
[] ?- and(if(not(and(not(p),not(and(q,r)))),and(not(and(not(p),not(q))),
    not(and(not(p),not(r))))),if(and(not(and(not(p),not(q))),
    not(and(not(p),not(r)))),not(and(not(p),not(and(q,r)))))).

OR-AND-NOT
[not(or(a,b))] ?- and(not(a),not(b)).
[and(not(a),not(b))] ?- not(or(a,b)).
[or(not(a),not(b))] ?- not(and(a,b)).
[and(or(p,q),or(not(p),q)), or(p,not(q))] ?- not(or(not(p),not(q))).
[and(and(or(p,q),or(not(p),q)),or(p,not(q)))] ?- not(or(not(p),not(q))).

IF-OR-NOT
[not(or(a,b)),if(not(a),b)] ?- ⊥.

Pelletier's propositional problems

[] ?- and(if(if(p,q),if(not(q),not(p))), if(if(not(q),not(p)),if(p,q))).

[] ?- and(if(not(not(p)),p),if(p,not(not(p)))).

[] ?- if(not(if(p,q)),if(q,p)).

[] ?- and(if(if(not(p),q),if(not(q),p)),if(if(not(q),p),if(not(p),q))).

[] ?- if(if(or(p,q),or(p,r)),or(p,if(q,r))).

[] ?- or(p,not(p)).

[] ?- or(p,not(not(not(p))))).

[] ?- if(if(if(p,q),p),p).

[] ?- if(and(and(or(p,q),or(not(p),q)),or(p,not(q))),not(or(not(p),not(q)))).

[if(q,r),if(r,and(p,q)),if(p,or(q,r))] ?- and(if(p,q),if(q,p)).

[] ?- and(if(p,p),if(p,p)).

[] ?- and(if(and(if(and(if(p,q),if(q,p)),r),if(r,and(if(p,q),if(q,p)))),
   and(if(p,and(if(q,r),if(r,q))),if(and(if(q,r),if(r,q)),p))),if(and(if(p,
   and(if(q,r),if(r,q))),if(and(if(q,r),if(r,q)),p)),and(if(and(if(p,q),
   if(q,p)),r),if(r,and(if(p,q),if(q,p)))))).

[] ?- and(if(or(p,and(q,r)),and(or(p,q),or(p,r))),if(and(or(p,q),or(p,r)),
   or(p,and(q,r)))).

[] ?- and(if(and(if(p,q),if(q,p)),and(or(q,not(p)),or(not(q),p))),
   if(and(or(q,not(p)),or(not(q),p)),and(if(p,q),if(q,p)))).

[] ?- and(if(if(p,q),or(not(q),q)),if(or(not(q),q),if(p,q))).

[] ?- or(if(p,q),if(q,p)).

[] ?- and(if(if(and(p,if(q,r)),s),and(or(or(not(p),q),s),or(or(not(p),not(r)),s))),
   if(and(or(or(not(p),q),s),or(or(not(p),not(r)),s)),if(and(p,if(q,r)),s))).

The Associativity Problems ("Asset")

1

[not(if(not(if(not(if(not(if(not(if(a,not(if(not(a),a)))),not(or(b,not(b)))))),
   not(if(not(not(if(not(if(a,not(if(not(a),a)))),not(or(b,not(b))))))),
   not(if(not(if(a,not(if(not(a),a)))),not(or(b,not(b))))))))))),
   not(or(c,not(c)))))))]
   ?-
   not(if(not(if(a,not(if(not(a),a)))),not(or(not(if(not(if(b,not(if(not(b),
   b)))),not(or(c,not(c)))))),not(not(if(not(if(b,not(if(not(b),b)))),
   not(or(c,not(c)))))))))))))).

2

[not(if(not(if(a,not(or(or(b,not(b)),not(if(not(a),not(not(a)))))))),
    not(or(or(c,not(c)),not(if(not(not(if(a,not(or(or(b,not(b)),not(if(not(a),
    not(not(a))))))))),not(not(not(if(a,not(or(or(b,not(b)),not(if(not(a),
    not(not(a)))))))))))))))]
?-
not(if(a,not(or(or(not(if(b,not(or(or(c,not(c)),
    not(if(not(b),not(not(b)))))))),not(not(if(b,not(or(or(c,not(c)),
    not(if(not(b),not(not(b)))))))))))),not(if(not(a),not(not(a)))))))))).

3

[if(not(if(not(a),not(if(not(if(a,not(not(a)))),not(or(b,not(b))))))),
    not(if(not(if(if(not(a),not(if(not(if(a,not(not(a)))),not(or(b,not(b)))))),
    not(not(if(not(a),not(if(not(if(a,not(not(a)))),not(or(b,not(b))))))))))),
    not(or(c,not(c)))))))]
?-
if(not(a),not(if(not(if(a,not(not(a)))),not(or(if(not(b),
    not(if(not(if(b,not(not(b)))),not(or(c,not(c))))))),not(if(not(b),
    not(if(not(if(b,not(not(b)))),not(or(c,not(c)))))))))))))))).

4

[or(or(a,not(if(not(if(a,not(not(a)))),not(or(b,not(b)))))),
    not(if(not(if(or(a,not(if(not(if(a,not(not(a)))),not(or(b,not(b)))))),
    not(not(or(a,not(if(not(if(a,not(not(a)))),not(or(b,not(b))))))))))),
    not(or(c,not(c)))))))]
?-
or(a,not(if(not(if(a,not(not(a)))),not(or(or(b,not(if(not(if(b,
    not(not(b)))),not(or(c,not(c))))))),not(or(b,not(if(not(if(b,not(not(b)))),
    not(or(c,not(c)))))))))))))))))))).

5

[not(if(not(if(not(if(not(if(a,not(or(a,not(a)))))),not(or(b,not(b)))))),
   not(or(not(if(not(if(a,not(or(a,not(a)))))),not(or(b,not(b)))))),
   not(not(if(not(if(a,not(or(a,not(a)))))),not(or(b,not(b)))))))))))))),
   not(or(c,not(c)))))]
?-
not(if(not(if(a,not(or(a,not(a)))))),not(or(not(if(not(if(b,not(or(b,
   not(b)))))),not(or(c,not(c)))))),not(not(if(not(if(b,not(or(b,not(b)))))),
   not(or(c,not(c)))))))))))).

6

[not(if(not(if(a,not(or(or(a,not(b)),not(if(not(a),not(b)))))))),
   not(or(or(not(if(a,not(or(or(a,not(b)),not(if(not(a),not(b))))))),not(c)),
   not(if(not(not(if(a,not(or(or(a,not(b)),not(if(not(a),not(b)))))))),
   not(c))))))))]
?-
not(if(a,not(or(or(a,not(not(if(b,not(or(or(b,not(c)),not(if(not(b),
   not(c)))))))),not(if(not(a),not(not(if(b,not(or(or(b,not(c)),
   not(if(not(b),not(c))))))))))))))))).

7

[not(if(not(if(a,not(or(or(b,not(b)),not(if(not(a),not(b)))))))),
   not(or(or(c,not(c)),not(if(not(not(if(a,not(or(or(b,not(b)),
   not(if(not(a),not(b)))))))),not(c)))))))]
?-
not(if(a,not(or(or(not(if(b,not(or(or(c,not(c)),not(if(not(b),
   not(c))))))),not(not(if(b,not(or(or(c,not(c)),not(if(not(b),
   not(c)))))))))),not(if(not(a),not(not(if(b,not(or(or(c,not(c)),
   not(if(not(b),not(c)))))))))))))).

8

[not(if(if(not(not(if(if(not(a),a),not(or(not(b),not(if(a,not(b))))))))),
   not(if(if(not(a),a),not(or(not(b),not(if(a,not(b))))))))),not(or(not(c,
   not(if(not(if(if(if(not(a),a),not(or(not(b),not(if(a,not(b))))))),not(c))))))))]
?-

not(if(if(not(a),a),not(or(not(not(if(if(not(b),b),not(or(not(c),
not(if(b,not(c))))))))),not(if(a,not(not(if(if(not(b),b),not(or(not(c),
not(if(b,not(c))))))))))))))).

9

[not(if(not(if(a,not(if(not(a),not(if(not(a),not(or(b,not(b))))))))))),
  not(if(not(not(if(a,not(if(not(a),not(if(not(a),not(or(b,not(b)))))))))))),
  not(if(not(not(if(a,not(if(not(a),not(if(not(a),not(or(b,not(b)))))))))))),
  not(or(c,not(c)))))))))]
?-
not(if(a,not(if(not(a),not(if(not(a),not(or(not(if(b,
not(if(not(b),not(if(not(b),not(or(c,not(c)))))))))),not(not(if(b,
not(if(not(b),not(if(not(b),not(or(c,not(c))))))))))))))))))).

10

[not(if(not(if(a,not(or(a,not(if(not(a),not(or(b,not(b))))))))),not(or(not(if(a,
  not(or(a,not(if(not(a),not(or(b,not(b))))))))),not(if(not(not(if(a,not(or(a,
  not(if(not(a),not(or(b,not(b))))))))),not(or(c,not(c)))))))))]
?-
not(if(a,not(or(a,not(if(not(a),not(or(not(if(b,not(or(b,not(if(not(b),
not(or(c,not(c))))))))),not(not(if(b,not(or(b,not(if(not(b),not(or(c,
not(c))))))))))))))))).

11

[or(or(a,not(if(a,not(or(not(b),not(if(not(a),not(b)))))))),not(if(or(a,not(if(a,
  not(or(not(b),not(if(not(a),not(b)))))))),not(or(not(c),not(if(not(or(a,
  not(if(a,not(or(not(b),not(if(not(a),not(b)))))))),not(c)))))))]
?-
or(a,not(if(a,not(or(not(or(b,not(if(b,not(or(not(c),not(if(not(b),
not(c)))))))),not(if(not(a),not(or(b,not(if(b,not(or(not(c),
not(if(not(b),not(c))))))))))))))).

12

[not(if(not(if(a,not(or(not(b),if(not(a),not(if(not(a),not(b))))))))),
    not(or(not(c),if(not(not(if(a,not(or(not(b),if(not(a),not(if(not(a),
    not(b))))))))),not(if(not(not(if(a,not(or(not(b),if(not(a),
    not(if(not(a),not(b))))))))),not(c)))))))))]
?-
    not(if(a,not(or(not(not(if(b,not(or(not(c),if(not(b),not(if(not(b),
    not(c)))))))))),if(not(a),not(if(not(a),not(not(if(b,not(or(not(c),
    if(not(b),not(if(not(b),not(c))))))))))))))))))).

13

[not(if(not(if(a,not(or(not(b),not(if(b,not(or(a,not(a)))))))))),not(or(not(c),
    not(if(c,not(or(not(if(a,not(or(not(b),not(if(b,not(or(a,not(a)))))))))),
    not(not(if(a,not(or(not(b),not(if(b,not(or(a,not(a))))))))))))))))))]
?-
    not(if(a,not(or(not(not(if(b,not(or(not(c),not(if(c,not(or(b,
    not(b)))))))))),not(if(not(if(b,not(or(not(c),not(if(c,not(or(b,
    not(b)))))))),not(or(a,not(a)))))))))).

14

[not(if(not(if(a,not(or(not(b),if(not(b),not(if(not(a),not(b))))))))),
    not(or(not(c),if(not(c),not(if(not(not(if(a,not(or(not(b),if(not(b),
    not(if(not(a),not(b))))))))),not(c)))))))))]
?-
    not(if(a,not(or(not(not(if(b,not(or(not(c),if(not(c),not(if(not(b),
    not(c))))))))),if(not(not(if(b,not(or(not(c),if(not(c),not(if(not(b),
    not(c))))))))),not(if(not(a),not(not(if(b,not(or(not(c),if(not(c),
    not(if(not(b),not(c)))))))))))))))).

15

[not(if(not(if(a,not(or(not(b),not(if(b,not(or(not(a),b)))))))))),
    not(or(not(c),not(if(c,not(or(not(not(if(a,not(or(not(b),not(if(b,
    not(or(not(a),b))))))))),c)))))))]
?-

not(if(a,not(or(not(not(if(b,not(or(not(c),not(if(c,not(or(not(b),
c))))))))),not(if(not(if(b,not(or(not(c),not(if(c,not(or(not(b),
c))))))))),not(or(not(a),not(if(b,not(or(not(c),not(if(c,
not(or(not(b),c))))))))))))))))))))))).

16

[not(if(or(not(if(or(a,not(if(a,not(not(a)))))),not(or(b,not(b)))))),
    not(if(not(if(or(a,not(if(a,not(not(a)))))),not(or(b,not(b)))))),
    not(not(not(if(or(a,not(if(a,not(not(a)))))),not(or(b,not(b)))))))))))))),
    not(or(c,not(c)))))))]
?-
not(if(or(a,not(if(a,not(not(a)))))),not(or(not(if(or(b,not(if(b,
    not(not(b)))))),not(or(c,not(c)))))),not(not(if(or(b,
    not(if(b,not(not(b)))))),not(or(c,not(c)))))))))))))).

17

[not(if(not(if(a,not(if(not(a),a)))),not(or(not(if(not(if(b,
    not(if(not(b),b)))),not(or(c,not(c)))))),not(not(if(not(if(b,
    not(if(not(b),b)))),not(or(c,not(c)))))))))))))]
?-
not(if(not(if(not(if(not(if(a,not(if(not(a),a)))),not(or(b,
    not(b)))))),not(if(not(not(if(not(if(a,not(if(not(a),a)))),
    not(or(b,not(b))))))),not(if(not(if(a,not(if(not(a),a)))),
    not(or(b,not(b)))))))))))),not(or(c,not(c)))))).

18

[not(if(a,not(or(or(not(if(b,not(or(or(c,not(c)),not(if(not(b),
    not(not(b))))))))),not(not(if(b,not(or(or(c,not(c)),not(if(not(b),
    not(not(b)))))))))))),not(if(not(a),not(not(a)))))))))]
?-
not(if(not(if(a,not(or(or(b,not(b)),not(if(not(a),
    not(not(a))))))))),not(or(or(c,not(c)),not(if(not(not(if(a,
    not(or(or(b,not(b)),not(if(not(a),not(not(a))))))))),
    not(not(not(if(a,not(or(or(b,not(b)),not(if(not(a),
    not(not(a)))))))))))))))))))).

19

[if(not(a),not(if(not(if(a,not(not(a)))),not(or(if(not(b),
   not(if(not(if(b,not(not(b)))),not(or(c,not(c))))))),not(if(not(b),
   not(if(not(if(b,not(not(b)))),not(or(c,not(c))))))))))))]
?-
if(not(if(not(a),not(if(not(if(a,not(not(a)))),
   not(or(b,not(b)))))))),not(if(not(if(if(not(a),not(if(not(if(a,
   not(not(a)))),not(or(b,not(b)))))),not(not(if(not(a),
   not(if(not(if(a,not(not(a)))),not(or(b,not(b)))))))))),not(or(c,
   not(c)))))).

20

[or(a,not(if(not(if(a,not(not(a)))),not(or(or(b,not(if(not(if(b,
   not(not(b)))),not(or(c,not(c))))))),not(or(b,not(if(not(if(b,
   not(not(b)))),not(or(c,not(c))))))))))))]
?-
or(or(a,not(if(not(if(a,not(not(a)))),not(or(b,not(b))))))),
   not(if(not(if(if(or(a,not(if(not(if(a,not(not(a)))),not(or(b,not(b))))))),
   not(not(or(a,not(if(not(if(a,not(not(a)))),not(or(b,not(b)))))))))),
   not(or(c,not(c))))))).

21

[not(if(not(if(a,not(or(a,not(a)))))),not(or(or(not(if(not(if(b,
   not(or(b,not(b)))))),not(or(c,not(c)))))),not(not(if(not(if(b,not(or(b,
   not(b)))))),not(or(c,not(c))))))))))]
?-
not(if(not(if(not(if(not(if(a,not(or(a,not(a)))))),not(or(b,not(b)))))),
   not(or(not(if(not(if(a,not(or(a,not(a)))))),not(or(b,not(b)))))),
   not(not(if(not(if(a,not(or(a,not(a)))))),not(or(b,not(b))))))))))),
   not(or(c,not(c)))))).

22

[not(if(a,not(or(or(a,not(not(if(b,not(or(or(b,not(c)),
   not(if(not(b),not(c)))))))))),not(if(not(a),not(not(if(b,
   not(or(or(b,not(c)),not(if(not(b),not(c)))))))))))))]

?-
not(if(not(if(a,not(or(or(a,not(b)),not(if(not(a),not(b))))))),
not(or(or(not(if(a,not(or(or(a,not(b)),not(if(not(a),not(b))))))))),
not(c)),not(if(not(not(if(a,not(or(or(a,not(b)),not(if(not(a),
not(b)))))))),not(c))))))).

23

[not(if(a,not(or(or(not(if(b,not(or(or(c,not(c)),
not(if(not(b),not(c)))))))),not(not(if(b,not(or(or(c,not(c)),
not(if(not(b),not(c))))))))),not(if(not(a),not(not(if(b,
not(or(or(c,not(c)),not(if(not(b),not(c)))))))))))))]
?-
not(if(not(if(a,not(or(or(b,not(b)),not(if(not(a),not(b))))))),
not(or(or(c,not(c)),not(if(not(not(if(a,not(or(or(b,not(b)),
not(if(not(a),not(b)))))))),not(c))))))).

24

[not(if(if(not(a),a),not(or(not(not(if(if(not(b),b),not(or(not(c),
not(if(b,not(c)))))))),not(if(a,not(not(if(if(not(b),b),not(or(not(c),
not(if(b,not(c)))))))))))))]
?-
not(if(if(not(not(if(if(not(a),a),not(or(not(b),not(if(a,not(b)))))))),
not(if(if(not(a),a),not(or(not(b),not(if(a,not(b))))))),
not(or(not(c),not(if(not(if(if(not(a),a),not(or(not(b),not(if(a,not(b))))))),
not(c))))))).

25

[not(if(a,not(if(not(a),not(if(not(a),not(or(not(if(b,
not(if(not(b),not(if(not(b),not(or(c,not(c))))))))),not(not(if(b,
not(if(not(b),not(if(not(b),not(or(c,not(c)))))))))))))))))]
?-
not(if(not(if(a,not(if(not(a),not(if(not(a),
not(or(b,not(b))))))))),not(if(not(not(if(a,not(if(not(a),not(if(not(a),
not(or(b,not(b)))))))))),not(if(not(not(if(a,not(if(not(a),not(if(not(a),
not(or(b,not(b))))))))),not(or(c,not(c))))))))).

26

[not(if(a,not(or(a,not(if(not(a),not(or(not(if(b,not(or(b,not(if(not(b),
    not(or(c,not(c)))))))))),not(not(if(b,not(or(b,not(if(not(b),
    not(or(c,not(c)))))))))))))))))]
?-
    not(if(not(if(a,not(or(a,not(if(not(a),not(or(b,not(b)))))))))),
    not(or(not(if(a,not(or(a,not(if(not(a),not(or(b,not(b)))))))))),
    not(if(not(not(if(a,not(or(a,not(if(not(a),not(or(b,not(b)))))))))),
    not(or(c,not(c)))))))))).

27

[or(a,not(if(a,not(or(not(or(b,not(if(b,not(or(not(c),not(if(not(b),
    not(c)))))))))),not(if(not(a),not(or(b,not(if(b,not(or(not(c),
    not(if(not(b),not(c))))))))))))))))]
?-
    or(or(a,not(if(a,not(or(not(b),not(if(not(a),not(b)))))))),
    not(if(or(a,not(if(a,not(or(not(b),not(if(not(a),not(b)))))))),
    not(or(not(c),not(if(not(or(a,not(if(a,not(or(not(b),
    not(if(not(a),not(b))))))))),not(c))))))))).

28

[not(if(a,not(or(not(not(if(b,not(or(not(c),if(not(b),not(if(not(b),
    not(c)))))))))),if(not(a),not(if(not(a),not(not(if(b,not(or(not(c),
    if(not(b),not(if(not(b),not(c))))))))))))))))]
?-
    not(if(not(if(a,not(or(not(b),if(not(a),
    not(if(not(a),not(b)))))))),not(or(not(c),if(not(not(if(a,not(or(not(b),
    if(not(a),not(if(not(a),not(b))))))))),not(if(not(not(if(a,not(or(not(b),
    if(not(a),not(if(not(a),not(b))))))))),not(c))))))))).

29

[not(if(a,not(or(not(not(if(b,not(or(not(c),not(if(c,not(or(b,not(b)))))))))))),
    not(if(not(if(b,not(or(not(c),not(if(c,not(or(b,not(b)))))))))),
    not(or(a,not(a)))))))))]
?-

not(if(not(if(a,not(or(not(b),not(if(b,not(or(a,not(a)))))))))),not(or(not(c),
not(if(c,not(or(not(if(a,not(or(not(b),not(if(b,not(or(a,not(a)))))))))))),
not(not(if(a,not(or(not(b),not(if(b,not(or(a,not(a)))))))))))))))))))).

30

[not(if(a,not(or(not(not(if(b,not(or(not(c),if(not(c),not(if(not(b),
not(c)))))))))),if(not(not(if(b,not(or(not(c),if(not(c),
not(if(not(b),not(c)))))))))),not(if(not(a),not(not(if(b,
not(or(not(c),if(not(c),not(if(not(b),not(c))))))))))))))))))))]
?-
not(if(not(if(a,not(or(not(b),if(not(b),not(if(not(a),not(b)))))))),
not(or(not(c),if(not(c),not(if(not(not(if(a,not(or(not(b),if(not(b),
not(if(not(a),not(b))))))))),not(c)))))))).

31

[not(if(a,not(or(not(not(if(b,not(or(not(c),not(if(c,not(or(not(b),c)))))))))),
not(if(not(if(b,not(or(not(c),not(if(c,not(or(not(b),c)))))))),
not(or(not(a),not(if(b,not(or(not(c),not(if(c,
not(or(not(b),c))))))))))))))))))))]
?-
not(if(not(if(a,not(or(not(b),not(if(b,not(or(not(a),b)))))))),not(or(not(c),
not(if(c,not(or(not(not(if(a,not(or(not(b),not(if(b,not(or(not(a),b)))))))),
c)))))))).

32

[not(if(or(a,not(if(a,not(not(a)))))),not(or(not(if(or(b,not(if(b,not(not(b)))))),
not(or(c,not(c))))),not(not(if(or(b,not(if(b,not(not(b)))))),not(or(c,
not(c))))))))))]
?-
not(if(or(not(if(or(a,not(if(a,not(not(a)))))),not(or(b,not(b))))),
not(if(not(if(or(a,not(if(a,not(not(a)))))),not(or(b,not(b))))),
not(not(not(if(or(a,not(if(a,not(not(a)))))),not(or(b,not(b)))))))))),
not(or(c,not(c))))).

Some simple Prolog proof-finders

The Prolog program SNAIL

```
%================================================================
% I.   BASIS CLAUSE
%================================================================
% trivial proofs:

proof(X,A,A) :-
     member(A,X).
%================================================================
% II.  INDUCTIVE CLAUSES
%================================================================
% IIa.  CLAUSES CORRESPONDING TO ELIMINATION RULES
%================================================================
% and_elimination:

proof(X,A,and_e(A,and(B,C),D)) :-
     member(and(B,C),X),
     delElement(and(B,C),X,Y),
     addElement(B,Y,Z),
     addElement(C,Z,W),
     proof(W,A,D).
%================================================================
% or_elimination:

proof(X,A,or_e(A,or(B,C),D1,D2)) :-
     member(or(B,C),X),
     delElement(or(B,C),X,Y),
     addElement(B,Y,Y1),
     addElement(C,Y,Y2),
     proof(Y1,A,D1),
     proof(Y2,A,D2).
%================================================================
```

```
%  not_elimination:

proof(X,#,not_e(#,not(P),D)) :-
        member(not(P),X),
        minor_proof(X,P,D).
%=============================================================
%  if_elimination:

proof(X,A,if_e(A,if(P,Q),D1,D2)) :-
        member(if(P,Q),X),
        minor_proof(X,P,D1),
        delElement(if(P,Q),X,Y),
        addElement(Q,Y,Z),
        proof(Z,A,D2).
%=============================================================
% The device of minor_proof is just to prevent loops:

?- dynamic asked/2.

minor_proof(X,P,D) :-
        asked(P,X),
        !,
        fail.

minor_proof(X,P,D) :-
        remember(asked(P,X)),
        proof(X,P,D),
        forget(asked(P,X)).

remember(X) :-
        assert(X).

remember(X) :-
        retract(X),
        fail.

forget(X) :-
        retract(X).
```

```
forget(X) :-
     assert(X),
     fail.
%=============================================================
% IIb.  CLAUSES CORRESPONDING TO INTRODUCTION RULES
%=============================================================
% not_introduction:

proof(X,not(A),not_i(not(A),D)) :-
     addElement(A,X,Y),
     proof(Y,#,D).
%=============================================================
% and_introduction:

proof(X,and(A,B),and_i(and(A,B),D1,D2)) :-
     proof(X,A,D1),
     proof(X,B,D2).
%=============================================================
% or_introduction:

proof(X,or(A,B),or_i(or(A,B),D)) :-
     proof(X,A,D).

proof(X,or(A,B),or_i(or(A,B),D)) :-
     proof(X,B,D).
%=============================================================
% if_introduction:

proof(X,if(A,B),if_i(if(A,B),D)) :-
     addElement(A,X,Y),
     proof(Y,B,D).
%=============================================================
```

End of SNAIL

The Prolog program SLUG

```
%================================================================
% I.  BASIS CLAUSE
%================================================================
% trivial proofs:

proof(X,A,A) :-
        member(A,X).
%================================================================
% II.  INDUCTIVE CLAUSES
%================================================================
% IIa.  CLAUSES CORRESPONDING TO ELIMINATION RULES
%================================================================
% and_elimination:

proof(X,A,and_e(A,and(B,C),D)) :-
        once(member(and(B,C),X)),
        delElement(and(B,C),X,Y),
        addElement(B,Y,Z),
        addElement(C,Z,W),
        once(proof(W,A,D)).
%================================================================
% or_elimination:

proof(X,A,or_e(A,or(B,C),D1,D2)) :-
        once(member(or(B,C),X)),
        delElement(or(B,C),X,Y),
        addElement(B,Y,Y1),
        addElement(C,Y,Y2),
        once(proof(Y1,A,D1)),
        once(proof(Y2,A,D2)).
%================================================================
% not_elimination:

proof(X,#,not_e(#,not(P),D)) :-
        member(not(P),X),
        once(minor_proof(X,P,D)).
%================================================================
```

```
%  if_elimination:

proof(X,A,if_e(A,if(P,Q),D1,D2)) :-
      member(if(P,Q),X),
      once(minor_proof(X,P,D1)),
      delElement(if(P,Q),X,Y),
      addElement(Q,Y,Z),
      once(proof(Z,A,D2)).
%===============================================================

% The device of minor_proof is just to prevent loops:

?- dynamic asked/2.

minor_proof(X,P,D) :-
      asked(P,X),
      !,
      fail.

minor_proof(X,P,D) :-
      remember(asked(P,X)),
      proof(X,P,D),
      forget(asked(P,X)).

remember(X) :-
      assert(X).

remember(X) :-
      retract(X),
      fail.

forget(X) :-
      retract(X).

forget(X) :-
      assert(X),
      fail.

%===============================================================
```

```
% IIb.  CLAUSES CORRESPONDING TO INTRODUCTION RULES
%==============================================================
% not_introduction:

proof(X,not(A),not_i(not(A),D)) :-
     addElement(A,X,Y),
     once(proof(Y,#,D)).
%==============================================================
% and_introduction:

proof(X,and(A,B),and_i(and(A,B),D1,D2)) :-
     once(proof(X,A,D1)),
     once(proof(X,B,D2)).
%==============================================================
% or_introduction:

proof(X,or(A,B),or_i(or(A,B),D)) :-
     once(proof(X,A,D)).

proof(X,or(A,B),or_i(or(A,B),D)) :-
     once(proof(X,B,D)).
%==============================================================
% if_introduction:

proof(X,if(A,B),if_i(if(A,B),D)) :-
     addElement(A,X,Y),
     once(proof(Y,B,D)).
%==============================================================
```

End of SLUG

The Prolog program NEWT

```
%===============================================================
?- dynamic failed/2.
%===============================================================
%  FAILURE FILTER
%===============================================================
proof(X,A,D) :-
      failed(A,X),
      !,
      fail.
%===============================================================
%  I.  BASIS CLAUSE
%===============================================================
%  trivial proofs:
proof(X,A,A) :-
      member(A,X).
%===============================================================
%  II.  INDUCTIVE CLAUSES
%===============================================================
%  IIa.  CLAUSES CORRESPONDING TO ELIMINATION RULES
%===============================================================
%  and_elimination:

proof(X,A,and_e(A,and(B,C),D)) :-
      once(member(and(B,C),X)),
      delElement(and(B,C),X,Y),
      addElement(B,Y,Z),
      addElement(C,Z,W),
      once(proof(W,A,D)).

proof(X,A,D) :-
      member(and(B,C),X),
      assert(failed(A,X)),
      !,
      fail.
%===============================================================
```

```
% or_elimination:

proof(X,A,or_e(A,or(B,C),D1,D2)) :-
        once(member(or(B,C),X)),
        delElement(or(B,C),X,Y),
        addElement(B,Y,Y1),
        addElement(C,Y,Y2),
        once(proof(Y1,A,D1)),
        once(proof(Y2,A,D2)).

proof(X,A,D) :-
        member(or(B,C),X),
        assert(failed(A,X)),
        !,
        fail.
%=============================================================
% not_elimination:

proof(X,#,not_e(#,not(P),D)) :-
        member(not(P),X),
        once(minor_proof(X,P,D)).
%=============================================================
% if_elimination:

proof(X,A,if_e(A,if(P,Q),D1,D2)) :-
        member(if(P,Q),X),
        once(minor_proof(X,P,D1)),
        assert(failed(A,X)),
        delElement(if(P,Q),X,Y),
        addElement(Q,Y,Z),
        once(proof(Z,A,D2)),
        retract(failed(A,X)).
%=============================================================
```

```
% The device of minor_proof is just to prevent loops:

?- dynamic asked/2.

minor_proof(X,P,D) :-
     asked(P,X),
     !,
     fail.

minor_proof(X,P,D) :-
     remember(asked(P,X)),
     proof(X,P,D),
     forget(asked(P,X)).

remember(X) :-
     assert(X).

remember(X) :-
     retract(X),
     fail.

forget(X) :-
     retract(X).

forget(X) :-
     assert(X),
     fail.
%================================================================
% IIb.  CLAUSES CORRESPONDING TO INTRODUCTION RULES
%================================================================
% not_introduction:

proof(X,not(A),not_i(not(A),D)) :-
     addElement(A,X,Y),
     once(proof(Y,#,D)).
%================================================================
```

```
% and_introduction:

proof(X,and(A,B),and_i(and(A,B),D1,D2)) :-
     once(proof(X,A,D1)),
     once(proof(X,B,D2)).
%=============================================================
% or_introduction:

proof(X,or(A,B),or_i(or(A,B),D)) :-
     once(proof(X,A,D)).

proof(X,or(A,B),or_i(or(A,B),D)) :-
     once(proof(X,B,D)).
%=============================================================
% if_introduction:

proof(X,if(A,B),if_i(if(A,B),D)) :-
     addElement(A,X,Y),
     once(proof(Y,B,D)).
%=============================================================
% FAILURE:

proof(X,A,D) :-
     assert(failed(A,X)),
     !,
     fail.
%=============================================================
```

End of NEWT

Please note that *SNAIL*, *SLUG* and *NEWT* are extremely simple and unsophisticated proof-finders.

Bibliography

A.R.Anderson and N.D.Belnap, Jnr., *Entailment: The Logic of Relevance and Necessity, Vol.1*, Princeton University Press, 1975

E.Beltrami, 'Saggio di Interpretazione della Geometria Non-Euclidea', *Giornale di Matematiche* 6, 1868; also in his *Opere matematiche* Vol.1 (Milano: Napoli, 1902) at p.379

W.W.Bledsoe and D.W.Loveland, *Automated Theorem Proving: After 25 Years*, American Mathematical Society, Providence, RI, 1983

I.Bratko, *Prolog Programming for Artificial Intelligence*, Addison-Wesley, 1986

W.F.Clocksin and C.S.Mellish, *Programming in Prolog*, Springer, 1981

A.Colmerauer, H.Kanoui, R.Pasero and P.Roussel, *Un Système de Communication Homme-machine en Français*, Research Report, Groupe d'Intelligence Artificielle Université d'Aix-Marseille II, 1973

S.A.Cook, 'The Complexity of Theorem-Proving Procedures', *Proc. 3rd Annual ACM Symposium on Theory of Computing*, 1971, pp.151-158

R.Dyckhoff, 'Contraction-Free Sequent Calculi for Intuitionistic Logic', Research Report CS/91/95, University of St Andrews (forthcoming in *The Journal of Symbolic Logic*)

M.van Emden and R.Kowalski, 'The Semantics of Predicate Logic as a Programming Language', *J. ACM* 23, 1976, pp. 733-742

K.Fine, 'Incompleteness for Quantified Relevance Logic', in ed. R.Sylvan, *Directions in Relevance Logic*, forthcoming

K.Fine, 'Semantics for Quantified Relevance Logic', *Journal of Philosophical Logic* 17, 1988, pp.27-59

T.Franzen, 'Algorithmic Aspects of Intuitionistic Propositional Logic', I and II, Swedish Institute of Computer Science Research Reports R87010B, 1987 and R89006, 1989

H.Friedman and R.K.Meyer, 'Can We Implement Relevant Arithmetic?', Technical Report TR-ARP-12/88, Automated Reasoning Project, Research School of Social Sciences, Australian National University, 1988

M.R.Garey and D.S.Johnson, *Computers and Intractability*, W.H.Freeman, San Francisco, 1979

K.Gödel, 'Über formal unentscheidbare Sätze der Principia Mathematica und verwandter Systeme I', *Monatshefte für Mathematik und Physik* 38, 1931, pp.173-198

K.Gödel, *The Consistency of the Axiom of Choice and of the Generalized Continuum-Hypothesis with the Axioms of Set Theory*, Annals of Mathematics Studies, no.3, Princeton 1940

A.Haken, 'The Intractability of Resolution', *Theoretical Computer Science* 39, 1985, pp.297-308

S.Jaskowski, 'Recherches sur le Système de la Logique Intuitionistique',*Actes du Congrès International de Philosophie Scientifique, VI Philosophie des mathématiques*, Actualités scientifiques et industrielles 393, Paris (Hermann & Cie.) pp.58-61

R.Kowalski, 'Predicate Logic as a Programming Language', *Proc. IFIP Congress*, North-Holland, Stockholm 1974

R.Kowalski, *Logic for Problem Solving*, North-Holland, 1979

D.Leivant, 'Syntactic Translations and Provably Recursive Functions', *Journal of Symbolic Logic* 50, 1985, pp.682-688

D.Miller and A.Felty, 'An Integration of Resolution and Natural Deduction Theorem Proving', *Proceedings aaai-86, Fifth National Conference on Artificial Intelligence*, Vol.1: Science, Morgan Kaufmann, Los Altos, 1986, pp.198-202

G.E.Minc, 'The Skolem Method in Intuitionistic Calculi', *Proceedings of the Steklov Institute of Mathematics 121, 1972: Logical and Logico-Mathematical Calculi, 2* (American Mathematical Society, 1974), pp.73-109

L.C.Paulson, 'A Generic Theorem Prover', *Journal of Automated Reasoning* 5, 1989, pp.363-397

J.Pelletier, 'Completely Non-Clausal, Completely Heuristically Driven Automatic Theorem Proving', Technical Report 82-7, Department of Computing Science, University of Alberta

J.Pelletier, 'Seventy-Five Problems for Testing Automatic Theorem Provers', *Journal of Automated Reasoning* 2, 1986, pp.191-216

J.Pollock, 'Interest-Driven Reasoning', *Synthèse* 74, 1988, pp.369-390

D.Prawitz, *Natural Deduction: A Proof-Theoretical Study*, Almqvist and Wiksell, Stockholm, 1975

J.A.Robinson, 'A Machine-Oriented Logic Based on the Resolution Principle', *Journal of the Association of Computing Machinery* 12, 1965, pp.23-41

J.A.Robinson, *Logic: Form and Function. The Mechanization of Deductive Reasoning*, Edinburgh University Press, 1979

G.Rose, *Jaskowski's Truth-Tables and Realizability*, Doctoral dissertation, University of Wisconsin, 1952

R.Schienes and W.Sieg, 'Searching for Proofs', to appear in *Proceedings of the 4th Annual Conference on Computers and Philosophy*

J.Slaney, 'Finite Models for some Non-Classical Logics, Technical Report TR-ARP-2/90, 1990; from Research School of Social Sciences, Australian National University

J.Slaney and G.Meglicki, 'MaGIC, Matrix Generator for Implication Connectives', Technical Report TR-ARP-10/89, August 1990; from Research School of Social Sciences, Australian National University

R.Statman, 'Intuitionistic Propositional Logic is Polynomial Space Complete', *Theoretical Computer Science*, 9, 1979, pp.67-72

L.Sterling and E.Shapiro, *The Art of Prolog*, MIT Press, 1986

N.Tennant, *Natural Logic*, Edinburgh University Press, 1978; 2nd revised edn., 1990

N.Tennant, 'Entailment and Proofs', *Proceedings of the Aristotelian Society* LXXIX, 1979, pp.167-189

N.Tennant, 'Perfect Validity, Entailment and Paraconsistency', *Studia Logica* XLIII, 1984, pp.179-198

N.Tennant, 'The Withering Away of Formal Semantics?', *Mind and Language*, vol.1, 1986, pp.302-318

N.Tennant, *Anti-Realism and Logic*, Oxford University Press, 1987

N.Tennant, 'Natural Deduction and Gentzen Sequent Systems for Intuitionistic Relevant Logic', *Journal of Symbolic Logic* 52, 1987, pp.665-80

N.Tennant, 'Truth Table Logic, with a Survey of Embeddability Results', *Notre Dame Journal of Formal Logic* 30, 1989, pp.459-484

N.Tennant, 'Delicate Proof Theory', in J.Copeland (ed.) *Proceedings of the Arthur Prior Memorial Conference*, forthcoming

N.Tennant, 'Intuitionistic Mathematics Does Not Need *Ex Falso Quodlibet*', typescript

P.B.Thistlethwaite, M.A.McRobbie, and R.K.Meyer, *Automated Theorem-Proving in Non-Classical Logic*, Research Notes in Theoretical Computer Science, Pitman, London and Wiley, New York, 1987

A.Urquhart, 'The Undecidability of Entailment and Relevant Implication', *Journal of Symbolic Logic* 49, 1984, pp.1059-1073

A.Urquhart, 'The Complexity of Decision Procedures in Relevance Logic', unpublished typescript

N.N.Vorob'ev, 'A New Algorithm for Derivability in the Constructive Propositional Calculus', *Trudy Mat. Inst. Steklov* 52, 1958, pp.193-225, English translation in *American Mathematical Society Translations* (2) 94, 1970, pp.37-71

Glossary

Names of systems of logic:

C — classical logic
I — intuitionistic logic
M — minimal logic
R — Anderson-Belnap relevance logic
LR — decidable subsystem of R obtained by dropping axiom of distributivity
IR — intuitionistic relevant logic
CR — classical relevant logic

In IR and CR, relevance is analysed differently than in R and LR. The former pair retain disjunctive syllogism, and place motivated restrictions on transitivity of deduction. The latter pair reject disjunctive syllogism and retain unrestricted transitivity of deduction.

Conventional notation for discussion of proofs:

$X?\text{-}A$ — deductive problem
X, Y, Z, etc. — sets of sentences
A, B, C, P, Q, R etc. — individual sentences
Π, Σ, Θ etc. — proofs

Replete representations of sentences:

$\gamma(P)$, 106
$\pi(P)$, 106

Notions used in metatheorems about relevance of premisses to conclusions of proofs:

$= (A; X)$, 85
$\neq (A; X)$, 85
$\pm (X)$, 85
$\nabla (A; X)$, 91
$\neq$-chain, 91
$\neq$-connected, 91

Logical operators (connectives):

$\neg$ — negation
$\wedge$ — conjunction
$\vee$ — disjunction
$\supset$ — implication

Notation in statement of discharge rules:

$\square$ — the subproof must contain an undischarged occurrence of the assumption indicated; and the application of the rule discharges *all* those occurrences

$\diamond$ — the subproof need not contain any undischarged occurrence of the assumption indicated; but *if* it does, then the application of the rule discharges *all* those occurrences

Index

absurdity rule, 4, 40
accessibility, 67
accessibility filter, 105
accessibility heuristic, 70, 105
accessible positive subformula, 44,
    65, 69
address, 103
adverting, 51
Anderson,A.R., 7
arboreal, 99
Asset, 186, 206
atomic accessibility filter, 70, 136
atomic accessibility heuristic, 71,
    138
atomising strategy, 57
attic-rules, 161
averting, 51
axiom of distributivity in R, 116

backgrounding redundant premisses,
    61
backgrounding strategy, 89, 138
backward-chaining, 170
bare oracle, 29
basic relevance filter, 85
Belnap,N.D., 7
Beltrami,E., 31
bottom-up search for proofs, 41
Bratko,I., 2

briefcase method, 89, 187

characteristic class of matrices, 32
choice problem, 60, 137
Church,A., 2
classical logic, 3
classical reductio, 4
classical relevant logic (CR), 6
classical rules of negation, 4
Clocksin,W.F., 2
cognitive science, 13
Colmerauer,A., 1
complete and bounded proof-finder,
    30
complete counterexample-finder, 33
complete proof-finder, 30
completeness, 188
completeness of Dyckhoff rules, 150
completeness-conserving constraints
    20
compossibility of constraints, 21
connectives, 1
con's of natural deduction systems,
    43
con's of sequent systems, 43
consequent-wary choice of condi-
    tional premiss, 169
consequent-wary choice of major pre-
    misses, 157
counterexample-finder, 31
countermodels, 15